Love and Electronic Affection

Love and Electronic Affection

A Design Primer

Edited by
Lindsay D. Grace

CRC Press is an imprint of the
Taylor & Francis Group, an **informa** business

First edition published 2020
by CRC Press
6000 Broken Sound Parkway NW, Suite 300, Boca Raton, FL 33487-2742

and by CRC Press
2 Park Square, Milton Park, Abingdon, Oxon, OX14 4RN

CRC Press is an imprint of Taylor & Francis Group, LLC

ISBN: 978-1-138-36724-1 (hbk)
ISBN: 978-1-138-36723-4 (pbk)

Contents

Editor

Lindsay D. Grace is Knight Chair of Interactive Media and an associate professor at the University of Miami School of Communication. He is vice president for the Higher Education Video Game Alliance and the 2019 recipient of the Games for Change Vanguard award. Lindsay is the author of *Doing Things with Games, Social Impact through Design* (CRC Press, 2019) and more than fifty peer-reviewed papers on games and related research.

He has given talks at the Game Developers Conference, SXSW, Games for Change Festival, the Online News Association, the Society for News Design, and many other industry events. He was the founding director of the American University Game Lab and Studio and the designer-developer behind several award winning games, including two affection games. He served as vice president and on the board of directors for the Global Game Jam™ non-profit between 2014 and 2019. From 2009 to 2013 he was the Armstrong Professor at Miami University's School of Art. Lindsay also served on the board for the Digital Games Research Association (DiGRA) between 2013 and 2015.

Editor

Contributors

Hermione Banger
Department of Media & Information
Michigan State University and Affinity Games, LLC
East Lansing, Michigan

Casey O'Donnell
Department of Media & Information
Michigan State University and Affinity Games, LLC
East Lansing, Michigan

Lindsay D. Grace
Interactive Media
University of Miami
Coral Gables, Florida

Stephanie Harkin
Department of Media and Communication
Swinburne University of Technology
Melbourne, Australia

Moyzhes Leonid
Center for the Study of Religion
Russian State University for the Humanities
Moscow, Russia

Alexandra M. Lucas
Freelance Game Writer & Narrative Designer
TenRed Studios

Renata E. Ntelia
Institute of Digital Games
University of Malta
Msida, Malta

Miguel Cesar Rodo
Japanese Studies
The University of Edinburgh
Edinburgh, Scotland

Karen Schrier
Games & Emerging Media
Marist College
Poughkeepsie, New York

Contributors

I

Patterns and Practice

CHAPTER 1

On a History of Love and Affection Games

Lindsay D. Grace

CONTENTS

INTRODUCTION

The reasons for a book about affection games and their design are plentiful. While games have proliferated in terms of the scale and complexity of the fictive wars they wage, the kinds of love they depict are still quite simple. While there are many great successes in war simulation (and also, in the simulation of racing cars or of exploring space), their equivalents in the domain of love and affection games are more scant.

Of all the things that games have modeled, love is perhaps one of the least completely explored. Most people would be hard-pressed to identify an affection game as intense as *Call of Duty* (Activision 2003) or *Wolfenstein 3D* (id Software 1992). So too they'd struggle to recall an affection game as widely popular as Risk (Hasbro 1957) or Monopoly (Hasbro 1935). Our studies of the most notable historical games, like chess, interpret them as games of war (Murray 1913). The very first line of Murray's 900-page examination of chess reads "historically chess must be classed as a game of war" (Murray 1913). Where in the history of play, is the love- or affection-focused canonical chess or Monopoly or *Call of Duty?*

If all is fair in love and war games, then love games need some support. The reality is that games are bereft of love as a subject or as an expression. There simply aren't as many games about love, as there are about war. There aren't even half as many affection games as war games (Grace 2017) as war games. When pressed, researchers and designers think of Truth or Dare or Spin the Bottle, games that while operationalizing some elements of affection are also clearly far less developed than chess or *Call of Duty*. Such play is also complicated by its marginalization—affection play is basement play or secret play. Players can execute hundreds of virtual soldiers in public eSports events, but kissing virtual characters remains a kind of taboo (Grace 2011).

Fundamentally, if a game researcher evaluates the number of opportunities players have to wage war, they far exceed the opportunities to express love and affection. If one of the many benefits of playing games includes imaginative practice (Brown 2009), then what does the imbalance between war and affection games mean for the society that plays these games and the culture that produces them?

At its most basic analogy, the culture of play in contemporary games looks far more like it was produced by Greek Spartans than Athenians, particularly in video games. Its culture of play is more about practicing the work of war than the labors of love. As a game industry we have excelled at producing engaging, thorough, and well-tuned experiences focused on the conflicts of war. What we have not done, is exploit the potential of games to involve love and affection.

The origin of this dichotomy may seem obvious. Games, particularly the modern video games, were not born from a love and affection industry. Instead, of course, they were born from the history of playing grand conflicts and recreations of war like *SpaceWar!* (Russell 1962), *1942* (Capcom 1984), and others. Even the history of role-playing games like *Dungeons and Dragons* traces its origins to war-gaming (Laycock 2015).

Likewise, the conflicts most common to the history of games were not ones at the scale of self. The conflicts in digital games from the 1970s through the 1990s rarely focused on conflicts of the intrapersonal or even interpersonal relationships. Instead they focused on waging war against invading armies of people and aliens. This is true even in the scale of conflict of that quintessentially-analyzed game, chess. While players may feel very personal relationships to their games and the game characters within them, the majority of historical game interactions seem to have been far less personal.

At least, that's the history most commonly attributed to games. In reality, there were some fairly personal hits. The historical experience of gaming was far more intimate than is commonly offered today. This chapter helps illuminate that history to explain how affection games have struggled to gain their place among the genre of games.

TECHNOLOGICAL EVOLUTION: LOVE AND AFFECTION

There are a variety of reasons for this pattern of impersonal interaction, perception of limited intimacy, and a lack of human love. Obviously the relatively impoverished opportunities for representation in low resolution technologies like the original *SpaceWar!* make it difficult to illustrate the complexities of personal relationships. Early digital games were too low fidelity to allow for responsible development of affection games, it might be argued.

While games like *Pong*, admittedly required two-person interactions that clearly must have involved some person-to-person interactions at the personal level, it could do little to offer a more representation-rich personal experience between player and computer. The subsequent big hits of arcade and console history biased away from two player experiences and scaled toward conflict at large scale. Most notably the historically noteworthy games, like *Space Invaders* (Taito 1978) and *Defender* (WMS Industries 1981), continue where *SpaceWar!* left off. Some might perceive this as a kind of representation of the players' developmental psychology, as players evolved their play styles to the paradigm of digital play (Grace and Spangler 2014).

Additionally, early generation arcade success biased toward the specific conflicts of life and death. Players through the years are far more familiar with the abstract notion of how many lives they have left than how many loves. It's important to recognize that "lives" as a concept is far more abstract than most players recognize. Generally, excluding cultural and religious beliefs like reincarnation, "life" is generally considered finite and singular by the North American developers that generated these early hits.

Yet players never balk at the idea of multiple lives because they understand each life as a new try. So too, love, could be portrayed as tries if love lives had been incorporated into such play.

Ultimately, the choice to focus on life and death situations, instead of love and love lost (or other themes), has mixed sources. These design choices may have to do with power fantasies of certain types of play, with who was playing, with who was designing, technical limitations, and more. To situate both the value and propensity for designing love and affection into games, this chapter outlines a design history to illuminate relevant threads and themes that effected the development of games focused on love and affection. It is an admittedly selected history that aims to explain why the rhizomes of love and affection, particularly in digital games, did not proliferate as well as other common lived experiences.

HISTORY: TECHNOLOGICAL LIMITATIONS IN REPRESENTATION

The first reason for a lack of love, it can be argued, is technological. Demonstrating the physical relationship between two objects in space is visually less challenging than representing love and affection. This is no more apparent than in *Pong* (Atari 1972). *Pong* is generally understood as a version of tennis. While the abstract representation of tennis is extreme (two rectangles and a square), the notion that the player is engaged in a kind of tennis volley is fairly easy to understand. The player understands a relationship between objects, recognizing that the three basic elements of tennis are a court, rackets, and a ball.

Yet, even tennis is more complicated than *Pong* represents. *Pong* doesn't have a net. *Pong* versions don't include a realistic representation of rackets, rather they include a rectangular abstraction of them. Nor do they include the complexity of tennis scoring. Even as a version of ping-pong, it falls short in its representation. With no net, limited ability to spin (a.k.a., put English on the ball), no angling, and a very simple table/court the game is a pretty substantial abstraction. It is a very simple simulation that cuts out core elements largely due to technical limitations.

Now imagine that *Pong* clone designers aimed to create something more complex and less related to object representation. Imagine for example, that the designer aimed to explore the complexities of co-parenting, aiming to describe the two rectangles as parents and the object they bounce between as child-rearing responsibilities. It is perhaps an appropriate analogy, as the responsibilities must be balanced and play ends

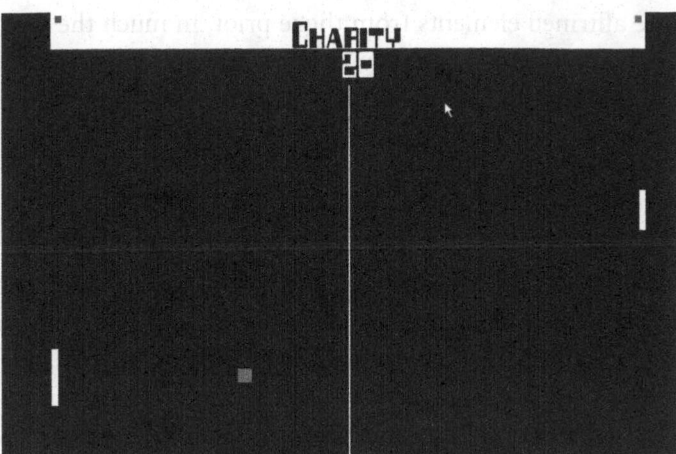

FIGURE 1.1 The Critical Gameplay Game, *Charity*, offers an alternative version of *Pong* where players are responsible for keeping the ball in play cooperatively, instead of competitively.

when either fails to meet their responsibility. This was the premise for my 2008 version of *Pong*, a cooperative version of *Pong* instead of a competitive version. It was named Charity and is shown in Figure 1.1. In such a simple game, the players are supposed to love the ball, sharing it between each other, instead of aiming to make it harder for the player to volley. It stands as a very simple example of an alternate trajectory in the history of games—one that preferred cooperation and support over competition and domination.

Historically, game designers repeatedly chose the competitive mechanic over the cooperative. Generally, when players played together they played against each other, or they played against the machine together. Many of the designers, whether aware of it or not, were working on an affirmative design premise (Raby 2008). They aimed to affirm the design assumptions of past games. The result is a myriad of computer interactions in games that are largely derived from a few precedents. *Pong*, for example, saw at least forty clones between 1977 and 1980 many of which resulted in lawsuits (Katxenbach et al. 2016). All of which continued the competitive mechanics. Later, mechanics like *Space Invaders* begot *Galaga* (Namco 1981) which set the standard for many space shooters (a.k.a., "schmups"). *Defender* informs later schmups, where designers combine invading wave mechanics (e.g., *Space Invaders, Galaga*) with more dynamic player movement to make games like *Gradius* (Konami 1985). Each subsequent game in the genre affirmed elements from those prior, in much the way a good product designer examines the competition, takes elements from it, and moves it forward. The same can be seen of platformers, first-person shooters, and a variety of action super genres that began as mechanics in the arcade.

Herein is the problem for the evolution of love from a technological perspective. In arcade games there was no precedent from which could have derived love and affection. There's no first love game in affection from the 1970s through the 1990s that provided enough financial precedent to encourage clones. There are many reasons for this, which are explored later in this chapter. In short, arcades didn't offer the audience, nor the time, for such experiences. There was little space for love, when so much of the alternative experiences were about surviving. They were also gender-biased play, with a history that moved them toward the affirmation of masculinity carried from the 1950s (e.g., guns and aggressive play). Modern understandings of gender have moved past these biases, but the history of games is still subject to them.

It's also important to admit that any kind of abstraction of love is a bit much to ask of players thirty years ago. The first arcade versions of *Spacewar!* were simply too complex for players to understand, resulting in relative failure when compared to rival releases. Between the challenges of relaying the complexities of love and affection and an audience that was entirely new to human-computer interaction, it was perhaps too much of a technological step to explore.

HISTORY: ADAPTING TO THE HUMAN-COMPUTER INTERACTION AND GENDER IDENTITY

The newness of human-computer interaction is perhaps the second reason for the dichotomy in growth between games that represent war and survival conflicts and those that represent love and affection. If games are the medium, the medium needed not only its technology to mature, but its audience's understanding of it to mature, too. From this perspective, games had to go through the equivalent of their silent film era. They first needed to appeal to whatever audience was interested in playing them, then to help the audience understand how much more they could do. The demographic reality of the arcade game is that in its infancy, that audience was largely male, North American, and maybe even a little drunk. It can't be forgotten that many arcade games, as a new technology, appeared in bars and as cocktail cabinets in the 1970s and early 1980s.

While the history of arcade games can be traced from a variety of trajectories, the one that most aptly fits the evolution of love and affection in games is that of the penny arcade. Before arcade games became the 1980s standard catapulting human-computer interaction into the everyday experience, there existed mechanical arcades. These mechanical arcades were first offered in the United States and later Europe as a low-cost amusement space. They offered moving picture machines before movies were common, testers for a variety of machine-based diagnostics (including early love testers), and amusements like flipper-less pinball machines.

The most germane of these were the love testers, which were found in midways and boardwalks of the early twentieth century. They were coin-operated electro-mechanical devices that are a small part of the mechanical history of digital games (Williams 2017). These love testers purported to combine the marvels of science with the power of the machine age to provide a novelty report of someone's love. Such devices sat near their more famed games indicating strength or skill. In the parlance of the day, a player might engage with these to impress their best gal—winning a prize and demonstrating their worthiness for further courting. Such devices were a kind of novelty aid for potential love and affection.

Penny arcades became the format that defined the first era of such public play. While penny arcades began as multi-gendered spaces, they became largely male (Huhtamo 2005). Why these spaces were dominated by males is more of a sociological question.

Given their growth in the United States, there are of course meaningful observations about gendered work and play dichotomies, which emphasize the notion that while males were allowed to have frivolous play, historically women were steered toward productive and social play (Chess 2009). If females wanted to be in the arcade, the combination of gender identity, social pressure, and norming may have discouraged them from attending.

What this arguably does to the arcade offerings is bias them toward the conflicts that appeal to their predominantly male audiences. The result is a combination of power-fantasy focused play that ultimately plays toward the gender stereotypes that are still present today about game players. Just as little boys were once steered toward playing with toy guns, the games in arcades focused on the same. The arcade in particular, as a kind of public play, was likely to feel the pressure of making sure it affirmed gender identities for their players. Young boys aimed to dominate at the games that supported their sense of domination. At least in public.

Such environments are reinforced by the financial realities of making and marketing an arcade game. Their largely male players wouldn't want to get caught playing the more feminine attributed games about managing relationships, playing house, or worrying about the needs of others. Doing so is the equivalent of a 1950s all-American boy, being caught playing tea party.

It's also important to recognize that games translated into other mediums. Both arcade and computer games borrowed their narratives and subjects from the writing of JRR Tolkien, science fiction, and other popular media. The subjects of games and their representations were borrowed from geek culture and informed by their popular-culture predecessors like dime store novels. It was no mistake that space shooters, like *Space Invaders* and *Defender*, ruled the arcade. They affirmed a playable experience of what many of their designers and patrons were reading and watching when they weren't playing games.

This is underscored by the ways in which player characters are situated in the conflicts of their games. The damsel in distress (so common to the situation and covers of the more lascivious dime store novels) finds its equivalent in games like *Super Mario Bros.* (Nintendo 1985) and *Donkey Kong* (Nintendo 1981).

The sole megahit of the 1980s that departed from these references was the Japanese game, *Pac-Man*. *Pac-Man* did so many things right; in hindsight, it was evident it would be a hit. It represented a character on screen, instead of merely showing a space ship, car, or other object. This made the experience a bit more personal. Players were made responsible for their Pac-Man's health. They tended to it simply by collecting food and avoiding conflict. Pac-Man had a mouth and needed to eat. That's it. Pac-Man is a character with needs and the player is their ward. One could argue that *Pac-Man* functions as a precedent for love games, as one of the earliest popular games requiring players to care for the needs of the player character. It can be argued that *Pac-Man* is a kind of parenting game, where players lovingly guide the character toward meeting its needs while avoiding that which threatens it.

What's most important to note about *Pac-Man* is not only that it was a giant success, but that its players spanned a wider demographic, by design. Its designer actively aimed at widening the demographic (Wade 2015). *Pac-Man*'s play hit a note with more people. While this is not clearly due to its relationship to themes that might be interpreted as part of love, it's worth noting. *Pac-Man* made money, lots of money. This economic reality is perhaps a harbinger to the contemporary game industry. Widely appealing games, ones that aim to do more than appease a narrow, but loyal, fan base can reap great rewards. *Pac-Man* can be viewed as a game about life and death and love. It is perhaps the best example of it in the pre–video-game-crash history of games.

Pac-Man also serves as an example of how abstract representation affords a variety of reads on the meaning and understanding of a game. *Pac-Man* can be a parenting game with loose relationships to love and affection, or a playable example of the greed and drug culture of the 1980s (Wade 2015). Much like the challenges of the uncanny valley (Mori, 1970), the benefit of early representation in games was that their abstract forms allowed for wider interpretation. As digital games work toward higher fidelity models (producing more characters richer in dialogue, action, and imagery), they are faced with the challenge of higher fidelity representations of love.

THE CULTURE OF GAME SUBJECTS

Ultimately, focusing games on the hobbies and media habits of fans of science fiction and fantasy limited the kinds of conflicts offered in games. They also required a kind of fantasy and science fiction literacy. If players weren't already familiar with the roles of an ogre, the power of certain spells, or the difference between a smart bomb and a laser, the experience of games had a steeper learning curve. In much the same way, consumers who don't understand the difference between "rouge" and "contour" might struggle to make a purchase at a cosmetics counter. These interests had gender connotations, but they were technically open to everyone.

All of these factors resulted in a fairly monolithic conflict set for games. Games, particularly those built in North America, offered playable experiences of many boyhood hobbies. Even when games came from other shores, namely Japan, they were influenced by that media. *Donkey Kong* (Nintendo 1981) is very much a reference to the *King Kong* movies—complete with representation of a helpless female caught in the clutches of the antagonist ape. Such references are replete with the racism and sexism of their eras. *Donkey Kong*, perhaps unintentionally, carries forward the sexist stereotypes with the racist analogy of taking the native, uncultured ape from jungle to city (Rosen 1975).

Whether intentioned or not, these early games affirmed the prior generation's views. Consider what happens when twenty- or thirty-year-old designers and developers aim to recreate the media of their youth. What happens when they reimagine, particularly without a critical lens, their first experiences with far away fantasies and epic films. They carry forth the simplest version of their memories, but that version often includes antiquated views.

If you're a young child watching *King Kong*, it's an adventurous film about a giant ape. If you're an adult it becomes something more complicated. This is the challenge of "hauntology" (Derrida 1994) that often affects game design (Grace 2019). The reference, whether intended or not, haunts the contemporary. While every game about a giant ape may not intend reference to *King Kong*, it is ultimately haunted by it. Ultimately, *Donkey Kong*'s character evolved independent of *King Kong*. But, recall that *King Kong*, it's origin at least, is in part a love story.

This perspective also makes the assumption that game designers were not actively avoiding love and affection in games, but instead perhaps ignorant of their bias against it. They were perhaps, seeking to affirm specific power fantasies or generally copying existing design challenges (technical or conceptual) in creating such play. The pattern of cloning prior success was not a matter of selection, but instead a product of financial realities and the ease of technological precedent.

Being critical of the designers of these early arcade games is not entirely fair to the reality of designing any playful system. In reality, love and affection as the focus of play is difficult in itself. It is difficult because it is culturally nuanced and sometimes deeply personal. Human-computer interaction continues to be a new relationship in society. One with which we are just becoming comfortable with how personal it is. The growth of mobile interactions and the myriad of personal data our mobile phones contain still creates a bit of tension for many users. The ease and personalization are enjoyed, but the worry is where to draw the line. When is too personal, too much? How much can a person trust a computer, and with what should they trust it? What happens when that computer fails a user, leaking their personal information or betraying that trust? What happens when the computer simply doesn't do what the user wants it to do? These are techno-cultural questions.

The questions of contemporary personal interactions with computers sound very much like the questions people ask as they enter into and maintain any relationship. The challenge with human-computer interaction is that these relationships have been developing not over weeks, months, or years, but instead over what will soon be lifetimes. Which is why, when reviewing the history of love and affection in games, it is perhaps unfair to criticize the industry for not offering or experimenting with it in more substantive ways. In reality during the early era of video game design and development, there were experiments with personal interactions within games. These were less common to arcade games, than, of course, in games for the personal computer. It was supposed to be a *personal* computer after all. The challenge was not so much in experimenting with love and affection, as finding compelling conflict from which to build a love-and-affection–focused game.

THE CHALLENGE OF DESIGNING CONFLICT IN AFFECTION GAMES

"Conflict" is another major challenge in the history of affection games. The vast majority of digital and analog games focus on conflict. Often players must right a wrong, destroy an evil invasion, collect that which is missing, and so on. The classic conflict in many historical games has been about the computer creating a conflict the player must correct. Non-player characters from *Donkey Kong* (Nintendo 1985) to *Q*bert* (Gottlieb 1982) were plagued by computer-controlled forces that brought conflict, not harmony, to the worlds in which the players interacted.

With a conflict-driven design approach, it's hard to ask questions about love and affection. Oddly love abounds in conflict, as evidenced in everything from the realities of parenting to the steamy scenarios of romantic novels. The challenge is, as mentioned, that there are few original experiments in love as part of the conflict in games. Instead, games might take the object or representation of love away from players as an inciting moment for them to engaging in the conflict. This was through the 1990s a common motivator for platformers and brawlers. Games often took the motivation of implied love—of kingdom or a non-player character—as their inciting moment. This might even include love of country or leaders, like the princess in *Super Mario Bros.* or the president in *Bad Dudes versus DragonNinja* (Data East 1988) or the kidnapped girlfriend in *Double Dragon* (Nintendo 1987). The sole genres to break this convention consistently were western and Japanese role-playing games.

Yet in each of these the love or object of affection is not central to the game's conflict. The player is not repeatedly seeking to gain the love (or affirm the love) of their princess, or their country, or their girlfriend. Instead, gamers are told, as minor setup, that this is why they are doing what they are doing.

In games, the *why* is not the same as the *action*. This is why many games can skip the *why* entirely and keep players compelled. Players don't need to know why the aliens are invading in *Space Invaders* to know they must shoot them. The players don't *know* why anthropomorphic mushrooms are attacking their Italian plumber—and generally they don't *care* why—when playing *Super Mario Bros.*

If love and affection are not central to the game, then it's hard to argue that it's an affection game. If the central conflict doesn't have to do with love or affection, then the game is likely simply about the subject of that conflict. This is fundamental to how we describe other genres in other media. A romantic film is a film in which romance is the central focus. An action film typically resolves the conflict through action, a horror film's conflict is set around some physical or psychological horror, and so on. There have been games in which love might be depicted, but few games in which love and affection are the focus.

Regardless, it's conceivable and demonstrable that conflict can come from love and affection—most obviously as conflicts about missing love, needing love, or having a desire for affection. There is even emerging evidence that players are interested in love and affection as a central conflict in games (Grace 2017). While it's not evident that Larry in the *Leisure Suit Larry* series (Lowe 1987) is seeking love, players are left to understand that the central conflict of the game is pursuit of affection. Al Lowe's *Larry* games are problematic in the context of this book simply because they share more with the comedy of the *Revenge of the Nerds* (Twentieth Century Fox 1984) film series than with the drama of the great love stories of their day. Suffice it to say that *Leisure Suit Larry*, and games like it, offered a peek into what might become of affection games. They include the operationalization of love and many of the traps discussed by the authors of subsequent chapters in this book.

Despite this history there is still limited evidence of love and affection in games. This is in part due to one great irony.

THE GREAT IRONY: LOVE AND AFFECTION FOR GAMES AND LOVE AND AFFECTION IN GAMES

There is of course the great irony in affection games. *Gamers love games.* They truly adore their experiences and their game character's experiences. They collect their experiences, sharing in that love in online communities, at conventions, and more. The love *of* games does not translate into love *in* games. That's the great irony. We love games, but we don't often love in games.

All of these reasons highlight what might be the next great opportunity in expanding game audiences and improving their engagement. You could argue that games have been stuck in a kind of Greek chorus formula. We've been making games that fit the same basic formula, particularly in mainstream, or AAA game development. The design formula is necessitated by large scale financial investments, by metrics that focus on initial scales, and so forth.

This is not the environment for mushy media, it is the environment that rewards high action, high intensity experiences. It's the environment that makes big budget action films, far more likely to succeed than whimsical romantic comedies. It's the environment that favors the epic win over the moving heartbreak. It's perhaps a product of humanness—of wanting to live a life that is full of success, instead of failure.

But the philosophical aspirations to incorporate more love and affection in games also abound. Love and affection are part of the reality of living. Games about simulating life and death, should probably incorporate one of the markers of a life well lived—a life with love. Those who want their game to be more lifelike, are likely to see the value in making their games more love-like.

Incorporating affection in games also affords for wider demographic appeal. Books and films have centered multi-million-dollar industries in all manner of love and affection, from romantic comedies and steam novels, to sincere explorations of how to love and when to stop. These range from fictive fantasies to non-fiction self-help. They help readers and viewers capture the heart of the one they desire, be better to the people around them, or survive the roller coaster of romantic ups and downs.

For those who love games, it's evident that love in games needs further development. The chapters in this book provide context for how love and affection in games has operated. It includes analysis of well-studied games like the *Dragon Age* series and in emotionally complex games like *Life is Strange*. These analyses are provided to help designers and researchers understand how to better offer love and affection in games.

BUT WHY?

With all these headwinds, the obvious question is why make affection games, or integrate affection into games at all. There's no guarantee they are going to sell. There is no guarantee they are even going to work.

But asking that question is a bit like asking why anyone paints, when we now have photographs. Or asking why we tell new stories, when we already have great stories. We should make affection games, because we haven't made enough.

If that's not a compelling reason, think more broadly about the economic pressures of any contemporary entertainment industry. If an industry doesn't grow, or show steady growth, it becomes a less attractive investment. Any company that isn't growing, might be perceived as dying. If there's nowhere else to go, then there's no reason to be a part of its future.

Affection games offer an opportunity to fill that space between a boyhood soldier fantasy and being an adult who fights to protect their family every day. It's the difference between winning the mate of your dreams because you bought a great new shirt and enjoying a lifetime of romance with the person of your dreams. As evidenced in several chapters in this book, it's an opportunity to widen the demographic audience of games. It's an opportunity to appeal across genders and gender identities. It's an opportunity for the medium to mature.

Affection games are a new future for games. They're one that better mates the human experience with the game experience. Quite literally, and figuratively. While there is a history of sex, and arguably, love-making in games, that history is largely vulgar, awkward, and often offensive. Or it is provided like a 1940s film, hinted at in the ever-too-common kiss in frame, followed by a slow pan away from the couple leaving the audience to imagine the love-making off-camera. By analogy, in terms of making-love in games, the industry floats between the dark alleys of red light districts few people would dare admit frequenting and sophomoric allusion.

In my years of writing, I've emphasized one of the great cultural contradictions in particularly North American views of sex and violence. We tolerate violence, which abounds in games, and abhor sexual content (Grace 2011). Censorship, for example, will allow depicted murder of many, but not the single exposure of a partially naked human body. Violence is mainstream, and sexual content is pushed to the edges.

But in nature, the opposite is true. Humans, like most of the animal world, needs one to keep going and the other is unnecessary for its survival. Humanity survives through its biology of reproduction, not through its violence against itself. If people stopped reproducing (a.k.a., having sex) humanity would end. If humanity stopped killing each other, humanity would go on just fine. Violence is not a natural necessity, save for the historical necessity of hunting animals for food. Reproduction is a long-term survival strategy.

In real life human-human interactions of affection and love are more common than gestures of violence. The average person gives more affection in a month, then they do violence. They hug, kiss, serve, and more in honoring their love of others than they do stab, shoot, or violate. In a given lifetime, people are more likely to carry love in their heart than a military weapon in their hands. If play is practice, practicing affection and love is likely of more value than the strategies of war and simulation that dominate many play situations.

So why then do we choose to make so many experiences of human-computer interaction about violence? Some might argue it's vicarious living through fictive worlds. It's about experiencing a world unfamiliar—about creating experiences only dreamed of. This may be true for a distinct population of players, but contemporary play belies this assumption.

Consider, for example, the walking simulators and other games that offer the mundane. Farm simulators, for example, may be the mundane experience of farmers, but the exotic experience of an urban dweller or child too young to do such work. So too, the reader of a romantic novel may indulge the mundane happenings of their fictive characters.

Moreover, anyone who has been in love likely recognizes that it is anything but mundane. So too, not everyone gets as much affection as they want. Just as not everyone gets to drive as fast as they want or lead an army of magical beings. Games can offer an other, and that other is entirely personally relative.

And then there's love-making. If you consider games to be a kind of wish fulfillment. Love-making is perhaps a more common wish than violence. It's hopeful that more people are dreaming of a great time in bed, then a great time murdering others. It seems more likely that healthy people are dreaming of being loved by millions, not hated by the millions of virtual families they destroyed in a murdering rampage. If power fantasies are sated through violence to virtual characters, then it seems other fantasy can be too. If we accept the premise that games are about wish fulfillment, are there not people who wish to be loved?

Perhaps the reality is that we, as a game design community, struggle to bring the medium up Maslow's pyramid of behavior motivation (1958). We are not exploring love, because we, or our players, or the industry, or the media around them, hold the gaming medium to the lowest common denominators. In doing so, games are held in the kind of impoverished simulation of staying alive, eliminating obstacles, and collecting the most basic needs. In short, players are bound to versions of survival horrors, whether they are starving sharks always looking to grow (Ubisoft 2016), rising criminals aiming to surmount the criminal underworld (Rockstar 2013), or fighting to live in any of the post-apocalyptic worlds.

Noah Falstein (2004) offered a view of game design that emphasized the notation of natural "funativity." He claimed that part of fun is derived from practicing the basic things that humans need, like hunting and collecting. How then does love and affection fit into this natural funativity? Is practicing love and affection part of living out fantasies or is it part of survival?

If games are about vicarious living, then why so much focus on the worst situations? The worst of humanity? Is there really an innate human desire to be the last person standing? Is there really some deep-seated need to destroy everyone and everything around us? Or, is it perhaps that we are still struggling against the tyranny of convention and affirmative design? That games are stuck in the loop of cloning past success with incremental innovation? That games were born from a tradition where love, in all its forms, was not a focus?

UNDERSTANDING THE TRAJECTORIES FOR LOVE AND AFFECTION IN GAMES

Game histories vary in their emphasis on where the video game industry came from. Some see a trajectory from pinball, electromechanical games, and the penny arcade (Williams 2017). In this way, the intersection of love and affection is actually a kind of bifurcation. Penny arcades, popular first in the United States and then later in England, introduced an entire generation to the notion of human-machine entertainment. The machines took some low value coin, a penny or nickel, and produced in the player a kind of joy if they subscribed to it. The player paid to play but got something in the real world they couldn't get elsewhere.

In the Victorian era, this experience was generally a moving picture or a variety of tests. These tests might be about your shooting accuracy, your health, or your ability to love (via love testers). Note, that penny arcades have both a film and game history. As the penny arcade grew, the history of film and games diverged. It wasn't long after the proliferation of the moving picture kinescopes and related technology, that they started showing racy and sexy figures. As Plunket (2008, p.252) recants from the public report of London's police articulating the character of images depicted in early penny arcades "a number of stereoscopic machines, which are also on view, however, are of a very highly objectionable character, consisting of photographs of women undressing, showing their underclothing, and sitting in certain postures in a highly suggestive manner, also there are some photographs of paintings of perfectly nude women." And so, the peep show was born as one of the predecessors to the video game arcade.

THE DELAYED MATURITY OF GAME ARCADES

Unlike their film neighbors, games on the penny arcade floors changed. They took the other route. They offered a different fantasy. This fantasy was eventually emblazoned on the glass backsplashes of pinball machines. The fantasy was one of power and of desirability. The games didn't provide a sexy peek, they offered the fiction of successes. Players could be mob bosses, with two beautiful woman each arm, or a race car driver with two bikini-clad women in their arms. The games were of course not without their sexy depictions (Figure 1.2).

FIGURE 1.2 Pinball machine art depicting sexualized females alongside non-sexualized males. From Williams' 1967 Beat Time and Gottlieb's 1978 Blue Note pinball games. (Photograph by Rob DiCaterino. Used with permission from https://www.flickr.com/photos/goodrob13/7273859468/in/photostream/.)

Of course, none of this is love. All of it is part of the long-running objectification of the female body. It's drowning in the male gaze. It encompasses all the stereotypes of gender disparity and the long running male dominance in both film and games. It's a sign of its time, and sadly, perhaps a sign of our contemporary times.

But it also hints at something. It hints at an interest in love. It hints at an interest in earning affection—at being so great at whatever the subject of the game was that the player would earn a kiss. Or that the player would earn the love and admiration of peers. It demonstrates this in the causal, fairly immature perspective of its audience. It does so from the perspective of young boys on the verge of becoming men.

This is an important observation. One that is evidenced in the scholarship on who spent the most time at these arcades (Huhtamo 2016). It's evident too in the largest ban in gaming history. Pinball spent thirty plus years at the edges of society. From the early 1940s until the mid 1970s, pinball parlors were illegal in New York, Chicago, and Los Angeles (Sternheimer 2014); partly because of their relationship to gambling. But also because they were considered a bad influence, as Sternheimer quotes the U.S. Supreme Court pinball machines were "in appearance quite innocent to the uninitiated and the gullible, unaware of the conniving malefactions that lurk behind it" (2014, 57).

The perception of pinball machines, during this era, was that they stole the hard-earned money of players. No such worry was extended to film in the United States. The result, among many other factors, could be equated to a kind of delayed development. Film grew, moving from the staid informed gimmicks of it's early work to the more mature visual language that propelled it toward being common entertainment.

Meanwhile, pinball and its game equivalents, were held back. Their growth was limited. They started as a kind of back-alley activity, born from the low-social standing of betting parlors and centers of vice. Then they were banned in major metropolitan areas in the United States. Their maturity was effectively delayed for thirty years. When they were let back in the daylight, in the 1970s, they were not only well behind their old film roommate, they were relegated to distinct audiences and a lower status in the media entertainment family. While the era of a fancy night out at the movies came and went, games were still relegated to dingy bars and hot cramped spaces full of t-shirts and sweat. When pinball died in the 1970s, it died in a room that shared more in common with a locker room than a living room. It died more like a basement dweller that was never given a chance at daylight, while its favorite sibling enjoyed a lifetime of mainstream adoption. Censoring games didn't help them mature, it delayed their development in a way that has left the industry playing catch up in its themes and portrayals. It's important to remember that some of the first arcade game companies, were pinball manufacturers like Gottlieb and Williams Manufacturing Company (later WMS Industries, WMS Gaming, and Midway Games).

But from the ashes of a declining pinball industry evolved the first arcade games. While products like *Spacewar!* and Higinbotham's *Tennis for Two* (1958) existed well before, the real introduction to video games for the average player happened with an arcade game. There they found a ball and paddle game, one that wasn't that different from pinball, named *Pong*. Both were about keeping the ball in play, both relied on rules from the physical world that children learn by age two or three, but master over a lifetime.

Within a few brief years, the industry rebounded with new titles and new content. The penny arcade was reborn as the video arcade and almost simultaneously, video games become living room or family room entertainment. The home console brought the digital game into the home, for even the most computer challenged. Screw two metal contacts into the antenna slot of a 1980s television and whole new worlds opened up. Thanks in a large part to Atari.

But Atari also opened up a new space for video games. It not only brought video games into many homes, mainstreaming the activity. It birthed a kind of independent developer. When Activision was founded by Atari developers who wanted personal credits for their games, it not only signaled a moment of maturation for the industry, it also created an opportunity for a variety of different game play. First, of course, Activision recognized the creative efforts of its makers, putting real credits for the work in games. It also allowed a whole lot of people to enter the industry and make games without having to work for the console manufacturer.

In the context of this book, it meant players didn't need to have computer savvy in order to play adult games. And adult games were offered. They were as crass, juvenile, and objectionable as any first foray would be. They were erotica games, that took the worst parts of the 1970s pornographic film rush and decanted them into pixelated monstrosities. They looked a bit like giving a horny pubescent boy a crayon and letting them draw everything they could think of after watching the most explicit parts of sexual and violent films like the 1970s release of *Caligula* (Hawes 2014). Yet like children, they seemed to miss the part about artistic aspirations and simply went for the shock factor.

The most famous of these was a product by Mystique, named *Custer's Revenge* (1982). Depicting rape and referencing the U.S. historical moment known casually as Custer's Last Stand, this was an unlicensed release. This game has special infamy. It's a low point for game design and a stain on video game history. Although a dearth of mediocre games for the Atari console created the great video game crash of 1983, games like *Custer's Revenge* did nothing to support the health of the industry nor the growth of mature content for video games.

As an industry, games had recently emerged from being grounded by pinball censorship when they started offering low-quality junk games like *Custer's Revenge* and Mystique's other offerings. Like a child who was still learning the rules, the industry transgressed cultural norms clumsily and immaturely.

Which brings another point to the challenge of love and affection in games. When game design flirted with love and affection in the past, it didn't go well. Its history includes rape, juvenile perspectives like *Leisure Suit Larry*, and overall a very one-sided view of affection. Not only is its history heteronormative, it's focused on sexual affections. It is limited in its portrayal of situations involving parental affection or friendly affection.

This may be in part because console game history is so closely coupled with arcade game history. They rose together and shared many of the same developers. Arcade games are by design punishing. They are meant not to give long satisfying experiences, but instead to take as many quarters as they can. They are designed to tease the player into submitting more money. They offer a peak of what may be and pull the player toward a little more. They are more like peep shows, than they themselves may recognize. In the 1980s and 1990s they offered a glimpse into another world that was time limited and titillating. Arcade games, more than home consoles and computer games, shared an income generating model akin to a peep show. If music television audiences were watching Madonna's peep show appearance in the music video "Open Your Heart" (Madonna 1985), arcade game players were watching screens bating them toward largely power fantasies.

Admittedly, this perspective is extraordinarily focused on the North American gaming experience. This is in part because, in reality, North American developers were a dominant part of the game industry until

Nintendo's Entertainment System landed in North America in 1985. There were obviously a few other successes, like Taito's *Space Invaders* produced in Japan before 1985, but North American developers were dominant.

Worldwide games had expanded, but the political standards for content were still being dominated by the North American game market. This is most evident in Nintendo North America's written policy for games on its console. In no uncertain terms, a game for the North American market had to pass Nintendo's censors (Arsenault 2008). If it didn't meet censorship guidelines, then it didn't get released. Nintendo offered the strict nannying that the game industry had unintentionally indicated it needed by producing its first immature content (ironically focused on mature themes).

Nintendo's censorship was in part due to the fact that games were marketed to children. The notion of love in games would for contemporary audiences seem inappropriate for such a young audience—particularly, any version of romantic love. Parental love, love of an object, or of a pet, would have been acceptable, but given the relatively new experience of human-computer interaction many situations were likely to draw critiques and confusion. Again, it was okay to indicate love of a game console or love of a game, but not necessarily love for the characters in it.

CONCLUDING THOUGHTS

The typical historical perspective of gaming never really talks about love and affection. Instead, it does what the industry did, which is aim at sex, not love or affection. There are practical reasons for this; the subtlety of love and affection are far harder to communicate in sixty-four pixels than space ships and tanks. Or that early game audiences were too drunk at bars (perhaps nursing the wounds of a lost relationship), or two young to understand these higher order experiences. Or perhaps, society simply wasn't ready for them, if they had been imagined. It was enough to ask players to understand human-computer interaction with out the complexity of love and affection in the digital space. Or perhaps the money-making time constraints of arcade games made such lofty aspirations untenable.

But, if a game like *Lim* can communicate the experience of being bullied through the movements of single blocks (2008), it seems we are at least at the point where love can be played in less time than it takes to give a *Call of Duty* weapons tutorial. If games like Jason Rhorer's *Gravitation* (2008) can give players a glimpse into the tensions of balancing the affections for family, while still rising to the call of a creative career, it's evident that love and affection in games is not only on the horizon but has emerged. At the least, it is evidence of potential.

Now, more than in the past, we are developing relationships with and through human computation. Beyond our reliance on dating apps, our long-distance relationships, and our increasingly connected world—we are playing with affection. We are doing so through dating simulation games, that let players flirt with the mundane and epic responsibility of creating and maintaining a relationship. While the first of these were about as transactional as a game of *Lemonade Stand* (MECC 1979), the evolution of these experiences is likely to continue to become much more complex. Before the power of machine learning algorithms encode and obscure the formulas of affection-based play, it's important to ask critical questions about designing love and affection.

Some researches foresee a future where this play is part of the robotic experience, imagining of course the oft-offered future of robots as romantic, sexual, or parenting partners. But before such realities develop, it seems necessary to gain a better understanding of the complexities of all range of love and affection.

As such, this book divides love and affection in games in much the way the very first publications in the field did. It looks at a kind of trajectory and considers the individual ways in which specific actions amount to playing with love and affection. Admittedly there are many, many other ways to slice affection. There are affectionate actions that are non-physical, like baking a cake or making a care package. In some cultures, the ways in which food is presented dictates a kind of affection. Given the relatively nascent character of this space, it's important to recognize that the writing in this book reflects a variety of cultural and cultural identity perspectives. These are in no way exhaustive, but they are designed to combine informed research and practice with inclusive intersectionality.

In closing, as you proceed through these chapters, I'd like to provide a disclaimer through anecdote. In my younger years, I frequented a few dance clubs often. In one club there was a man at least three times the age of most party goers. He was jovial, and everyone loved him. He started wearing a jacket that read, Dr. Love.

By writing and editing this book, I am in no way interested in becoming Dr. Love (in games). Instead, as counterpoint to the many, many ways in which games have become exceedingly good at mimicking war, this book is offered to show how games could be better at love and affection. If the 1960s ethos of "make love not war" is a mantra to live by, then perhaps in the games world, "making love games, not war games" might be the twenty-first century's mantra for bringing games into the future.

This work aims not to belittle the high-quality games of war that have been designed, but instead to encourage designers away from the life-and-death scenarios which have a finite audience to the life-and-love scenarios that might move the medium toward its aspirations as an historically great medium. This book does not aim to declare a single minded, one solution fits all how-to on designing love and affection in games. Instead it aims simply to help the reader understand the ways in which love, and its variety of expressions, can find presence in everything from single developer indie games to multimillion-dollar AAA games series. It also aims to remind researchers of how such work needs further investigation. Whether it's to better understand how games become more inclusive, to unearthing the effect of playing stories versus reading and watching them, this research pulls a dimension of game design into conversation that has until recently had limited critical analysis.

At the least, it's hoped that this book might inspire a few more Dr. Love's to be the life of the design party.

REFERENCES

1942. Capcom. 1984.

Arsenault, D. "System profile: The nintendo entertainment system (NES)." In Mark J. P. Wolf (Ed.), *The Video Game Explosion: A History from Pong to PlayStation and Beyond*, pp. 109–114. Greenwood Press, Westport, CT, 2008.

Bad Dudes versus DragonNinja. Data East. 1988.

Brown, Stuart L. *Play: How It Shapes the Brain, Opens the Imagination, and Invigorates the Soul*. Penguin, 2009.

Call of Duty. Activision. 2003.

Castle Wolfenstein 3D. Id Software. 1992.

Chess, Shira. "License to play: Women, productivity, and video games." PhD diss., Rensselaer Polytechnic Institute, 2009.

Custer's Revenge. Mystique. 1982.

Defender. WMS Industries. 1981.

Derrida, Jacques. *Specters of Marx: The State of the Debt, the Work of Mourning and the New International*. Routledge, New York, 1994.

Donkey Kong. Nintendo. 1981.

Double Dragon. Nintendo. 1987.

Falstein, Noah. "Natural funativity." *Gamasutra.com*. 2004. https://www.gamasutra.com/view/feature/130573/natural_funativity.php.

Galaga. Namco. 1981.

Grace, L. D. "Discomfort design: Critical reflection through uncomfortable play." *17th International Symposium on Electronic Art (ISEA)*, Istanbul, Turkey, September 14–21, 2011.

Grace, L. D. "Love, lust, courtship and affection as evolution in digital play." In *Proceedings of the 11th Digital Games Research Association Conference (Digra 2017)*, Melbourne, Australia, 2017.

Grace, L. D. Hauntology, the Penumbra, and the Narratives of Play Experience, 25th International Symposium of Electronic Art (ISEA), Gwangju, South Korea (2019).

Grace, L. D., Spangler, B. "The psychology of play: Understanding digital game evolution through developmental psychology." In B. Li and M. Nelson (Eds.), *Society for the Advancement of Digital Games*, Santa Cruz, CA, London, 2014. http://www.fdg2014.org/proceedings.html and https://dblp.org/db/conf/fdg/fdg2014.html. ISBN: 978-0-9913982-2-5.

Gradius. Konami. 1985.

Grand Theft Auto. Rockstar Games. 2013.

Hawes, W. *Caligula and the Fight for Artistic Freedom: The Making, Marketing and Impact of the Bob Guccione Film*. McFarland, London, 2014.

Huhtamo, E. "Slots of fun, slots of trouble: An archaeology of arcade gaming." In Raessens and J. Goldstein (Eds.), *Handbook of Computer Game Studies*, pp. 3–21, MIT Press, Cambridge, 2005.

Huhtamo, E. "Amusement arcade." In R. Guins and H. Lowood (Eds.), *Debugging Game History: A Critical Lexicon*, pp. 21–28, MIT Press, Cambridge, 2016.

Hungry Shark World. Ubisoft. 2016.

Laycock, J. P. Dangerous games: what the moral panic over role-playing games says about play, religion, and imagined worlds. University of California Press, 2015.

Lemonade Stand. MECC (Minnesota Educational Computing Consortium). 1979.

LIM. Merrit Kopas. 2008, http://www.gamesforchange.org/game/lim/.

Lowe, Al. "Leisure suit Larry in the land of the lounge lizards." *Sierra On-Line* (1987). https://store.steampowered.com/app/763970/Leisure_Suit_Larry_1__In_the_Land_of_the_Lounge_Lizards/.

Mori, M. "The uncanny valley." *Energy* 7, no. 4 (1970): 33–35.

Madonna. "Open Your Heart" [Video], True Blue. Warner Bros. 1985. https://www.youtube.com/watch?v=snsTmi9N9Gs.

Maslow, A. H. "A Dynamic Theory of Human Motivation." In C. L. Stacey and M. DeMartino (Eds.), *Understanding Human Motivation*, pp. 26–47, Howard Allen Publishers, New York, 1958.

Monopoly. Hasbro. 1935.

Murray, H. J. R. *A History of Chess*. Clarendon Press, London, 1913.

Plunkett, J. "Selling stereoscopy, 1890–1915: Penny arcades, automatic machines and American salesmen." *Early Popular Visual Culture* 6, no. 3 (2008): 239–255.

Pong. Atari, 1972.

*Q*bert*. Gottlieb. 1982.
Raby, F. "Critical design." In M. Erlhoff and T. Marshall (Eds.), *Design Dictionary*, pp. 94–96, Birkhäuser Basel, Basel, Switzerland, 2008.
Revenge of the Nerds. 20th Century Fox. July 20, 1984.
Risk. Hasbro. 1957.
Rohrer, J. *Gravitation*. 2008. http://hcsoftware.sourceforge.net/gravitation/.
Rosen, D. N. "King Kong. Race, sex, and rebellion." *Jump Cut* 6 (1975): 7–10.
Sternheimer, K. *Pop Culture Panics: How Moral Crusaders Construct Meanings of Deviance and Delinquency*. Routledge, New York, 2014.
Space Invaders. Taito. 1978.
Spacewar! Steve Russell. 1962.
Super Mario Bros. Nintendo. 1985.
Tennis for Two. William Higinbotham. 1958.
Wade, A. "Dots, fruit, speed and pills: The happy consciousness of Pac-Man." *Journal for Cultural Research* 19(3) (2015): 248–261.
Williams, A. *History of Digital Games: Developments in Art, Design and Interaction*. Routledge, Boca Raton, FL, 2017.

CHAPTER 2

On the Origin and Definition of Digital Affection Games

Lindsay D. Grace

CONTENTS

Understanding the origin of affection games and defining them is more an exercise in interpretation than history. One of the fundamental dilemmas in understanding affection games is not only determining what constitutes an affection game, but also in following their reporting, archiving, and tracking. In short, there is no ultimate guide to affection games in academic literature. There isn't a cannon of play, nor is there a clear record of what games were played, when they were played, and who played them in the context of affection games. This is of course a product of the games themselves. If affection game history begins with the first physical kisses in games, or the first historical hugging play, few of the players were likely to recognize the significance of such play. More likely, even fewer were eager to report it.

To offer some standard for defining affection games in the digital space I have formerly defined affection games as requiring one of the four fundamental affection verbs (Grace 2013) as the means to accomplishing the primary goal in the game:

- Flirt
- Kiss
- Hug
- Make-love (a.k.a., have sex)

This outline and definition are useful in describing the subset of digital affection games in the casual and mobile space but does not appropriately support the wider range of affection available in games. It is a way to understanding "affection" as an operation that is often, but not entirely, embodied in digital representation. It is a simplified definition useful in describing the simplified representations of affection common to the most basic affection games.

However, it fails to support the wider range of games involving affection. This is because it is about the embodied expression of affection, but not the intent of affection. In the case of parental affection for example, it is true that a parent may kiss or hug their child, but parental affection involves more than that. Parental affection might involve doing something for a child or giving a gift. So too, the acts of expressing interest or appreciation for someone involves much more than flirting, kissing, and hugging them. For this reason, its useful to think of the wider range of affections that are likely to express themselves in games. These include:

- Supporting: as in providing consolation or other supportive acts;
- Giving: as in gifts, time, or other resources and creations;
- Taking: as in responsibility, burdens, or other acts of service; and
- Collecting: acquiring earnable resources.

The truth is that affection can quickly involve an extraordinarily wide set of actions, especially when ascribed to a variety of situations. Dying, as in the sacrifice a parent might make to help their child survive, can become an act of affection. While this is all true, the fundamental dilemma is how to turn this complexity into something easily discerned. Much like attempting to write a reductive, analytical description of love, defining what constitutes an affection game can quickly become awkward and ill-fitting.

This is why it's useful to discern between *affection games* and *affection in games*. To keep things simple, an affection game is a game whose primary intent is not earning affections, but instead the expression of those affections as the primary activity of the game. If games are about goals, obstacles, and obstructions (Grace 2019), then an affection game prescribes affection as the solution to those problems. Reductively, that has commonly been flirting, kissing, and making love. That doesn't mean there isn't space for more, just as game verbs like "rewind time" were novel before their implementation.

The easiest way to understand this is to the consider some of the most common affection games in the analog space. Spin the Bottle, has two game verbs, "spin" and "kiss." The player spins the bottle, it points to two people in the circle, and they kiss. This is an affection game. The act of kissing is a dominant action in the game.

A game in which players are afforded the ability to kiss isn't an affection game, unless the kissing is the way the problem in the game is solved. So, if a fighting game rewards players with a kiss, that game isn't an affection game unless those kisses somehow resolve the main conflict in the game. This particularly definition is dissatisfying to some. Admittedly, it narrows the universe of "affection games," versus "games with affection." But that's okay, as sometimes to understand something it's important to winnow it down to its smallest set to examine its pieces.

Herein is the problem with widening the definition of affection games. If "supporting," for example, is considered an affection verb, then suddenly many, many, many games become affection games. Every game in which the player is supporting the success of a player character or non-player character, could be interpreted as supporting the needs of that character. If the player helps a non-player character by completing a mission, is that truly an act of affection, an errand, or a job? If "caring for," without the context of an affection framing conflict is added to the definition, then nearly every game is an affection game.

In reality, it's likely the best games of the future will offer many game verbs, of which the affection verbs are only a part. Just as there might be some kissing in action films, or some fighting in a romance novel, the verbs are part of a complete formula. Their genre remains the same, action and romance respectively, despite the addition of some affection.

This definition is probably most disconcerting to individuals who want to place dating simulations in the domain of affection games. This definition doesn't preclude dating simulations from being categorized as affection games. It also doesn't place *all* dating simulations in the category of affection games. Instead it does what any functional pragmatic definition does, it provides a line that allows for clarity while still accepting exceptions to the rule.

There are other ways to define affection games. One could choose to use a content-specific approach, which might bias toward including any game in which affection is dominant as an affection game. The fundamental problem there is that content in games and other media does not define the genre or type. Games in the *Grand Theft Auto* franchise (2013) have lots of car content, but they'd never be confused with other car-content-focused games like car racing simulations.

A critical inquiry into affection itself complicates the understanding of affection verbs. Not all sex is performed out of affection. Not all kisses have affection linked meaning or intent. The reality is that in studying and designing affection in games, there needs to be some line drawn to understand the difference between affection and all other play that orbits it. To do so, some careful, but necessary simplifications are made in the hopes that the work of understanding affection games can move forward. As the following section illuminates, the headwinds to understanding affection games are already fairly substantial. In a headwind it's often easier to move a narrow subject forward, than to head through it with a wide and amorphous one. Focusing affection games narrowly, then recognizing that it's understanding supports wider development and inclusion helps move the entire practice forward.

Ultimately for clarity, it's somewhat useful to widen the scope of affection games to include all games for which the central conflict of the game is resolved through the repeated execution of an affection game verb. This means that when Mario seeks the princess in *Super Mario Bros.* (1985), he is not involved in an affection game because he's running and jumping his way through the conflict. But, in a dating simulation, where the player must repeatedly flirt with the subject of their affections to remain in the game—that's an affection game. If Spin the Bottle is played without kissing, it ceases to be an affection game.

UNDERSTANDING AFFECTION GAMES

One of the earliest modern catalogs of affection games comes from a small paper published by the world-renowned researcher, Brian Sutton-Smith. Sutton-Smith's paper, "The Kissing Games of Adolescents in Ohio" (1959) offers a list of twenty-two kissing games his study group of high schoolers and college students admitted to playing in the 1950s. The specifics of these games are outlined in the paper but include contemporary carry-overs like Spin the Bottle. The work is a fascinating peek into the affection play of a 1950s United States before the liberal 1960s.

What's perhaps even more interesting than the content of the paper is its significance in research literature. It is one Sutton-Smith's least cited works. When compared to any of his seven books, its mere twenty-nine citations (as of the writing of this book) make it one of the least cited of his writings by a wide margin. It's also worth noting that Sutton-Smith never published another study of kissing or affection games again.

Affection games are not merely an under-researched space, it is somewhat of what a dark horse topic. There are many ways to speculate the why. Studying what children do behind closed doors, as Sutton-Smith had done, can be discomforting research potentially colliding with privacy and minor protection laws. It might read as frivolous, in much the way the study of games was once considered (and to some remains) an unnecessary line of inquiry. For some areas of affection games, they have become taboo topics, relegated to a kind of red-light district of research.

Yet understanding affection play, and the smaller subset of affection games, offers opportunities to interpret emerging problems in general society. The affection games Sutton-Smith researched were part of the development of those player's understanding of human-human relationships. They were part of how such players learned about their bodies and about courtship. In a world where population decline effects many industrial nations including the United States (Livingston and Cohn 2012) and Japan (Tsuya 2015) an understanding of courtship and its origins can be useful. As family roles, responsibilities, and gender dynamics shift—affection becomes an important element to understand. With these shifts, come changes in courting rituals, in identity, and responsibility, that call for affection play research.

Likewise understanding affection games seems increasingly important as the world in which people operates changes. The expression of affection is complicated by the growth of autism spectrum diagnosis, which may affect affection experiences (Shana and Byers 2016). Evidence indicates that work with computer meditated interactions can aid children with autism spectrum disorders (Stanton et al. 2008). Others have investigated programs aimed at improving affection expression between parents and children with autism (Cullen and Barlow 2002). The increase in cross-cultural collaborations changes the ways in which people express affection between individuals. The evolution toward recognizing wider gender and sexual identities changes the meaning and previous norms of affection play.

In short, understanding affection games helps capture changing elements of society, offering opportunities to understand origins and view effects.

COURTSHIP

For these reasons, the best historical understanding of affection games is really a product of a few non-game disciplines. Anthropologists have done some of the work of game studies researchers and historians, by taking note of courtship rituals. Informally, courting rituals include the games people play to express interest, typically romantic or with the intent of marriage. From an anthropological perspective these activities may involve games, but as with the writing of this book, anthropologists who did this work weren't necessarily looking at these activities as games explicitly—at least in terms of design.

The activities of courtship, and their associated play, are part of the many activities the contemporary world might simply describe as dating. In reality, dating itself is an evolving set of cultural standards that involve much more than the date event itself. Courtship includes the lead in and lead out. Its research asks questions about how cues are communicating for everything from intent and interest to rejection. For a further understanding of courtship, reading *From Front Porch to Back* Seat (Bailey 1989) and *Courtship* (Cate and Lloyd 1992) for an American perspective is a good orienting start. More recently, *Coming of Age in South and Southeast Asia* (Manderson et al. 2002) outlines a Southeast Asian perspective.

CASE STUDIES

Case studies provide an opportunity to see theory in practice. They demonstrate how the ideas of affection play resolve into practice. Generally real-world case studies in affection games fall into two categories—evolved games and designed games. Evolved games are the games that develop less out of the specific intention of a game designer and more out of the innate interests or behaviors of the players. In design terms they are a kind of participatory design, without a distinct designer present, or where the designer is the psychological and cultural constraints or influences that shape the play. They are what turns bobbing for apples or chew the string, into a kissing game. They are what turns seven minutes in a dark closet into an opportunity to explore sexuality, or an opportunity to reject it. Evolved games also include the individual instincts that turn playing with dolls (GI-Joe, Barbie, or Street Fighter II characters) into a romantic or affectionate escapade.

On the other end of the spectrum are designed games. These are the games produced with the explicit intention of creating affection play. They are intentioned designs, informed by explicit design decisions. In the digital space, some pronounced examples are games like:

- *Big Huggin'*: Hug a giant teddy bear controller to help it past it's obstacles (Grace 2013)
- *Kiss Controller:* Players use controller inserted in the mouth to kiss while playing a variety of games (Nam 2013)
- *Dark Room Sex Game:* A non-visual, audio only game in which players must please the other by moving a Wii controller in rhythm with sexual sounds (*Copenhagen Game Collective* 2009)
- *Smooth Operators:* two player cooperative kissing game (Heydeck Games 2013)

The first three of these examples are not only affection games, but embodied affection games. They involve controllers that function in the physical world as part of the affection game. There is much potential in this space, which extends far beyond the red-light elements of teledildonics (Liberati 2017) toward the potential for affection to deliver new types of play.

More mundane examples of affections games are listed on websites like GirlsGoGames.com, which offers more than sixty games in its kissing category (https://www.girlsgogames.com/games/kissing) and nineteen in its flirting category. These same types of games are offered in mobile game spaces like Google Play and to a lesser degree, Apple's iOS App store. More tangentially they also, arguably, include games like *Unicorn Makeout Mania* (SoftwareSoft 2013), a game in which players compete to have two unicorns kiss aggressively. It's part kissing game, part fighting game, so it's interpretation as an affection game is complicated.

While Sutton-Smith's work (1959) illuminates affection games in its era, it is by no means the only collection of such case studies. My prior writing on affection games provides case studies in the casual and mobile games space (Grace 2015). It's also useful to read reflections like *Game Love* (Enevold and MacCallum-Stewart 2014) and *Digital Love: Romance and Sexuality in Games* (McDonald 2017) to understand the wider context of these case studies.

But the aforementioned case studies are largely focused on affection games, not affection in games. For case studies in affection in games, the most prolific genre is role playing. While it may seem obvious that role playing games offer affection (it's role play after all), it's important to note that part of the motivation for incorporating affection in role play games is not only to solidify the fiction of another world, but to increase the diversity of audience. The case studies on *Dragon Age* contained in this book help illuminate how this is done.

Other case studies in this book help showcase the most recent and significant uses of affection in games. Combining historical case studies with contemporary case studies helps a designer and researcher chart the trajectories of such play. It can be useful in understanding where affection games are likely to go next, as well as recognizing potential design gaps offer opportunity for new play.

UNDERSTANDING AFFECTION GAMES FROM THE WAY PEOPLE PLAY

To understand affection games, it can be useful to ask questions about how players play with affection. This approach is not about identifying games specifically designed for affection, but instead in imagining the ways in which games not intended for affection become affection games. So, while a researcher could aim at understanding the types of affection play engaged by children playing with dolls, for example, few people have proposed such research in the space of games and affection.

That is to say, that part of the history of affection games starts merely with the addition of affection to games for which affection was not a primary focus. A role-playing game in which players evolve the play from the conflicts of war toward the affection of love is one such imagined example. One can image that children playing with G.I. Joe or Transformers concoct storylines that involve romantic interest and affection. Likewise, while arguably still in the domain of playing with dolls, such play can and has included aspirational and affirmational scenarios that include affection. This has become a focus of substantial research (Bretherton 2014).

This is one of the key elements of understanding affection games. Affection games involve the imagined. Much like the contemporary view of romance, they require players to commit to a fiction that carries with it much of the contemporary view of what is and isn't affection.

Which of course returns us to the conundrum of understanding the origins of digital affection games. It may be that some of the first digital affection play involved making two characters from *Double Dragon* (1987) look like they were kissing, instead of fighting. It might be the imagined fictions of a basement *Dungeons and Dragons* game. Such imagined histories are of course dissatisfying to researchers, no matter how true they may be. At best they can only be proven with anecdotal interviews and player histories.

Instead, what we as researchers commonly do is find a moment where the intent is evident—where something is created, commemorated, or documented in a way that indicates that it is seminal. To do this, distinct lenses must be adopted to understand the origin of digital affection games.

If the first academic recognition of affection as the core focus of games is the origin, then Sutton-Smith's catalog of kissing games may well be that first instance. Sutton-Smith, a well-recognized play researcher, ventured into the closed-door spaces of adolescent kissing games to provide a snapshot of their activities. In reality, those games clearly existed before his work.

Yet, Sutton-Smith identifies other games that have been made into common digital experiences. The most common of which is Spin the Bottle. Spin the Bottle has been translated into digital form numerous times as shown in Figure 2.1.

FIGURE 2.1 A collection of Spin the Bottle games available as mobile app on Google Play's store.

But there are many other games that have not been copied into the digital space. The five most-popular affection games played among college students are listed below, as demonstrated in Sutton-Smith's study:

- Spin the Bottle (91% of college respondents played);
- Mistletoe Kissing (83% of college respondents played);
- Post Office (70% of college respondents played);
- Winks (23% of college respondents played); and
- Chew String (34% of college respondents played).

It's worth noting that few of these games have been converted into digital experiences.

Yet the challenge with tracing the history of such games from analog to digital is that they don't necessarily emphasize the defining features of digital affection games. Carrying a game history from the analog to the digital has some important limitations. For one, it doesn't do a good job of supporting the history of elements and experiences born solely from the digital space. While, for example, chasing the history of *Pong* to tennis seems evident, tracing the history of any first-person shooter game to some analog equivalent becomes a little harder. More to the point, tracing the history of a games involving time manipulation, for which there is limited analog equivalent, becomes even harder.

This is where it might be useful to consider a history of affection games that begins with the digital games themselves.

DIGITAL GAMES AS DIGITAL AFFECTION GAME HISTORY

One of the primary challenges to understanding the history of "digital affection through games" is that it has taken a long time for digital play to actively engage in affection as the core goal of a game. While it's true that one could attribute affection as early as the automated love letters produced by computer in *1952* (Strachey), the reality is that getting a computer to emote or feign affection is not really an affection game. An affection game, by definition, is much more about facilitating affection between player and computer, or at the least orbiting the space of a play experience in which affection is the goal.

From this perspective it could potentially be argued that *Eliza* (O'Dell and Dickson 1984) is the first digital affection game. While the experience itself is a somewhat playful opportunity to receive the intellectual advice of a fairly basic AI system, its potential description as an affection game comes from the game verbs it supports. Players could, despite the experience's goals, flirt (or at least attempt to flirt) or otherwise offer affection to the computer. While these weren't the explicit goals of the experience, their support at least affords the ability for players to experiment with affection.

Yet, admittedly, a critical voice might correctly identify that simply because a player can attempt affections in an experience, doesn't mean it's an affection game. Defining *Eliza* as an affection game, would then mean that any such game supporting a myriad of verbs might also be labeled as such. This would allow early versions of *Dungeon* (Daniels et al. 1979) to be called affection games simply because the player was allowed to use affection verbs.

This is where one of the fundamental tenets of affection games becomes most evident. It is not enough to have not designed against affection. It is not enough to define an affection game as any game that allows affection. Because, quite simply, there is no consent.

ON COMPUTER CONSENT, CONSENTING ALGORITHMS, AND AFFECTION PLAY

To some it might seem absurd to think about consenting algorithms, but in a world that has matured its understanding of consent, a consenting algorithm is perhaps the most important way to understand true design for affection. That is to say, instead of merely initiating an interpretation of digital affection with games that were likely to conjure affection play, it's important to understand design intention. Coercing the non-player characters in a game into affection situations is not affection at all. At its best it is a misunderstanding of affection, in much the way an uninvited kiss intended as a greeting is a kind of violation. Intent is in the grey areas of affection, the most important place to begin to understand affection.

To understand the history of affection games and to understand their design from a digital perspective, it's important to seek the first games that actually intended to afford for such affection. This of course skips crass examples like *Custer's Revenge* (Mystique 1982), which by most accounts is a game of violence, not love. What's left are games that aim to develop relationships, to allow players to understand the needs of the game characters, and to develop relationships that mature into consent and accepted affection.

In the early history of digital games, where players were merely trying to develop an understanding of how to play games and designers were struggling with eighty-column resolutions and sixteen color palettes, this seems like a tall order. While there may have been love expressed for the characters in *Q*bert* (Gottlieb 1982), for example, players were not allowed to express those affections as part of the game. In a world full of action, the nuances of affection and love had little space.

That is until the first hints of affection started to appear in choose-your-own-adventure games. Such games had a history in role playing games and in narrative that understood that a story was more than action and result.

It's almost impossible to say with any certainty when the primary affection verbs first appeared in games. What's more likely useful to a designer of love and affection in games is to understand how they have evolved over the years.

Such a history emphasizes the notion that there is no distinct moment but instead an evolution toward more clear and nuanced affection. By analogy, if a game studies researcher aimed to understand the history of shooting in games, they might start with the *Spacewar!*, because players were supposed to shoot each other. This is clear in the dynamics of the game. But then, what's the next shooting game. Is it *Pong*, because the ball shoots between players? Is it *Space Invaders*, because it's the most popular game after *Spacewar!*? How does that history move clearly from *Spacewar!* to *Call of Duty*, without also referencing games that explored perspective, that provided inventory systems, explored narrative, simulated war, etc. Every history of digital games is a bit messy as influence between designs is never as linear as a simple one-to-one relationship.

There is no first kiss in video games but instead a variety of moments that moved it toward its current state of affection. In part, because it's likely some of the first affection games were experienced in dark rooms, designed in secret, and shared in the equivalent of the red-light districts of bulletin board systems. Because such play has taboo elements, its history is muddled with rumor, limited research, and obfuscated elements.

This is particularly important in considering affection in games, versus affection games. It is technically easier to track affection in games, as there are distinct moments where games offer affection in games. The 1981, *Softporn Adventure* (Benton 1981), as the predecessor to *Leisure Suit Larry*, is one such example that has survived the routine demolition of virtual red-light districts. In it, evidence of early affection in games is available, but there is little proof that it is the first. It's also worth noting that affection in games may have been the product of an evolved game inspiring or effecting a designed game. For those interesting in independent games, it's safe to say that the year 2013 seems to be one of the highlights of the history of independent affection games. The number and variety of such games seems to have blossomed in that time (Grace 2013), but the history is muddled.

UNDERSTANDING AFFECTION GAMES AND PSYCHOLOGY

The relationship of mechanics in games is like relationships, also complicated. The task of a designer is often to make the complicated, simple. Doing so allows complex ideas to become programmable algorithms. For this reason, it's useful to come up with a simple model for understanding the digital evolution of games. From experience and analysis of game history, one of the easiest ways to simplify the evolution of digital affection games is to consider them in the context of psychology.

The dynamic between human and computer, is relatively new to humanity. It is a dynamic that is evolving quickly and one for which there is little precedence. If poets, psychologist, biologists, and others have spent generations trying to understand love and affection, it's a bit much to ask game designers to quickly be able to encode it into algorithms and play experiences that not only feel right, but are also engaging.

As such, it makes sense to lean on research that has already explored love and affection in methodological terms. That is, designers need to find work in other fields that formalizes an understanding of love and affection and then convert such understandings into playable experiences.

MASLOW

Most undergraduates and many an arm-chair psychologist are familiar with the work of Abraham Maslow. As a result, the notion of Maslow's hierarchy of needs, or informally Maslow's pyramid, is clear. As people in their own lives move up or down the hierarchy of needs, they change their levels of wants and needs. At the bottom of the pyramid, a person is worried about basic survival needs. They are worried about eating and drinking and finding shelter. These are our basic needs as organisms, shared by humans and the lowest creatures on the food chain. At the top of the hierarchy, are more abstract needs, like, unsurprisingly, love and being able to love.

Maslow's hierarchy provides an interesting perspective for understanding affection in games. In short, early games were largely focused on the bottom of the pyramid. Early play was about survival. Players attempted to survive crossing the road in *Frogger* (Konami 1981). They attempted surviving an invading hoard of aliens in *Space Invaders*. Or they fled ghosts hunting them down through a maze in *Pac-Man* (Namco 1980).

These games let players practice the bottom of the hierarchy of needs. Player characters needed to eat (Pac-Man) or they needed to stay alive (Frogger). While not every game in early game history fell neatly into this characterization, many popular games did.

But, as the practice of game design evolved, so too did the player character's needs. Digital play moved from basic physiological needs, like surviving toward needs of safety. Players were offered resource management games, in which strategies could be raised from simply staying safe all the way up to building resources to ensure that safety. These games largely came from the history of war gaming as an economic game. These games assumed personal safety and offered the players an opportunity to think more long term. Early examples include the games *Lemonade Stand* (1979) and *Oregon Trail* (MECC 1974), although their original release dates and the dates at which they became popular can be misleading. Both became more popular many years after their release, when games like *Pac-Man* and *Frogger* had already succeeded. These games moved play up Maslow's pyramid toward the focus of this book—love and affection. Players of *Oregon Trial*, for example, had a family to worry about.

In Maslow's view, people can't worry about love and belonging until they are able to assure their own physiological needs and safety. To afford love and affection, play had to evolve. Players needed to first experience games that helped them understand physiological needs in game. Then they learned how to manage resources, and ultimately, they became capable of practicing love and affection as play experience.

This is one way to not only understand the history of games, but also to understand the design of such games. If players are focused on the bottom of Maslow's pyramid, then they are going to struggle to worry about things at the top. If a game is a survival horror, there will always be a tension between the top of the pyramid and the bottom. This doesn't mean that a game can't achieve the appropriate balance of these needs. Instead it's important to recognize that such a game is a complex balance that requires the player moving focus from survival to safety to love.

The later chapters in this book work to help game designers and writers understand how this is done, primarily by analyzing the successes and failures of major games like *Life is Strange* (Dontnod Entertainment 2015).

UNDERSTANDING A CULTURE OF CHARACTERS AND GAME LOVE

Yet another lens from which to understand love and affection in games is through the perspective of love of characters. That is to say that love for a character, or feeling and expressing affection toward a game character, fits the constraints of affection in game spaces. This can range from the affections expressed about in-game characters, to the pragmatic expression of affection in games toward characters. Players might love *Q*bert* or *Pac-Man*, but they might also spend game currency to buy an avatar a gift, give them a kiss, or more.

This is important to recognize, as much of the work in thinking about love and affection in games focuses on the portrayed affections. It considers how a player might make their player character emote affection or act in a loving way toward a non-player character. What such work does less frequently is ask how designs afford the player the ability to express affection from player (not player character) toward non-player or player characters. This is a tough lens to put in historical terms. Does it start with the first time a player declared that they love Pac-Man, because they love playing *Pac-Man*? Does it start when the player buys a better controller, to more effectively navigate the player character through their world? Does it start when players move to protect a virtual character, perhaps failing to complete a game to avoid harm to the virtual character? Does it start with fan art, depicting game characters?

The other problem with asking such questions is recognizing the moment of affection. Games are generally considered inanimate. They are created objects. Shintoism supports the notion that all inanimate objects have an energy, much like humans and animals. The four million or more people who practice Shintoism are primarily in Japan. Japan, as a country, is a significant producer of video games. It is reasonable to consider that the notion that games and game characters are worthy of affection has some, at least tangential, link to Shintoism.

Of course, the history of digital games in western culture views love of an inanimate objected and designed things differently. It decidedly views love and affection of people and living creatures as distinct from those of imagined or designed characters. In these cultures, loving *The Adventures of Tom Sawyer* (Twain 1876), is really about loving a book, which in turn is really about loving the writing of its author. This is ultimately is ascribed to liking, if not loving, the author. How then do game characters receive love from such a culture?

Does love and affection in games then arise when Nintendo popularizes the Nintendo Entertainment System and potentially brings the cultural elements of Shintoism to its players? This is, at best, a stretch. Instead, while analyzing love and affection for characters, it might be most effective to think about the cultural shift that moved games toward the kind of love and affection applied to fictional characters. The kind of perspective that shifted on-screen characters from odd abstractions to loveable Italian plumbers like Mario in *Super Mario Bros.* (Nintendo 1985) and frustrating archetypes like *Donkey Kong* (Nintendo 1981).

CONCLUSION

This chapter aimed at illuminating the many lenses from which affection games and affection in games can be understood. It provides the basic jumping off points from which any researcher or designer should engage in a more complete understanding of affection games. As this book is a primer, there is far more to be explored than will fit within these pages. However, each of the chapters offers a combination of these lenses to interpret and outline heuristics for the design of affection in games.

REFERENCES

Bailey, B. L. *From Front Porch to Back Seat: Courtship in Twentieth-Century America*. JHU Press, Baltimore, MD, 1989.

Benton, C. *Softporn Adventures*. Online Systems. 1981.

Bretherton, I. ed. *Symbolic Play: The Development of Social Understanding*. Academic Press, Orlando, FL, 2014.

Cate, R. M., and S. A. Lloyd. *Courtship*. Sage Publications, 1992.

Cullen, L. and J. Barlow. 2002. "'Kiss, cuddle, squeeze': The experiences and meaning of touch among parents of children with autism attending a touch therapy programme." *Journal of Child Health Care*, 6(3), 171–181.

Custer's Revenge. Mystique. 1982.

Daniels, B., D. Lebling, M. Blank, and T. Anderson. *Dungeon*. Commodore/PET. 1979. https://ifiction.org/games/playz.php?cat=1&game=386&mode=html.

Dark Room Sex Game. Copenhagen Game Collective. 2009.

Double Dragon. Nintendo. 1987.

Donkey Kong. Nintendo. 1981.

Enevold, J., and E. MacCallum-Stewart, Eds. *Game Love: Essays on Play and Affection*. McFarland, 2014.

Frogger. Konami, 1981.

Grace, L. D. "Affection Games in Digital Play: A Content Analysis of Web Playable Games." *DiGRA Conference*. 2013. http://www.digra.org/wp-content/uploads/digital-library/paper_359.pdf.

Grace, L. D. "Big huggin: a bear for affection gaming." In W. E. Mackay, S. Brewster, and S. Bødker (Eds.), *CHI'13 Extended Abstracts on Human Factors in Computing Systems*, pp. 2919–2922. ACM, New York, 2013.

Grace, L. D. "Objects of Affection: Kissing Games on Mobile Devices." In B. Li and M. Nelson (Eds.), *Foundations of Digital Games*, Society for the Advancement of Digital Games, Santa Cruz, CA, 2015.

Grace, L. D. *Doing Things with Games: Social Impact Through Play*. CRC Press, Boca Raton, FL, 2019.

Grand Theft Auto IV. Rockstar Games. 2013.

Lemonade Stand. MECC (Minnesota Educational Computing Consortium). 1979.

Liberati, N. 2017. "Teledildonics and new ways of 'Being in Touch': A phenomenological analysis of the use of haptic devices for intimate relations." *Science and Engineering Ethics*, 23(3), 801–823.

Life is Strange. Dontnod Entertainment. 2015.

Livingston, G., and D'Vera Cohn. "U.S. birth rate falls to a record low; decline is greatest among immigrants." In *Pew Research Social and Demographic Trends*, November 29, 2012. https://www.pewsocialtrends.org/2012/11/29/u-s-birth-rate-falls-to-a-record-low-decline-is-greatest-among-immigrants/

Manderson, L., P. Liamputtong, and P. Liamputtong Rice, eds. *Coming of Age in South and Southeast Asia: Youth, Courtship and Sexuality*. No. 30. Psychology Press, 2002.

McDonald, H. *Digital Love: Romance and Sexuality in Games*. AK Peters/CRC Press, Boca Raton, FL, 2017.

Nam, H. Y. "Game controller using kiss." U.S. Patent 8,439,755, issued May 14, 2013.

Nichols, S. and E. S. Byers. 2016. "Sexual well-being and relationships in adults with autism spectrum disorder." *Autism Spectrum Disorder in Mid and Later Life*, 248–262.

O'Dell, J. W., and J. Dickson. 1984. "Eliza as a 'therapeutic' tool." *Journal of Clinical Psychology*, 40(4), 942–945.

Oregon Trail. MECC (Minnesota Educational Computing Consortium). 1974.

Pac-Man. Namco. 1980.

*Q*bert*. Gottlieb. 1982.

Smooth Operators. Heydeck Games. 2013.

Softporn Adventure. Online Systems. 1981.

Stanton, C. M., P. H. Kahn, R. L. Severson, J. H. Ruckert, and B. T. Gill. "Robotic animals might aid in the social development of children with autism." In *2008 3rd ACM/IEEE International Conference on Human-Robot Interaction (HRI)*, pp. 271–278. IEEE, 2008.

Strachey, C. "MUC Love Letter Generator (1952)." *Ferranti Mark* 1. https://en.wikipedia.org/wiki/Strachey_Love_Letter_algorithm. Last modified July 27, 2018.

Super Mario Bros. Nintendo. 1985.

Sutton-Smith, B. 1959. "The kissing games of adolescents in Ohio." *Midwest Folklore*, 9(4), 189–211.

Tsuya, N. O. "Below-replacement fertility in Japan: Patterns, factors, and policy implications." *Low and Lower Fertility*, pp. 87–106. Springer, Cham, 2015.

Twain, M. *The Adventures of Tom Sawyer*. Oxford University Press, Oxford, 2007 [1876].

Unicorn Makeout Mania. SoftwareSoft. 2013.

CHAPTER 3

On Flirting Games and In-Game Flirts

Lindsay D. Grace

CONTENTS

OF ALL THE TRADITIONAL affection game verbs, "flirting" is the most nuanced. It is so nuanced in the real world that many people miss it entirely. It is subtle, except when it's not. It is a signal for something more, without explicitly indicating the more. "Flirting" in its dictionary definition is really simply behaving amorously, without serious intent. But it also includes the notion of expressing casual or superficial interest. It is perhaps the least committed of the amorous game verbs and the most abstract.

Perhaps unsurprisingly, flirting even has multiple wikiHow articles, ranging from how to flirt with real-life females (Schewitz 2019), men (wikiHow Staff 2019), and through a video game (Wikihow Staff 2018). The steps range in number from as few as ten and as many fourteen. This is at least a hint that it's a deliberate action, one that some people plan and research. The how-to, or mechanics, of flirt are far less clear than the basics of giving a kiss or hug.

The mechanics and efficacy of flirting are so culturally intertwined that it's almost futile to try to separate them. An effective flirt is as much a product of time and place, as it is person, context, and randomness. Despite this seemingly amorphous character, there are some rules from which game design can borrow to formalize the ambiguities of flirting. While it might seem that flirting is one of the more abstract affection verbs, it's also one of the social cues that there might be a something more amorous in the future. But, as its definition hints, there's no promise, only potential.

Why then, would a book aiming to help designers and researchers understand the generally-unexplored space of affection games start with flirting? It's simple. It's where many of the other affections start. Flirting, from the literature is cueing (Gersick and Kurzban 2014). It is a sign that something more is about to start.

In my past writing about game design, I illuminated five essential elements of every game (Grace 2019). If a game lacks one of these, or they are ill-defined, the play experience is more likely to be a play experience and not a full game. The five elements that differentiate play (kicking a ball on a field) from games (football and kickball) are: competition, implements, territory, inventory, and rules.

In the play of flirting, territory is everything. What flirting does is cue those involved with the flirt that the play space has been entered. It signals the start of something different. In the animal world, this might be done through a bird's dance, or the gestures of a mammal's body. In the human world, it might be similar physical cues (a.k.a., body language), but it might also include how something is said in online chat, or the way someone dances at a bar. But what's important is to understand that flirting is a part of a territory.

To enter the flirt state is to enter the territory of flirt. This territory has a variety of demarcations. Typically, it can't be too serious, or it ceases to be playful. It can't be too aggressive, because that ceases to keep the levity to which flirts are ascribed. The edges of flirt are perhaps more ambiguous than its start. A wink as a flirt might read as an invitation, but following a flirt with a declaration of love or proposal of marriage is likely to cross the line. That is of course, subject to a whole other set of cultural and context cues. Any creative could imagine a situation, perhaps among long-time friends, or as part of a comedic first meeting, in which the same flirt fails or flies.

RECOGNIZING FLIRTS: ON CONSENT IN PLAY SYSTEMS

The human brain is admittedly complex, and so too are the ways in which it interprets information. Not every flirt is noticed, and not every flirt is invited. As is apropos to such work, this book focuses on consensual situations. In this context that means flirts must be intended. It also assumes that when discussing flirts between players, those flirts are consented.

It should go without saying, flirting without consent is not just creepy, it can even be illegal (a.k.a., sexual harassment). This is why the focus of this chapter centers on the notion of *flirting with*. Flirting with implies some modicum of consent or agreement between those involved in the flirt. Even in the case of human-computer flirting, the ideal situation is that the computer system has been designed to accept (a.k.a., consent) to such flirting. The moral and theoretical complexities of this consent—how it's expressed and what it means—are worthy of a book unto itself. It could be argued that until a developer explicitly designs such intention and invitation into an algorithm, there is no clear consent.

Likewise, one might argue that consent—by developer intention, player use, and any autonomy given the system—are all independent, especially when considering machine learning and artificial intelligence systems. In short, just as there is understood to be an age of consent for humans, it could be argued that computer systems are not at their developmental age of consent. It could also be argued that those last sentences are entirely baseless claims, not worthy of further discussion. In short, we have a long way to go before there are clear definitions of "consenting computer systems" in play. While systems might consent in terms of input validation or security, our relatively immature history of human-computer relationship means we are still seeking to understand "consent" in play systems.

To focus these explorations, it's easiest to assume that each flirting interaction is about players flirting between players in a system that allows players to consent to such interactions, or with players flirting with a system that consents to such interaction by design and algorithmic intention. This is what is meant by flirting with, not flirting at or toward. By doing so, it implies a two-part system that not only expresses the flirt, but recognizes the flirt. By analogy, when that bird shows its feathers as a mating cue, it is only a complete mating cue if seen and recognized by its recipient. Otherwise it's a little dance or flutter, not a flirt. Hence, for humans to flirt with each other through play—or to flirt in human-computer interaction play—the flirt must be communicated and received.

The English language supports this perception simply. Flirting is done *with*, not *to*, its subject. Even the old expression, flirting with death, is understood this way. That's because flirting is very much like play. Just as people are played with, flirting is done between people, not to people.

This means as a case study in designing affection it's a particularly apt place to start. To effectively flirt takes at least two consenting people. It may only take only one to start a flirt, but like a volley, it's only true when it is recognized and an attempt to return is applied.

This is particularly important in both understanding the history and identification of flirting and flirt-enabled games. Some games allow, or susceptible to, flirts at, not with. The earliest text adventure games, for example, allowed players to communicate whimsical flirts, but the systems were not typically designed to accommodate much of a volley. The player could attempt a verbal flirt or offer a game verb as a command that might imply some kind of flirt. In the end, the system did little to return the flirt. If a player types "I find you very attractive" as the opening move in the 1976 version of *Colossal Cave Adventure* (1977), the response is "all I understood is that you wanted to take inventory." The system responds as a computer would, all business and clearly no volley.

Later games, such as *Leisure Suit Larry* (1987) or some of the other Sierra Entertainment games are obvious examples. The *Larry* series contained many situations involving versions of flirting. While an alternate version of the *King's Quest* franchise, *King's Quest III: To Heir is Human* (AGD Interactive 2011) contained small moments using a character known anonymously as Barmaid. She provided extra-marital flirt dialogue and rewarded the player character with a lute if he played it for her. But such games were designed with flirting in mind. They are part of consenting systems. Their systems expected players to flirt.

And of course, this is where the notion of digital flirting becomes so complicated. If it takes two to flirt, then what's left for the computer? In the history of computer dating, there was of course plenty of flirting through the computer. In the history of simulations like *Eliza* (Weizenbaum 1966), there was likely some flirting with the computer. In the first move of the simulation, players are prompted with "Hi! I'm Eliza, What's your problem." If the player responds, "I'm in love with you," the response is an awkwardly mechanical "Did you come to me because you are in love with I?" Yet the system is much more accommodating to the player response "I'm in love," to which it responds "How long have you been in love?" Yet in a new session, if the player responds to the initial prompt, "What's your problem" the conversation almost always takes a flirtatious trajectory as shown in Figure 3.1.

If the player continues along these lines, the algorithm takes a turn. If the player responds, "I love you" when responding to the psychoanalytic

```
Would you like a transcript? (Y/N)

ELIZA -- an interactive parroting

From Creative Computing magazine;
adapted for the IBM PC by Patricia Danielson and Paul Hashfield;
readapted for Inform by Ricardo Dague.
[type "shut up" to end]


Hi! I'm Eliza. What's your problem?

>I think you're beautiful
Do you really think so?

>Yes
Are you sure?

>Very much so
Say, do you have any psychological problems?

>_
```

FIGURE 3.1 The *Eliza* interactive experience responses when attempting to flirt with the system.

problems, the result is a direct "we were discussing you—not me." Eliza accepts some flirts, but in much the way it's designed to respond as a mature, professional counselor. Out of context, and noting only the first interactions, it might seem the player is afforded a kind of successful flirt. This ambiguity comes from the arguably positive response "do you think so" which could be read as inviting more compliments (i.e., tell me more). It could also be read as a less-inviting mechanical read (i.e., is that what you're thinking). Either way, the end result of the interaction is all business, with an abrupt closure to the player's attempted flirt. This after all, is a business relationship in the fiction of the *Eliza* system.

WHAT THEN CAN A DESIGNER DO TO SUPPORT "FLIRTING WITH"?

One way to answer this question is to follow the example of other game designers who have aimed to translate human nature, psychology, or sociology into playable experiences. When Will Wright sought to design the complexities of human wants and desires into Sims games, he used the writing of Abraham Maslow on the hierarchy of needs (Maslow 1943), and Charles Hampden-Turner's *Maps of the Mind* (1982). So too, as designers seek to involve flirting in games, the simplest solution is to borrow from the experts. Specifically, to examine the formal formulas, patterns, and dynamics that researchers have developed to explain flirting. Adapting these into playable models, is one the most ready-made ways to incorporate flirting into playable experience. Such formal models and evaluations exist in three specific research collections. These are game theory, varied sociology, and self-help books.

The first is the formal research of game theory. This Nash-born set of game theories (Nash 1950) seeks to understand the logical conclusions to a variety of human interactions, including the pursuit of mates (their terms not mine). In short economic theorists offer formulas for the balance of risk versus reward in flirting among other courtship activities. These have a variety of names and common representations, often based on game theory dynamics like the Prisoner's Dilemma and Waiting for Mr. Perfect.

The second is a variety of individual research trajectories that seek to understand the ways in which flirting works in general society. These are less about formalizing how they are done than how they are used. Elaine Hall (1993), for example, researched gendered table service in restaurants to understand perceptions of good service. One highlight of such research is the notion that female servers performed a "job flirt" in restaurants. The research highlights the role of gender, gender expectations, and customer expectation.

Such research can serve the game and narrative design community well. Consider for example, the notion that a non-player character can be considered a kind of service industry worker. Non-player characters keep players in games, so engendering an NPC with the ability to do a job flirt, might mean the difference between player retention and player withdrawal. From this one perspective, the game designer can borrow from the playbook of table service job flirts. Restaurant research, among others, can inform game design. Of course, there's a lot of research on flirting in many disparate social science areas. This book wouldn't be worth much if it didn't make that research a little easier for its readers. As such the following are highlights of a few key findings that appear ready to integrate into game design:

- **Flirtations as prelude and mechanic:** Cunningham and Barbee (2008) offer a model for the hypothetical phases of relationship initiation which they describe thus:

  > relationship initiation begins with the biology (such as gender and temperament), background (such as culture), motives, and expectations of each person. Similarly, our model begins with *prioritize desires*, which focuses on how salient motives and expectations affect the courtship sequence as a function of a

variety of individual and social variables. This first stage has an impact on subsequent flirtation and courtship stages, which we term (b) attract attention, (c) notice and approach, (d) talk and reevaluate, and (e) touch and synchronize, that follow in the dance of courtship. The model is offered as an organizational heuristic rather than as a fixed sequence of actions.

- **Models of miscommunication:** Henningsen (2004, 481) works to examine how miscommunications occur in flirting interactions, noting that gender identity differences effect perceptions. The research notes that:

  Men tend to view flirting as more sexual than women do, and women attribute more relational and fun motivations to flirting interactions than do men. No gender differences emerge for esteem, exploring, or instrumental motivations. This dynamic is likely useful to gender specific design, especially when trying to accurately portray flirting in game.

- **Opening dialogue and flirting:** Weber et al. (2010, 185) conducted a study with more than six hundred college students to understand which of ten opening lines were was most appropriate and effective:

  Results indicated that participants rated the third-party introduction and direct introduction opening lines as the most appropriate … direct compliments, humor attempts, and cute-flippant lines were rated as equally inappropriate and ineffective.

In the most academic terms, flirting can be categorized as part of interpersonal communication. That means there is an entire body of literature about its communication and interpretation that spans more than twenty years. While the research into body language is more likely to help animators and motion capture actors, small budget games can also find use in the cues that support the physical human expression of a flirt.

More recently, research into pragmalingusitics and sociopragmatics could be stretched to include the recognition of flirting and aligned social cues. As the number of people with autism spectrum disorder (ASD) increases, these fields, and the relationship to perceived and recognize affection becomes even more complex. To be clear, understanding affection games is not only about design deeper experiences, it's also about bridging experiential gaps, translating experiences, and supporting individuals who may express affection differently than the romantic novels of the twentieth century described. Recognizing that players may be on the autism spectrum, means that designers may need to find multiple ways to communicate the sociopragmatics of a flirt. It also means there is opportunity for games to educate players and support their experience both in and outside of the game.

The third collection of literature, if it can be called that, rests with the variety of self-help guides and self-described gurus of flirt. While this might be generously described as informal research, it offers an opportunity to understand very specific, if not always healthy, views of flirting. They can serve as a kind of baseline set of mechanics.

While much of the literature in this space is considered popular psychology, or simply pop-writing, it's useful to consider how such work aims to formalize in accessible terms some of the more complicated ideas evaluated by other researchers. Of these, one well-praised collection is Gary Chapman's *Love Language* (2009). These books aim to explore and explain a primary thesis that each person has a love language through which they both express and understand love.

In Chapman's terms these languages are:

1. ***Words of affirmation:*** using words to build up the other person. "Thanks for taking out the garbage." Not—"It's about time you took the garbage out. The flies were going to carry it out for you."
2. ***Gifts:*** a gift says, "He was thinking about me. Look what he got for me."
3. ***Acts of Service:*** Doing something for your spouse that you know they would like. Cooking a meal, washing dishes, vacuuming floors, are all acts of service.
4. ***Quality time:*** by which I mean, giving your spouse your undivided attention. Taking a walk together or sitting on the couch with the TV off—talking and listening.
5. ***Physical touch:*** holding hands, hugging, kissing, sexual intercourse, are all expressions of love.

(Chapman 2009, 14)

While this can be applied beyond flirting, it's useful to start with their application to games through flirting. This is because flirting is an initiative act, and as such, those who seek specific love languages are likely to express first through their language of preferences. If a person understands love through providing gifts, for example, they might provide a gift as a way to cue flirting.

For game design this might express itself in a variety of ways. When deciding how to afford a player the ability to flirt with another player or a non-player character, the player may be given options that equate to their love languages. They might be allowed to:

- To give a flirtatious gift;
- To do a flirtatious act of service;
- To speak flirtatiously;
- Touch in a flirtatious way; or
- To spend a significant amount of time with another player or non-player character.

These are particularly evident in the content of role-playing games, where virtual currency, and player–non-player character encounters, and player-player interactions abound. Large virtual worlds, such as *World of Warcraft* or the formerly popular *Second Life* are evident spaces in which such activities are readily available and apparent.

It is of course, no surprise that varying levels of flirting and relationships exist in these worlds. Many of these activities are also the foundation verbs of and activities of relationship Sims. In the most complex relationship Sims, players develop their relationships through very similar activities. In networked play, many of these affordances are simple enough to create. If players can exchange in-game items, then it's likely that the language of gifts is supported. If they can cooperate or share resources, quality time (e.g., working together on a game task), the acts of service (doing a game task for another player) may be supported. Likewise, physical touch, while often virtually presented, are likely available through in-game representation.

That's the good news for designers. What becomes more difficult is keeping an eye on these affordances when the environment is not a role-playing game or virtual world. When the player might be experiencing a kind of relationship simulation, but the relationship is not the key goal in the game. A *Call of Duty* player (Activision 2003) for example, could receive a gift from a non-player character that implies a kind of flirt. But in so doing this by design, the players who reads such action as a flirt are more likely to be those who bias toward gifts as love language. So, if a non-player character hands one player a great weapon with a wink, some players may have preferred that the character had gone on the mission with them or given them a hug before they left.

In turn, for those who design relationship Sims, it's easy to provide an unbalanced set of love languages. Players may be annoyed or disconnected from a game that's largely about earning the affection of a non-player character through gifts, when what they want is the non-player character to do an act of service (e.g., provide some in-game currency). There are many ways to evaluate this interplay, between love languages and player need, but ultimately the designer has to divine how such flirts are going to be perceived.

What the love languages framework provides is a way to think of player action across the spectrum of expressions. Instead of merely thinking of flirtatious things to say, as is common in some games, or the ability to give an object, a wider assortment of flirts may appeal to a wider audience. This applies across the spectrum of player interactions. If players can flirt with other players through the game's system, they might engage with the play space more, in much the way that people go to bars and clubs because they are often appropriate play spaces for flirting. In terms of player to non-player character interactions, the opportunity to entice a player toward affections for the game characters might be amplified if the nonplayer character is speaking the player's love language. Algorithmically this could be done by self-identification or by opportunities to make choices at the start of the game that help identify the player's own biases in receiving and communicating love as discussed in Chapman's title (2009).

Consider this in the context of virtual worlds like the old *Second Life*. As players created relationships in the world, the environments affordance dictated their abilities. While players did get *Second Life* married, the environment's constraints dictated how those marriages began and ended. Flirts in that environment were encoded as gifts, expressions, and virtual body language. Technically, in much the way that someone could build service into *Minecraft*, there were opportunities for players to do acts of service. Players could build something for another player or help a player do something. This is a flirting activity that is supported by the designed experience, although not explicitly built into the experience as closely as speech. It's likely that effective designers who support more varied means of expression will find more players content with the experience. But it's also important to note that in systems that warrant it, players seem to find a way to meet their love language needs through the system. That is, of course, save for touch, which is at best virtual-touch in the game.

GAME EXAMPLES

It's obviously useful to use existing games to understand how flirting has been effective or ineffective. This book contains an entire section of case studies that aims to illuminate all the varied elements of love and affection as they relate to both major AAA releases and independent games. Therefore, this chapter concludes with two simple case studies as a way to examine how the concepts in this chapter play out. These case studies are not provided as critique of the individual works, but instead as an opportunity to understand how games have explored flirting in relation to this chapter's content. It's an opportunity to look backward, as a way of plotting a path forward.

SCHOOL GIRL FLIRT

The easiest game to start with is the simplest. *School Girl Flirt* (Girls Go Game 2009) is one of several clones for a common game mechanic. In the game the player's goal is to flirt with as many non-player characters as possible. Each time they flirt they collect those non-player characters, who trail behind them in a lustful daze. This game, and its clones, all have the same basic mechanic. Players are basically engaged in a shooting mechanic, where they must capture their victims, sometimes while competing with others.

This game removes all the nuance of flirting in an almost juvenile naiveté that emulates a childlike perspective of flirting. Much like a doe-eyed middle-schooler who thinks they've fallen in love with a classmate, the player need only stare to capture the heart of the other. This game is as simple in its depiction of flirting as it is in its understanding. From the mechanics of these games, flirting is a kind of tag. Targets are sighted. They have no choice but to fall victim to the flirt. They are not flirted with, they are flirted at. Flirting is not a product of some dynamic as much as they are subject to the seduction. The result is a simple kind of seductive power fantasy—one look from the player character and all males are theirs. This is not a complex game.

Yet even in this simplicity is a series of encoded values that illustrate how complicated analysis of such work can be. First note that the goal is merely to collect the attention of these flirt victims, with no intention of doing anything more with them. The goal of the game is to catch-and-keep, not catch-and-release. It also hints at no further steps. The flirt is the endgame for each target. There is no date, no hug or kiss, no further aim. This is a collecting game. It simply happens to uses flirting as its primary game verb.

Second, is the way in which the game encodes gender competition. Player's resource limitations are only time and energy. The only threat to a player's performance is wasting time on less than desirable males and the competition. This encapsulates a very specific view of gender competition. The victims of the flirt have no choice but to succumb. The competition, has no choice but to compete using her own abilities. At no point do the genders interact otherwise. The females never talk to other females, nor do they ever talk to the males. There is no space in this game for negotiation or for expressing a love language. There is only the flirtatious stare and its power to catch the attention of its victim.

What this game illustrates is that even in the simplest of games, there is much to be understood and interpreted about specific philosophies on flirting (and love). This is so before characters are developed, relationships managed, or any other mechanics offered. As a case study it helps illuminate that even with the simplest of mechanics and the most basic game goals, much is communicated about values in play.

THE SIMS

The Sims franchise is an interesting case study in that while the game contains flirting, it is not often thought of as an affection game. In juxtaposition to *School Girl Flirt* and it's clones, it is a very big game with much more content, far more complexity, and a richer collection of game verbs. It contains plenty of affection, but in the literature, people often focus on the psychological and sociological models of the game. This is in part because the game focuses so much on meeting needs, and those needs are not always about affection. It's also because despite the anthropomorphic qualities of the non-player characters, they tend to be perceived as complex dolls rather than characters. They speak a language distinct to the themselves, and in the early Sims versions in particular, act less like autonomous beings and more like pets. Obviously, of the five love languages, the one that's surprisingly least developed in the *Sims* is words of affirmation.

Sims is (as it has been described in the past) a kind of doll or pet management game. The result is that player affections toward Sims is much more like the love of a parent to a child, or an owner to a pet. The player is in charge of meeting the needs of the Sims, but not of involving themselves romantically with the Sims. For this reason it's a reasonable subject for the analysis of player-computer love and affection in a parent-child framing. More thorough analysis of parenting love and affection is examined in Chapter 5, "Would You Kindly Parent?: Parenting, Caretaking, and Love in Games," by Dr. Karen Schrier.

REFERENCES

Call of Duty. Activision, 2003.

Chapman, Gary. *The Five Love Languages: How to Express Heartfelt Commitment to Your Mate*. Moody Publishers, Chicago, IL, 2009.

Colossal Cave Adventure. William Crowther and Don Woods. 1977.

Cunningham, M. R., & Barbee, A. P. (2008). Prelude to a kiss: Nonverbal flirting, opening gambits, and other communication dynamics in the initiation of romantic relationships. In Sporecher, S., Wenzel, A., and Harvey, J., (Eds.), *Handbook of Relationship Initiation*, pp. 97–120, Psychology Press, New York, 2008.

Eliza. Joseph Weizenbaum. 1966.

Gersick, Andrew, and Robert Kurzban. "Covert sexual signaling: Human flirtation and implications for other social species." *Evolutionary Psychology* 12, no. 3 (2014): 147470491401200305.

Grace, Lindsay D. *Doing Things with Games: Social Impact Through Play*. CRC Press, Boca Raton, FL, 2019.

Hall, Elaine J. "Smiling, deferring, and flirting: Doing gender by giving 'good service.'" *Work and Occupations* 20, no. 4 (1993): 452–471.

Hampden-Turner, Charles. *Maps of the Mind*. Macmillan Publishing Company, New York, 1982.

Henningsen, David D. "Flirting with meaning: An examination of miscommunication in flirting interactions." *Sex Roles* 50, no. 7–8 (2004): 481–489.

King's Quest III: To Heir Is Human. AGD Interactive. 2011.

Leisure Suit Larry. Sierra Entertainment. 1987.

Maslow, Abraham H. "A theory of human motivation." *Psychological Review* 50, no. 4 (1943): 370.

Nash, John F. "Equilibrium points in *n*-person games." *Proceedings of the National Academy of Sciences* 36, no. 1 (1950): 48–49.

Schewitz, Sarah. "How to Flirt with Women", May 15, 2019. wikiHow https://www.wikihow.com/Flirt-With-Women

School Flirting Game. Girls Go Games. 2009. https://www.girlsgogames.com/game/school-flirting-game

Weber, Keith, Alan K. Goodboy, and Jacob L. Cayanus. "Flirting competence: An experimental study on appropriate and effective opening lines." *Communication Research Reports* 27, no. 2 (2010): 184–191.

wikiHow Staff, "How to Flirt on a Video Game with Online Players", January 20, 2018, https://www.wikihow.com/Flirt-on-a-Video-Game-With-Online-Players

wikiHow Staff, "How to Flirt with a Guy", November 9, 2019, wikiHow https://www.wikihow.com/Flirt-with-a-Guy

CHAPTER 4

In the Mood for Love

Embodiment and Intentionality in NPCs

Renata E. Ntelia

CONTENTS

This chapter examines the experience of romantic love between a player and a non-playable character (NPC) in the context of single-player avatarial games. "Romantic love" is to be understood here as the experience of being in love with someone. As such, it is demarcated from other types of love, (e.g., love for friends, family members, divine love, etc.). In this chapter, it is argued that for a game to successfully afford the experience of romantic love there are two main challenges that need to be addressed. One is the embodiment of the NPCs and the other is their intentionality. This means that the game should provide for NPCs that are to be perceived by the player as autonomous subjects with their own intentions and goals rather than passive bodies that cater to the player's agency. The argument is built upon embodied perception, Merleau-Ponty's phenomenology, and Sartre's existentialism. It is finally argued that this challenge will eventually be overcome by artificially generated agents rather than fictional, designed characters.

INTRODUCTION

Olli Tapio Leino (2015) in "I know your type, you are a player: Suspended Fulfillment in Fallout: New Vegas" discusses three types of love that can be afforded in video games. He calls those three types of love (1) vicarious love, (2) fictional love, and (3) love in bad faith. According to him, vicarious love is felt by the player when they see themselves as distanced from the romantic relationship, which takes place between the avatar and the NPC. Fictional love, on the other hand, is when the player feels romantic attraction for an NPC while being aware of the NPC's fictionality, namely that they are not real so the only romantic relationship the player can have with them is in the context of role-playing. The last type of game love is defined by Leino as love in bad faith, which means that the player refuses to acknowledge the fictionality of the NPC by refraining from participating in those in-game actions that will shatter their illusion that there can never be a real romantic relationship between the player and the NPC.

Using *Fallout: New Vegas* as his example, Leino describes how he purposefully avoided interacting with the NPC Rose of Sharon Cassidy during his playthrough so as to sustain the illusion of having the possibility of a real romantic affair with her. He compares his experience to that argued by Sartre as bad faith. He contends that this experience of romantic love is the closest to a real relationship a player can have in a video game and that it is a medium-specific experience different from other media, which offer de facto fictional romances. He argues that even love in bad faith sooner or later is transformed to vicarious or fictional love, exactly because it is very fragile: a single interaction with the game system can potentially disrupt this experience in the same way that bad faith cannot be sustained for long in the physical world as well.

Notwithstanding the different experiences of romantic love the player can have in games, Leino's argument stems from the same fundamental premise: there can never be an authentic romantic love relationship for the player with an in-game entity. For Leino, this is due to the ontic difference between the player and the NPC. This reality is what the player tries to forget when they are acting in bad faith. But what exactly is this ontic difference? Leino connects it with the NPC's, Cassidy's in this case, fictionality. As a fictional character, Cassidy has certain limitations, which deny the player the romantic fulfillment of their attraction to Cassidy or any other NPC: "The knowledge of Cass as less than real implies knowledge of the impossibility of fulfillment and as such is prone to killing the uncertainty characteristic to romantic attraction, hence revealing the feelings of anticipation as plain pretense" (Leino 2015).

Leino pinpoints the fictionality of the NPCs in the same way that Aarseth talks about the difference between virtual and fictional in relation to doors in digital games. Aarseth (2007) argues that in digital games there are some doors that can be opened, which are then virtual, and some that are only decorative, which are fictional. Following the same rationale, Leino contends that NPCs are both virtual and fictional: in some aspects, they can be interacted with so that makes them virtual while in some others they cannot so they are fictional. In the player's falling in love with them they are fictional because, according to Leino, the player cannot fulfill their romantic attachment to them. In this sense, he calls this type of love fictional, since it is formed with a fictional character. Leino does not call the emotion experienced by the player fictional but only the object of the player's affection: "qualities of emotions do not necessarily have anything to do with the qualities of the actually existing object of the emotion" (Leino 2015).

Thus, Leino concludes that a person can fall in love with a fictional entity, yet this cannot be an authentic romantic love because if a person knows that they are in love with a fictional being then they are aware that their love can never be fulfilled. This claim demands closer consideration. It is argued that it surpasses Leino's game example and can be examined for drawing conclusions for human-player to NPC romantic interactions in single-player, avatarial games in general. Avatarial is understood in the sense of a game that includes a visible, in whole or in part, body which is controlled by the player and an implied, most of the times at least, second body, which constitutes the camera body; this second body follows the playable character and can be directly controlled by the player or not (Rehak 2003, 109). Indicative titles of avatarial games that include player-NPC romance are: the *Witcher* series (CD Project Red 2007–2015), the *Mass Effect* series (BioWare 2007–2012), *Batman: The Telltale Series* (Telltale Games 2016), *Heavy Rain* (Quantic Dream 2010), *Life is Strange* (Dontnod Entertainment 2015), and *Catherine* (Atlus 2011).

How exactly does the fictionality of the NPCs in such games not allow the fulfillment of authentic romantic love? Leino does not go into detail when it comes to this; the NPCs' inability to have a romantic relationship is explained by their fictionality. Here, the ontic difference between the real player and the fictional NPC is further analyzed. The argument revolves around two main anchors: one is the embodiment and the other is intentionality. It is argued that these two aspects constitute the NPC's fictionality when it comes to romantic love and as such challenge the ability of games to offer an authentic romantic love experience between a player and an NPC.

PHYSICALITY AND EMBODIMENT

The first aspect, embodiment, is arguably the most overt. The player possesses a physical body and the NPC does not. To experience romantic love is usually tightly connected with its embodied aspect. Evolutionary psychologists, biologists, and neurologists having examined the physiology of humans argue that romantic love is an evolutionary system in the human brain activated by certain hormones and amino acids (Fisher et al. 2002; Sternberg and Weis 2006; Bartels and Zeki 2000; Beauregarda et al. 2009; Langeslag et al. 2012). As a physiological system romantic love is connected to reproduction and sexuality, therefore physicality constitutes a significant part of its experience (Platek et al. 2006; Fisher 1997; Meyer et al. 2011; Jones 1996). At the same time, the poetics of romantic love speaks of a different story. Platonic love is a whole attitude towards love, in which physicality is refused (Price 1981). Romantic love as a literary genre is founded in works, in which "love did not have as its aim either carnal pleasure or reproduction" (Paz 1995, 90). This becomes more prominent in the Romantic era, during which love is treated in the duality of the beautiful and the sublime (Eldridge 2001).

Nevertheless, as Mario Praz notices the sublimity of the romantic object of desire is an experience infused with terror, pain, and mortality—all of which constitute a testimony to one's own physical body (1951). In the same fashion, platonic love does not negate the physicality of lovers. The lovers choose not to contemplate the physical traits of their relationship because they are very well aware that they are there. The possibility of platonic love turning into physical is always present (Secomb 2007; Plato 2018). Instead, the NPC's physicality is never a given. It is not that the player chooses not to notice the physicality of the NPC but rather the player must refrain from thinking that the NPC is not a physical being so as to retain as much as possible the illusion of a romance. This is indeed an ontological difference between the physical player and the virtual love interest. Yet does this affect the perception of the NPCs by the player as embodied agents they can fall in love with? I argue that human players indeed perceive virtual characters as embodied agents due to embodied perception.

Following a cognitive neuroscience perspective, Morrison and Ziemke (2005) examine how human players relate to computer game characters. They argue that when we play a video game our brains transform figures on a flat screen to embodied characters. As they explain this is due to the mechanism of visuo-affective mappings, which "transform visual information about someone else's emotional state into similar emotional dispositions of our own" (73). Visuo-affective mappings compliment the already known visuomotor mappings "when objects in the coordinate system of external space are transformed into a coordinate system of which the body and its effectors (e.g., hands, arms) are at the center," and visuotactile mappings "in which visual and touch information become integrated into the brain's representational body schema" (74).

Gallese (2005) explains in more detail the neuroscientific workings of embodied perception. We perceive the space surrounding our body, our peripersonal space, the space which our body can act upon and affect, in a different fashion than the extrapersonal space. We do not visually code peripersonal space using a Cartesian or another geometrical system. Instead, our peripersonal space is a motor space, a space which we perceive by a "simulated motor action directed towards a particular spatial location" (26). Our body moves in the space it acts in and not in a predefined space of coordinates. Experiments further support these findings by showing that in the case of peripersonal space the spatial location of an object perceived by brain neurons has dynamic properties according to the change in time because it is a motor space and hence susceptive to time. According to Gallese action and spatial awareness are connected: "Vision, sound, and action are parts of an integrated system; the sight of an object at a given location, or the sound it produces, automatically triggers a 'plan' for a specific action directed toward that location" (27). This plan, according to him, is a "simulated potential action" (27). This means that we perceive our peripersonal space by what action plans it can sustain.

As Gallese remarks: "It is interesting to note the closeness of the view emerging from single neuron recordings, and the philosophical perspective offered by phenomenological philosophers on space perception" (2005, 27). Indeed, phenomenological space connects perception with movement; from Husserl and Heidegger to Gadamer, Sartre, and Merleau-Ponty (Zahavi 2002). Building on Husserlian and Heideggerian phenomenology, Merleau-Ponty (1962) set perception as the means by which we experience our world. According to his theory, we are by default subjects of perception and intentionality, intended actions that is, and this is how we experience existence, which is being in the world. He has argued that we perceive our world around us by the tasks we perform with our body. Our phenomenal body structures our world in accordance with its intentional relations with the objects around it. People perceive the world not as an ideal concept, but as a process of making meaning of their bodily intentions; their world exists based on their bodily actions. As a result, the body perceives both the world functioning as a subject and at the same time the body itself as the object of this making meaning process.

This body is not the fixed body of human anatomy. It is a lived body that has the ability to expand and extend. Merleau-Ponty gives an example of this in the walking stick of a blind man. For the blind man, Merleau-Ponty concludes, the stick is now part of his body, thus his body does not stop at his hand anymore but rather at the end of his stick providing him with expanded intentionality and perception of being. In the words of Merleau-Ponty, "the blind man's stick has ceased to be an object for him, and is no longer perceived for itself" (1962, 165). The same applies to instruments and tools. Merleau-Ponty describes how when a secretary masters the blind system of writing on a typewriter, the typewriter stops being an object for her body, but instead constitutes an extension of her bodily abilities that affords a novel intentionality and perception: "To get used to a hat, a car or a stick is to be transplanted into them, or conversely, to incorporate them into the bulk of our own body" (166). Then the stick and the typewriter are no longer perceived objects but instruments that augment our perception: "a bodily auxiliary, an extension of the bodily synthesis" (176).

Applying Merleau-Ponty's theory to video games, Rune Klevjer (2012) argues that the same workings are at play when we experience a game world. According to him, the avatars in games function as extensions of the players' body that allow them to extend their own bodies inside the screen. He particularly calls them "proxies" of the physical body inside the game world, since when the player controls an avatar the avatar is not any more an object on itself but an extension of the body of the player on screen (30). Klevjer describes the control of avatars like controlling a marionette, through which the bodily actions of the player are extended to the screen, on the environment of the marionette, enabling the player to inhabit by proxy the avatar's world.

For Klevjer, the in-screen extension demands an alteration of materiality that is essentially unique. When Merleau-Ponty says that for the blind man his body used to be here, where his fingers end, but with his stick his body is now there, at the point of his stick, both here and there reside in the same physical world. That is not the case with digital games. Klevjer contends that this is where the simulation of digital games lies; in the conceit of the continuation of tangibility. Nevertheless, I argue that this pretense of materiality does not affect the extension of the body, since this extension is a matter of perception. After all, although Merleau-Ponty had not anticipated a phenomenon like digital games, his theory is not limited by physicality: "The word 'here' applied to my body does not refer to a determinate position in relation to other positions or to external coordinates, but the laying down of the first co-ordinates, the anchoring of the active body in an object, the situation of the body in face of its tasks" (1962, 115).[1]

Merleau-Ponty may have conceived his theory based on the physical world, yet he did not consider it a prerequisite. On the contrary, it is the ability to manipulate one's body according to one's own intentions that attributes the state of worldness to the surrounding environment: "I can, therefore, take my place, through the medium of my body as the potential source of a certain number of familiar actions, in my environment conceived as a set of manipulanda" (1962, 120). Thusly, if we can act upon an environment to achieve certain tasks, then we immediately experience this environment as our world. We only need a body to *anchor upon* objects within this environment. In that sense, digital games offer the potentiality of worlds the player can inhabit, as they are environments the player can perform actions in. The fact that digital games are images on a flat-screen makes no difference to our perception. Since we can act on this space we perceive it as our peripersonal space, the space of our embodied actions.

This argument is supported by the neuroscientific application of Morrison and Ziemke mentioned before. They contend that our perception works the same way when we perform tasks in our physical world and "when we navigate through apparent positions in a game world, using the joystick to act upon objects within the game world as if our veridical hands were actually in that world's space" (Morrison and Ziemke 2005, 74). How does this relate to the player's treating NPCs as embodied agents? This is

---

[1] Heidegger's term would be *Geworfenheit*, being thrown into the world (1967, 135). For a more comprehensive application of the term to digital games see Vella and Gualeni (2019).

explained by the visuo-affective mappings referenced by Morrison and Ziemke, which are activated when we experience the emotional responses of others, in a virtual or the physical world. The cognitive workings of this are discussed in the following section.

AGENTS OF EMBODIMENT

Our embodied perception described above is equally responsible for our perception of other bodies as intentional beings, namely agents of intended actions. This again is connected with our body schema described by Gallese (2005). Our social coexistence demands that we are able to interpret the goals and intentions of the other bodies we share our environment with. This is a useful survival skill that we are able to achieve by relying once more on the simulation model we use to perceive our own movement and space. In other words, when we see someone performing an action our respective motor schema is activated as if we are the ones performing this action (Gibbs 2005, 35). By this translation of third-person observation to first-person perspective, we can apply to this action the goals and intentions we associate with this particular motor schema (Gallese 2005, 35). In this capacity, we perceive the embodied agents around us not simply as bodies performing actions but, as Gibbs contends, as: "volitional agents capable of entertaining, similarly to us, an agentive intentional relation to the world" (35–36). As such the other body becomes more than a representational system of behaviors, it becomes a person; or in phenomenological terms, the other does not merely have a body but they are a body, namely an "embodied subjectivity" (Zahavi 2007, 72).

Research has shown that humans and humanoids possess bimodal neurons called mirror neurons which help them perceive the actions of others as their own actions and thus understand them: "Action observation causes in the observer the automatic simulated re-enactment of the same action" (Gallese 2005, 32). This is true not only when humans perceive the actions of others but also their emotional responses: "We are not alienated from the actions, emotions, and sensations of others, because we entertain a much richer and affectively nuanced perspective of what other individuals do, experience, and feel" (31). For example, there is a common activation in our brains related to pain, disgust, touch, and fear when we both feel the emotions and see others experiencing them (Morrison and Ziemke 2005, 76). What is of particular importance for the current argument is that based on neuroimaging studies the brain area related to spatial cognition "did *not* differ between viewing agents in the real and virtual worlds" (Ziemke 2005, 74). That means that even though real and virtual worlds activate different networks of the brain, probably because of the "differences in the visual realism of the scenes" (74), our perception of others as embodied agents of enactment and emotional reactions does not differentiate between materialities.

Still, our brain system exhibits more intricate nuances. An fMRI study performed by Buccino et al. (2004) found that the mirror system responses of human participants did not differ significantly when they watched other humans, dogs, and monkeys biting food. Different networks were activated when the same subjects observed the objects performing activities that were species-specific: talking, barking, and lip-smacking respectively. It seems that our human brains tend to understand embodiment based on tasks that they have associated with their own embodiment, tasks that they perform with their own body. Biting food for a dog and a monkey is a motor-scheme similar to how humans bite their food. On the other hand, humans do not bark nor smack their lips.

Hence, we recognize as embodied an agent that manipulates their bodies in a fashion similar to ours, no matter if this agent shares our ontology or not. We perceive them as such because this is how we can relate to them, by bringing along our own perception and consciousness, which are bound by our embodiment and physicality. It is in this capacity that I can perceive the consciousness of the others. In Merleau-Ponty's words: "The other consciousness can be deduced only if the emotional expressions of others are compared and identified with mine, and precise correlations recognized between my physical behavior and my 'psychic events'" (1962, 410). How this transformation works depends on our biology, culture, and personal experience (Gibbs 2005). It is highly influenced by the degree of expertise of the subject on the performed action. Familiarity helps people translate bodily movements and emotional responses of others better (Gallese 2005). The general direction is, however, that we are far more likely to anthropomorphize other agents than the other way around (Basu and Dickstein 2018; Turner 2017; Roffe and Stark 2015). We simply look for agents that resemble us everywhere because this is how we perceive our world. It is much easier for us; it is perception in the first instance.

Understandably, realism plays an important factor in facilitating our perception of designed others as embodied agents. Rigid movement of a robot arm causes less identification with one's own arm movement (Morrison and Ziemke 2005, 77). Morrison and Ziemke make that connection to videogames: "It is intuitively obvious that the realism of display would play a part in the extent to which the user becomes engaged in the game world" (2005, 77). At the same time, not only does our perception influence virtual agents but virtual agents influence our perception (77). In the same fashion that our body can be augmented and/or added upon by tools, our constant exposure to virtuality can broaden our perception to include manifestations of embodiment that go beyond our physical world. In the same vein that typography created the typographic man of McLuhan (2011), virtuality may create the virtual human.

EMBODIED DESIGN

To bring this back to romance in digital games, the lack of physicality of NPCs does not deem them de facto fictional as romantic partners to our perception. They may not possess a physical body, but our perception of them allows us to bestow them with a body similar to our own. Verisimilitude is understandably important so as to eventually overcome the effect of the uncanny (Tinwell 2015). What is equally important is how virtual bodies can be perceived by the human player as bodies for love or, more difficult still, as bodies in love. The design, the mechanics, and the narrative can help facilitate or shatter this perception. Kirsh (2013) argues in favor of a human-computer interaction design, which will take an embodied perspective. He specifically argues that embodied cognition in digital design may open ways for us to think in new ways that are now inconceivable.

His rationale follows the principle that our interacting with tools changes the way we both think and perceive the world around us. Referencing neurophysiological, psychological, and neuropsychological research, he contends that the use of tools changes our body schema and our perception of space. This change is manifested despite the ontology or materiality of the tool: "our sense of where our body boundaries are, and what in space we can affect can be altered through telepresence and teleimmersion" (2013, 8). In this sense, we can employ digital tools and as such perceive digital space as the space of our action. The digital tools not only allow us to manipulate a materiality beyond our own but "in addition to altering our sense of where our body ends each tool reshapes our 'enactive landscape'—the world we see and partly create as active agents" (3). In other words, according to the tool we are using we perform our being in the world—for example, when one is holding a pen they experience their world as the accumulation of everything that can be written upon and at the same time since they can perform writing actions with the object they are holding they perceive it as a pen.

The more familiar and capable one becomes with the tool, their perception of the world changes as well. This is a dynamic process of expertise: "the concepts and beliefs we have about the world are grounded in our perceptual-action experience with things, and the more we have tool-mediated experiences the more our understanding of the world is situated in the way we interact through tools" (2013, 3). Kirsh borrows this position that people experience their environment by the ways it allows them to interact with it from Gibson, who introduced the term affordances (1966). The more actions we can perform with our bodies the more affordances our environment provides (e.g., if you can juggle you can see an object as affording juggling) (Kirsh 2013, 3). Gibson did not mention tools in his theory, yet as Kirsh suggests since the world is perceived in relation to the action repertoire of the perceiver, then "with a tool, the action repertoire is increased to include tool-enabled actions, so there ought to be new affordances to perceive" (9).

Kirsh connects perception with goals (2013, 10), bridging the gap of Gibsonian exegesis with phenomenology and embodied enactment, a definition proposed by Varela et al. (2016) according to which the world is a product of co-creation with an agent when this agent acts in a goal-oriented manner. Kirsh argues that designers create enactive landscapes: a structure that includes a "set of possibilities that can in principle be brought into being when an agent interacts with an underlying environment while engaged in a task or pursuing a goal" (2013, 11). This is not new in game design. Game environments incorporate game objects and/or objectives that afford certain actions the players can perform (McBride-Charpentier 2011; Cardona-Rivera and Young 2013). The added value of embodied cognition, besides providing a solid theoretical and scientific background, is that it explains how humans interpret the behavior of other agents with whom they share this virtual environment.

As it was argued before, when we see someone performing an action we translate this to as if we were the one performing this action. This is not only a matter of visual perception but of sensory interpretation in general. More importantly, we not only experience the other person's action as if it were our own but by doing so we apply certain goals, intentions, and sense to this action. This is our way of understanding the behavior of others in our social environment and based on this knowledge we can also predict behavioral patterns that will eventually be executed by others. In digital games, where the other agents inside the game world are designed, if we want the players to perceive NPCs as romantic agents, then they must perform and exhibit romantic intentions in an environment that affords actions we associate with romantic love.[2] The NPCs not only have to look as real as possible; they must allow through their actions, reactions, and interactions with the player and the environment to be perceived as bodies in love.

Grace (2017) explains that the type of involvement that games allow between the player and the NPC also affects the player's experience of them. As such, NPCs may afford the experience of romantic love if the player can interact with them romantically. This is not as straightforward as it may sound, however. What does romantic interaction entail? For some games, it is to include game verbs that are culturally associated with romantic love, such as flirting, kissing, hugging, and making love. These are the mechanics used in different variations in the *Sims* series (Maxis 2000–2019) for example, or in *Singles* (Rotobee 2003–2005).

Here one needs to note that the inclusion of a verb that implies romantic involvement does not solve the challenge as such. Having reviewed a vast corpus of affectionate games, Grace (2017) remarks how popular flirting games make use of the affectionate verbs just like a shooting game; the action of the verb is directed from the player to the NPC yet instead of the player throwing bullets, knives, and punches, they now throw kisses and hugs until they find their target and/or achieve their goal. A similar design is for the player to be collecting points through various in-game actions, which in turn increase the approval of the NPC until the player manages to win them over and/or unlock their romantic story tree path; a design choice used predominantly in dating Sims and otome visual novels, like *Clannad* (Key 2015) and *Hatoful Boyfriend* (Mediatonic 2014).

In those approaches, the NPC is a passive object to the player's agency. Such an implementation of romantic love and affection trivializes and simplifies the experience of love. This brings us eventually to the second issue pertaining to the games' inability to offer an authentic romantic relationship between a player and an NPC, namely the NPCs' lack of intentionality. As it was argued above, NPCs' ontic difference in terms of physicality can be overcome because our perception helps us, if not forces

[2] An interesting perspective on this is Doyle-Myerscough's analysis of intimacy in *The Last Guardian* (2019). It does not concern romantic love per se but intimacy is arguably a facet of it. Doyle-Myerscough describes how the gameplay of *The Last Guardian* helps build intimacy among the player, the playable character, and the NPC, which is an animal in this case.

us, to bestow embodiment to any agent that resembles us and shares our enactive space. The game design can facilitate this perception by means of verisimilitude and affording agency and embodiment to NPCs; meaning that the NPCs should be designed as bodies performing tasks in a world on the basis of their own specific goals, means, and intentions.

For romantic love, in particular, NPCs should be designed as intentional romantic interests or partners for the player. This is arguably the biggest tension between the physical player and the virtual NPC because NPCs as designed and coded behavior cannot bear the proof of intentionality for us to perceive them as intentional beings. In this capacity, the inclusion of romantic love in games is inherently challenging because the game must actively create and maintain the illusion that the agents the player interacts with are capable of intention and romantic love for that matter. In the following section, the NPCs' lack of intentionality is further explained by drawing on Sartre's existentialism.

EXISTENTIALIST LOVE

For Leino (2015), authentic romantic love is defined by reciprocity between two free human beings. What does Leino mean by that? Leino treats romantic love under the lens of Sartre's existentialism. Expanding on phenomenology, Sartre (1956) starts from the thesis that being is nothingness, in the sense that there is no one way to be. In actuality, we are not being at all. Our actions define our conduct but not our being. In this regard, one's existence is constantly in virtuality (i.e., fluidity between modes of being, which are never one's own being). At the same time, one's conduct is highly deterministic in nature by forces beyond one's control. Sartre takes the example of a homosexual man, whom he calls a pederast. The pederast, according to Sartre, is a pederast because he has the tendency to be one: "To the extent that a pattern of conduct is defined as the conduct of a pederast and to the extent that I have adopted this conduct, I am a pederast" (64). At the same time, a pederast can deny being a pederast while behaving as a pederast, because he does not will himself to being a pederast: "But to the extent that human reality cannot be finally defined by patterns of conduct, I am not one" (64).

Sartre differentiates between being and behaving. More precisely, he differentiates between the unconscious deterministic behaviorism of the human beings and the conscious actualization of one's being. In this, he follows Freud's distinction between the id, the unconscious, and the ego, the conscious (1956, 50). For Sartre, we are the ego but not the id, yet this ego is a series of phenomena rather than a fixed totality. As a result, ontologically our ego is nothing. We will it to existence by establishing our psychic phenomena in a conscious reality. The pre-existence of the id notwithstanding, one is free to be conscious of their being not being the id despite conducting the behavior dictated by the id. The homosexual's behavior is determined, as Sartre claims. Nonetheless: "he has an obscure but strong feeling that a homosexual is not a homosexual as this table is a table or as this red-haired man is red-haired" (1956, 64). For Sartre, our freedom, despite our predetermined conduct, resides in our consciousness, which realizes that our being is nothing.

The same applies to how we perceive the consciousness of the others and how they perceive ours. We perceive their conduct but their consciousness is always absent for us, because it is nothing, a thing in potentia: "It is the object always present as the meaning of all my attitudes and all my conduct—and always absent, for it gives itself to the intuition of another as a perpetual question—still better, as a perpetual freedom" (1956, 61). This duality of existence finds its way also in romantic love. Sartre argues that what the lover wants is to essentially capture the consciousness of the other, their freedom that is: "It is certain then that the lover wishes to capture a 'consciousness'" (366). It is not the physicality of the other, but rather "it is the Other's freedom as such that we want to get hold of" (367). By that Sartre means that the lover wants to conquer the beloved not because of their psychological determinism. At the same time the lover does not want a love out of conscious choice alone either: "Who would be satisfied with the words, 'I love you because I have freely engaged myself to love you and because I do not wish to go back on my word'" (367).

It is in this human condition of oscillating between the determinism of the id and the nothingness of the being that Sartre sees love finding its expression. In Sartre's love one does not seek either; they instead seek this contradiction of constant instants: "In love it is not a determinism of the passions which we desire in the Other nor a freedom beyond reach; it is a freedom which plays the role of a determinism of the passions and which is caught in its own role" (1956, 367). Or in other words, the beloved must will themselves into being in accordance with the lover or rather for the lover. As existence is willingness into being, in love this willingness must find its limitation on the face of the lover. The lover "wants to be placed beyond the whole system of values posited by the Other and to be the condition of all valorization and the objective foundation of all values" (369).

Love, as Sartre explains it, is not in the world. Instead, it makes the world depending on the beloved, this specific Other. When the lover demands love they do not demand an object to be given: predefined behavior or conscious freedom. They demand an actualization of being, a particular willingness that is born specifically for them and by its birth it limits the willingness of the beloved as its point of reference and determination: "I must no longer be seen on the ground of the world as a 'this' among other 'thises,' but the world must be revealed in terms of me" (1956, 369). Cleary sums Sartre's take on love by suggesting that "loving is intentional: it is love of and sparked by someone" (2015, 112). In this understanding of love, loving is a free action. Anything else would make the beloved "no more than a robot" (2015, 106).

Love in this existential context poses indeed a significant challenge when it comes to mediating romantic love in digital games. This is because NPC's perceived intentionality when it comes to love is falling in love with a generic other and not the nominal player in their individuality. In actuality, in most digital games the player has no problem understanding that an NPC is in love. Their coded behavior is quite clear following the paradigm of other romantic love mediations or simulating human psychology and behavior as we know it. The challenge is to show the player that an NPC is in love with *them*; that their coded behavior is not to exhibit a set of actions that the player will perceive as their having fallen in love but as their having fallen in love with the player as in their unique subjectivity.

Leino's ontic difference between player and NPC is, in fact, this lack of freedom that plagues the NPC. The NPC cannot will itself into being in love. It may conduct itself as a person in love would, yet this conduct remains strictly that: conduct and not being. In this regard, the NPC remains always a coded behavior but of a different determinism than that of the human player. More importantly, the NPC does not possess the means to will the specific otherness constituted in the player. The NPC is designed to fall in love with a generic other. On the other hand, the player themselves cannot freely choose the actualization of their being. In order to experience the love offered by the game, they need to execute predetermined commands. If they do not, then their own willingness results to nothing. In the context of games, Sartre's nothingness takes on a different or added meaning. It is not the nothingness in the sense of infinite possibility. It is the nothingness of the absolute non-existence.

In the game *Dragon Age: Origins* (BioWare 2009) the player can romance different in-game characters. The player uses some crude mechanics to make the NPCs fall in love, like giving them gifts, which increase their approval, which is measured in a numbered bar below their name in the player's inventory. These mechanics are only part of the problem. If the game implemented a more sophisticated design the player could not see them at all.[3] But they would still be there, in the sense that the code of the game demands certain commands so as to execute specific parts, in this case, the NPC's behavior to the player. If the player does not do A, then the NPC will not do B. The player must necessarily perform certain in-game actions so as to activate the command for the NPC to fall in love.

This translates the process of the NPC falling in love with the player into a puzzle with a quantifiable outcome of true or false (Kelly 2015). Or, as Khandaker-Kokoris (2015) suggests, the player should manipulate the code to get the romance as a reward: "Press the correct sequence of buttons in order to get them to sleep with you." It is then argued that the real challenge games need to address when mediating love is to conceal from the player this mechanistic approach that corresponds to the NPC doing B no matter who performs A. In other words, in games and in any context that a human agent perceives coded behavior, the challenge is for the system to make the human agent perceive this behavior as caused by and directed exclusively to this individual human.

INTENTIONAL BEING

That being said, how does this approach account for players who argue that they feel something akin to romantic love with an NPC? Waern (2015) recounts fora entries by people describing their *Dragon Age: Origins* experience. As Waern references, players detail their romance experience as having fallen in love with characters that the players themselves call non-real. They even recount instances of jealousy when they watch images and videos of their chosen beloved with other players' avatars online. There are people who feel guilty when they romance one character while being in an established relationship with another character. The same happens when they choose to romance a different character in their second playthrough; they say that they cannot resist their first love and end up romancing the same companion again despite their original plan.

Players can indeed feel strong emotions for virtual characters, which they themselves describe as love. They are positively aware that those characters are not real but they still love them. Whatever love for those players

[3] Arguably, the other installments in the series incorporate more subtle mechanics without managing, however, to overcome the challenge discussed here, see: *Dragon Age 2* (BioWare 2011); *Dragon Age: Inquisition* (BioWare 2014).

is, they argue that they feel it for virtual characters. They do not use any other word; they say *love*. The feeling and/or experience they have come to know as love from their personal life is the same as what they feel in the game world. Since they call it love it means that what they themselves consider and perceive as love, erroneously or not, is ascribed to their experience both in the physical world for other physical beings and in the virtual world for virtual NPCs.

How can this happen? Waern explains this phenomenon with the term "bleeding," which has primarily been used within role-playing communities and expresses the experience by a player of their thoughts and feelings being influenced by those of their character and vice versa. In order to achieve that from a game design perspective, game designers build role-play scenarios, in which the distinction between player and character is deliberately blurred, or they emotionally manipulate their players so as not to be able to fully distance themselves from their characters.

As Waern notes "bleed" is a vague term that demands further refinement if one is to use it to describe the experience of love in a game context. She distinguishes between: "a *bleed-in* effect, when the player's emotions and personality traits affect the way the role is performed, and a *bleed-out* effect when the player cannot distance himself/herself from the (simulated) emotions of the character" (2015). As such, Waern situates the bleeding of romantic feelings in the interplay between players who are already willing to emotionally engage with a game and a game design that facilitates this engagement. She attributes this player willingness to the safety of romantic experience in games. She claims that this practice is similar to the idolization of male celebrities by female teenagers: "it offers a relatively safe form of romance in situations where you are not prepared or able to engage in a real one." She particularly contends that "*Dragon Age* allows us to fall in love safely and just a little."

Waern raises many essential issues pertaining to romantic love in games. Her bleeding exegesis, however, positions romance in digital games only as a pretense. In Waern's piece, the fictionality of the romance in games is a given, the romantic experience the games offer is never treated as being on equal terms with the real-life experience. It is seen as a safe substitute for people who are not ready or unable to feel the real thing. The romantic experience in games is portrayed as the result of a suspension of disbelief by the player in the context of role-playing. Based on Waern's account, the players are very eager to experience romance in games, but in order to do so they must be ready to consciously delude themselves that what they experience is real when it is not. In this effect, the players do not fall in love in the context of games; they play the role of someone in love.

For the players to be able to feel love in a game, the game should include agents that can love. To understand the logical steps of this argument, one must connect Sartre's existential love with the embodied perception of other agents discussed in the previous section of this chapter. For that, a key term is Merleau-Ponty's "intercorporeality" (1962). Following on his theory that we have a body that inhabits a world, it is through this body that we experience our world and we make meaning of it, a process through which our consciousness is shaped. However, our subjectivity, namely our subjective perception, is not an entity in isolation that comes to know objects in the world. Instead, our subjectivity is constantly informed by our relation to the objects of our perception including other bodies of the world we inhabit: "I have the world as an incomplete individual, through the agency of my body as the potentiality of this world" (408).

Thus, each one of us is a person in virtuality constantly actualizing themselves by relating to the world and the agents in it; not by objective relation, but by intentional relation, meaning by doing and behaving intentionally, in simpler words through interaction. For Merleau-Ponty, this comparison and identification can only be achieved intentionally, as in actively, meaning through a movement of my body towards the other and theirs towards me. As long as we stay inactive our consciousness and thus the consciousness of others remains incomplete, a thing in potentia. It is in this context of intercorporeality that we experience love. As Diprose contends, Merleau-Ponty "does not think love or sexual desire is any different in structure to personal existence in general" (2002, 90).

We have a body and because we have a body we can have a world and in this world we can love. Yet, we can only love as a conscious experience when this love is realized in this system of intercorporeality we share with the other bodies of our world. This is a matter of reciprocity not in the sense of reciprocation but potentiality. We can know love by loving. This loving is an intentional loving towards another person. This person is another person because we recognize our own behavior in their behavior. If their behavior cannot actualize the potential of love then we cannot actualize our love and we cannot have a conscious experience of love in this world.

When Wearn suggests that in games we can fall in love in a safe way, the safety lies in our inability to experience love in its full actualization. We may experience something akin to love but because the agents in this game world cannot offer love then our sentiment can reach up to a certain point, after which it remains virtual since the intercorporeality afforded by the embodied agents inside the game world does not allow for romantic love. This is why Leino calls love in games love in bad faith. According to Sartre when one practices bad faith, one "is hiding a displeasing truth or presenting as truth a pleasing untruth" (1956, 47). Its difference from the lie is that in bad faith "it is from myself that I am hiding the truth" (47). So when we play a video game we are practicing love in bad faith because we are hiding from ourselves the truth that we cannot actualize our experience of love since the agents that are available for our intercorporeality in this world cannot afford romantic love. We may perceive them as embodied agents but when it comes to their capacity to love, they are proven to be no more than passive objects. In this, what we feel for them may be better compared to the feelings of attachment we have for non-human entities or items we care for. When we say that we love our car the emphasis is given on the attachment we experience because we allocate time and resources to it. Equally, while playing the game we spend a lot of time and energy for or with the NPC. It is then understandable that we grow attached to it, which is a facet of love. Romantic love, however, demands reciprocity that the in-game agents cannot afford.

What Leino deems fictional love in games is when we are aware that we cannot experience romantic love in games and we accept it for the type of experience that it is; safe and just a little as Waern suggests. As Leino argues, this experience of love in bad faith is intrinsic to the medium of games. Leino sees medium-specific love as being in bad faith but, in actuality, it is also his fictional love that is medium-specific since it is not a different experience but rather a different conscious stance towards the same experience. Even when we accept that our love cannot be actualized because we target it toward a fictional character, it is not the same experience as that obtained from other media that include fictional characters in love.

The discrepancy lies in the point of perception of the player as part of the game world. They are not witnesses as in other media; they actively actualize the game world through their body, which makes them subjects of this world. As argued above, in digital games the player extends their physical space to the virtual space that affords their actions towards certain tasks and goals. In most games, this expansion is facilitated by a playable character (PC), through which the player experiences the game world. This PC can vary from an empty vessel as vague as a mouse cursor to a fully fleshed-out character that the player has little or no ability to adapt to their own personality. In all cases, the embodiment that the PC allows the player enables a fusion of subjectivity, a subjective perspective onto the game world that continues dynamically throughout the play session.

Vella has coined the term "ludic subject," which "is not a pre-existing character that the player finds ready-made and simply steps into (though it can be, and often is, tied to a scripted diegetic character)" (2014). Instead, the ludic subject is an amalgamation of the player's subjective stance in the game world infused with the features, abilities, and limitations of the PC: "As such, the ludic subject is composed of the set of player's subjective experiences of engaging with the game world from the standpoint of the ludic subject-position, and is only brought into being by the player's playing." In this phenomenological regard, it is impossible to talk about the PC and the player in clearly demarcated terms: "the player simultaneously inhabits a subjective standpoint internal to the game world (the ludic, or virtual, subjectivity) and her own subjective standpoint as an individual external to the game world."

Our experience of the game world is always part of our subjectivity. In romantic love, if the PC falls in love as part of the game then we perceive it subjectively as our falling in love. Or rather as our self, actualized in this game world through avatarial embodiment with the PC, falling in love. Yet as was argued before, this self of ours cannot experience romantic love in the game world because the intercorporeality afforded in this game world does not allow for such an experience. This experience is the same no matter if we acknowledge it or not, acting in bad faith that is. As such, the inability to experience romantic love becomes a facticity of the medium instead of a practice afforded or imposed by the game system.

This becomes apparent in the other type of love that games include, which is what Leino calls "vicarious love" (2015). In vicarious love the player is not part of the experience of love anymore, it is instead the PC and the NPC who are falling in love. In this type of love the player is no longer a subjective agent inside the game world but instead experiences the game world as a "fly on the wall." This is the type of love that games offer when they withdraw control from the player; when the player's actions do not affect the game world, most commonly in cutscenes, a point in which the player releases the mouse/keyboard/joystick and consumes the game world through their eyes and ears in a passive manner similar to watching a film. Indeed, during this time the game abandons the most distinguishing feature that discerns it from other media: the cybernetic loop between the player and the system.

For example, in the game *Nier: Automata* (Platinum Games 2017) the love story between androids 2B and 9S mostly develops in cutscenes, when the game reclaims control from the player. Whether this story is romantic love or not is open to interpretation, which makes it an interesting case of how games can include thought-provoking and nuanced stories and characters. The challenge is to offer an uninterrupted experience of this to the player rather than constantly alternating between story progression and gameplay.[4] Since they are the non-ergodic parts of the game that contain the vicarious love, the gameplay is then found to not be able to afford any authentic experience of romantic love.[5] Once the player regains control, their subjectivity meshes with the playable character and thus transforms a fictional experience to a cybernetic experience. As such, the experience of romantic love should become cybernetic itself for a game to offer it. What exactly I mean by that is explained in the following section, in which I argue that for games to overcome the challenge of the intercorporeality discussed above, the game should include artificial agents rather than fictional ones.

ARTIFICIAL OTHERS

From the above, it can be deduced that the ability of games to offer subjective agency to their players works against their capacity to afford romantic love experiences. The player by embodying a virtual self in the game world cannot actualize this self's intention toward romantic love because the other agents inside this world do not provide bodies that allow it by constituting designed behaviors and not intentional beings. Undoubtedly intuitive game and narrative design that helps cover this lack of intentionality of NPCs is a valid way for games to overcome this challenge and provide an almost seamless illusion of romantic love; a feat that will become increasingly easier as technological means advance. At the same time, the fact that NPCs are coded behavior cannot be addressed by design alone. Instead, it is argued that games may eventually be liberated from the constraints of artificiality not by concealing it but rather by embracing it.

Ravenet et al. (2016) in explaining models of emotion for NPCs contend that the NPCs' behavior in games is usually scripted so as to avoid blocking

[4] As aptly described by Chris Crawford (2003, 260): "The story itself is non-interactive, and the game itself lacks dramatic content. You interact with the non-narrative game, then see some non-interactive story, then interact some more with the game, then see more story, and if you alternate between the two fast enough, it becomes an 'interactive story'—right?"

[5] Ergodic in the sense of demanding extranoematic effort to be accessed, see Espen J. Aarseth (1997, 1).

the player's progress. This results to their acting "as emotionless robots that are only here to obey the rules of the game; they do not adapt their behavior to the current game situation, giving no sense of engagement in their interaction with the player" (139). As they argue, in most games the non-interactive parts of the game show NPCs with powerful emotional behaviors, yet during interactive phases, they lack autonomy. No matter how large the trees of possibilities the developers can code, this scripted approach, while being realistic for a specific context, cannot go very far in terms of adaptability and variability during the play session. They propose instead the application of generation models for autonomous virtual characters. These models can be data-driven or literature-based, both of which have their advantages and disadvantages: data models are costly and in need of large sets of data but are more adaptable and can evolve with new data, while models based on literature from the human and social sciences are less costly and more enriched, however, they do not provide the same level of adaptability and variability as the data models (146).

Essentially, what Ravenet et al. suggest are agents of artificial intelligence that are generated and evolve beyond the immediate control of the human, developer and/or player. In this way, digital games as cybernetic systems have the capacity to overcome the boundaries of fictionality. Specifically, digital games have been argued to work on a cybernetic feedback loop, which describes the circulatory communication between the game system and the player (Gazzard 2011; Bogost 2006; Sicart 2008; Stang 2019; Newman 2002). Friedman (1999) defines the concept as: "The constant interactivity in a simulation game—the perpetual feedback between a player' choice, the computer's almost instantaneous response, the player's response to that response, and so on—is a cybernetic loop" (137).

This is a medium-specific quality of digital games due to the fact that they are manifestations of a cybernetic system as coined and defined by Wiener (1948). Wiener revolutionizes the term "cybernetics," which originally meant having a goal and taking action to achieve that goal, in two important ways. First, he connects goals with communication between systems. In order for one to know whether they are reaching or have succeeded in their goal, they need information from their environment, which is what Wiener calls "feedback." Second, he argues that both animals (biological systems) and machines (non-biological or artificial systems) can operate according to cybernetic principles. This is an explicit recognition that both living and non-living systems can have a purpose.

In human-computer interaction, we then have the communication between two willful systems that exchange information toward a certain goal, which can either be shared or not. In this light, digital games can be seen as the medium or space of communication between those two systems—the human player and the artificial machine, in a constructed context, which includes a set of goals, some predefined, scripted, and embedded in the design, some others emergent in the course of this cybernetic loop of communication. The agents in this space can themselves be designed and/or emergent. Scripted agents, as previously argued, convey realism because they are based on human representation. At the same time, they cannot overcome their fictionality. Instead, emergent agents, agents of the willful machine, are artificial because they are generated by a simulation model, yet they can overcome the boundaries of representation by showing adaptability, variability, and evolution. In this capacity they become bodies actualized in the face of their tasks, fulfilling the condition of Merleau-Ponty's intentionality. They become intentional embodied agents.

The subsequent question is whether this artificial intentionality can include romantic love. According to Sartre's approach described before, love is the mode of being born out of our wanting a certain person. How can this be translated into a simulation model? Some research has been done outside of digital games in the field of robotics, which has taken on the special term "lovotics": love and sex with robots. Cheok et al. (2016) explain how the lovotics robot works: "The artificial intelligence of the Lovotics robot includes three modules: the Artificial Endocrine System, which is based on the physiology of love; the Probabilistic Love Assembly, which is based on the psychology of falling in love; and the Affective State Transition, which is based on human emotions" (308). The authors comment on how larger input by human users will lead to more realistic physical interactions with the robots since their models can be better configured. Digital games constitute an appropriate medium for data collection since they are more cost-efficient than building an actual robot, human players freely engage with them, and they provide a relatively contained and thus safe context for human-machine communication.

Safety in this sense opens up a discussion that goes beyond the mere technological advances of the field. There are certain ethics arising from building an artificial other programmed to manipulate human feelings "in order to evoke loving or amorous reactions from their human users" (320). This can take a very pragmatic approach, as for example whether loving and having sex with a robot can be held legally liable in marriage dissolution court cases as a form of cheating (Cheok et al. 2016, 321). Depending on the applicable law, this can cause legitimate tensions; for example under Sharia law adulterers found guilty may be subject to bodily or even capital punishment (321). A solution to this ethical problem is said to be "having robots designed in such a way as to incorporate feelings of heartbreak together with the goal of caring for those in its owner's circle of friends and relatives" (321). In other words, the goal is to build artificial others that go beyond inspiring feelings of love by simulating human responses to agents that can choose to experience love themselves.

CONCLUSION

This chapter discusses the experience of romantic love between a human player and a non-playable character (NPC) in single-player avatarial games. It expands on Leino's argument that digital games cannot offer an authentic romantic relationship due to the ontic difference between the player and the NPC. It is specifically argued that this ontic difference is to be understood in two aspects: the first one is the embodiment and the second is intentionality. The first aspect concerns the lack of physicality of NPCs. Romantic love is an experience associated with physicality and in the case of digital games the player is a physical being while the NPC is not. For this, it is argued that despite NPCs not being physical bodies, players perceive them as such. This argument is framed by drawing from embodied perception.

Research has shown that we perceive the space around our body, our peripersonal space, according to the actions we can perform in it, in other words, it is the space of our actions. In this sense, we perceive the space of the game as our peripersonal space as long as we can perform actions in it. In this, embodied perception coincides with phenomenology, as this is explained in the work of Merleau-Ponty. Merleau-Ponty contended that we perceive our world by our intentional actions within this world by our body. This phenomenal body can be extended and expanded through tools. Applying Merleau-Ponty to digital games, Klevjer has argued that through the controllers we expand our body to the screen of the digital game. When we play digital games, we are then expanded bodies that include the space of the digital game.

In this space, we encounter other agents, whose behavior and actions we perceive using the same mechanisms for perceiving the agents in our physical space. As with objects which we perceive according to which actions they afford when we observe the actions of others the sama motor-schema is activated in our brain as if we were the ones performing this action. This enables us to attribute intentions, goals, and aspirations to others and foresee their behavior. This applies to emotional reactions as well. Further research has shown that this motor-schema is at work even when we encounter non-human or virtual/fictional agents. Especially when it comes to virtual agents, verisimilitude facilitates our perception of them as embodied agents together with their performing actions that match our own motor-schema and/or our own emotional reactions.

Specifically for romantic love, for a player to perceive an NPC as a body for love and/or in love, the NPC must look like a human as much as possible but also perform actions associated with romantic love. This leads to the second aspect of tension between a physical player and a virtual NPC, namely the NPC's inability to choose romantic love. This freedom of choice is described under Sartre's existentialism. Sartre argues that in love we are neither psychological determinism nor conscious choice alone. Instead, when we are in love we will ourselves into being in accordance and for the person we are in love with. In this sense, love is always intentional for a specific person, who has sparked this emotion in us.

NPCs cannot choose to love the player in their uniqueness since they are coded behavior. Their actions are rather reactions to certain commands the player executes; any player for that matter. This inability of the NPCs to intentionally choose to love the player makes the experience of romantic love in digital games unattainable. The reason for this is explained by Merleau-Ponty's concept of intercorporeality. According to this understanding, our own conscious experience of the world is always a thing in potential. We are virtual beings, who are actualized by our intentional interaction with the objects in our world and the other agents in it. In the physical world we are able to feel love because the other agents around us can feel love; not in the sense of reciprocation but as potentiality. On the contrary, the agents in a digital game we interact with cannot feel love. As such, we as well cannot actualize our potential for love in its full force while acting in the game world.

For this reason, as long as digital games do not include agents that can choose love, games will not be able to offer an authentic romantic love experience to the human player. Understandably, clever game design can help cover this limitation but it is argued that this challenge cannot be surpassed by mere design alone. Instead, it is suggested that rather than games focusing on veiling the NPCs fictionality, a more fruitful direction is to embrace their artificiality more broadly. This means that games should incorporate artificially generated agents that can adapt and evolve beyond the limited control of the human developers and players. The subsequent question is whether and how these artificial agents will eventually reach a point of consciously feeling romantic love towards a human player.

This is primarily a technological question but opens up discussions for legal and ethical matters as well. Still, the relation between a human agent and an artificial other remains an anthropological question as much as ever. Once upon a time, Frankenstein strove to create an artificial human being. In the end, he created a monster because his creation could not afford love. Digital games offer us the space to perceive, engage with, and potentially love otherness. In this, they also let us explore, understand, and eventually love humanness as well.

REFERENCES

Aarseth, Espen J. 1997. *Cybertext: Perspectives on Ergodic Literature*. Baltimore, MD: The Johns Hopkins University Press.

Aarseth, Espen. 2007. "Doors and Perception: Fiction vs. Simulation in Games." *Intermédialités* 9: 35–44. https://doi.org/10.7202/1005528ar.

Atlus. 2011. *Catherine*. Sega. Microsoft Windows et al.

Bartels, Andreas and Semir Zeki. 2000. "The Neural Basis of Romantic Love." *NeuroReport* 11, no. 17: 3829–3834.

Basu, Gautam Thakur and Jonathan Michael Dickstein eds. 2018. *Lacan and the Nonhuman*. Switzerland: Palgrave Macmillan.

Beauregarda, Mario, Jérôme Courtemanchea, Vincent Paquettea, and Évelyne Landry St-Pierre. 2009. "The Neural Basis of Unconditional Love." *Psychiatry Research: Neuroimaging* 172: 93–98.

BioWare. 2007. *Mass Effect*. Microsoft Game Studios. Microsoft Windows et al.

BioWare. 2009. *Dragon Age: Origins*. Electronic Arts. Microsoft Windows et al.

BioWare. 2010. *Mass Effect 2*. Electronic Arts. Microsoft Windows et al.

BioWare. 2011. *Dragon Age 2*. Electronic Arts. Microsoft Windows et al.

BioWare. 2012. *Mass Effect 3*. Electronic Arts. Microsoft Windows et al.

BioWare. 2014. *Dragon Age: Inquisition*. Electronic Arts. Microsoft Windows et al.

Bogost, Ian. 2006. *Unit Operations: An Approach to Videogame Criticism*. Cambridge, MA: The MIT Press.

Buccino, Giovanni, Fausta Lui, Nicola Canessa, Ilaria Patteri, Giovanna Lagravinese, Francesca Benuzzi, Carlo A. Porro, and Giacomo Rizzolatti. 2004. "Neural Circuits Involved in the Recognition of Actions Performed by Nonconspecifics: An fMRI Study." *Journal of Cognitive Neuroscience* 16, no. 1: 114–126.

Cardona-Rivera, Rogelio E. and R. Michael Young. "A Cognitivist Theory of Affordances for Games." 2014. *Proceedings of DiGRA 2013: DeFragging Game Studies* 7. www.digra.org/wp-content/uploads/digital-library/paper_74b.pdf.

CD Projekt Red. 2007. *The Witcher.* Atari. Microsoft Windows et al.

CD Project Red. 2011. *The Witcher 2: Assassins of Kings.* CD Project. Microsoft Windows et al.

CD Project Red. 2015. *The Witcher 3: Wild Hunt.* CD Project. Microsoft Windows et al.

Cheok, Adrian David, David Levy, and Kasun Karunanayaka. 2016. "Lovotics: Love and Sex with Robots." In *Emotion in Games: Theory and Praxis*, edited by Kostas Karpouzis and Georgios N. Yannakakis. Switzerland: Springer, 303–328.

Cleary, Skye. 2015. *Existentialism and Romantic Love.* New York, NY: Palgrave and Macmillan.

Crawford, Chris. 2003. "Interactive Storytelling." In *The Video Game Theory Reader*, edited by Mark J. P. Wolf and Bernard Perron. New York, NY: Routledge.

Diprose, Rosalyn. 2002. *Corporeal Generosity: On Giving with Nietzsche, Merleau-Ponty, and Levinas.* Albany, NY: State University of New York Press.

Dontnod Entertainment. 2015. *Life is Strange.* Square Enix. Microsoft Windows et al.

Doyle-Myerscough, Kaelan. 2019. "The Monster Has Kind Eyes: Intimacy and Frustration in The Last Guardian." *Invisible Culture* 30. https://ivc.lib.rochester.edu/the-monster-has-kind-eyes-intimacy-and-frustration-in-the-last-guardian/.

Eldridge, Richard. 2001. *The Persistence of Romanticism: Essays in Philosophy and Literature.* Cambridge, UK: Cambridge University Press.

Fisher, Helen E. 1997. "Lust, Attraction, and Attachment in Mammalian Reproduction." *Human Nature* 9, no. 1: 23–52.

Fisher, Helen E., Arthur Aron, Debra Mashek, Haifang Li, and Lucy L. Brown. 2002. "Defining the Brain Systems of Lust, Romantic Attraction, and Attachment." *Archives of Sexual Behavior* 31, no. 5: 413–419.

Friedman, Ted. 1999. "Civilization and its Discontents: Simulation, Subjectivity and Space." In *On a Silver Platter: CD-ROMs and the Promises of a New Technology*, edited by Greg M. Smith. New York: New York University Press.

Gallese, Vittorio. 2005. "Embodied Simulation: From Neurons to Phenomenal Experience." *Phenomenology and the Cognitive Sciences* 4: 23–48.

Gazzard, Alizon. 2011. "Unlocking the Gameworld: The Rewards of Space and Time in Videogames." *Game Studies* 11, no. 1.

Gibson, James J. 1966. *The Senses Considered as Perceptual Systems.* London: George Allen & Unwin LTD.

Gibbs, Raymond W. Jr. 2005. *Embodiment and Cognitive Science.* Cambridge, UK: Cambridge University Press.

Grace, Lindsay D. 2017. "Love, Lust, Courtship and Affection as Evolution in Digital Play." *Proceedings of DiGRA 2017* 14, no. 1. www.digra.org/wp-content/uploads/digital-library/123_DIGRA2017_FP_Grace_Affection.pdf.

Heidegger, Martin. 1967. *Sein und Zeit*. Tübingen: Max Niemeyer Verlag.

Jones, Doug. 1996. "An Evolutionary Perspective on Physical Attractiveness." *Evolutionary Anthropology* 5, no. 3: 97–109. doi:10.1002/(SICI)1520-6505(1996)5:3<97::AID-EVAN5>3.0.CO;2-T.

Kelly, Peter. 2015. "Approaching the Digital Courting Process in Dragon Age 2." In *Game Love: Essays on Play and Affection*, edited by Jessica Enevold and Esther Maccallum-Stewart. Jefferson, NC: McFarland & Company. Kindle edition.

Key. 2015. *Clannad*. Sekai Project. Microsoft Windows et al.

Khandaker-Kokoris, Mitu. 2015. "NPCs Need Love Too: Simulating Love and Romance, from a Game Design Perspective." In *Game Love: Essays on Play and Affection*, edited by Jessica Enevold and Esther Maccallum-Stewart. Jefferson, NC: McFarland & Company. Kindle edition.

Kirsh, David. 2013. "Embodied Cognition and the Magical Future of Interaction Design." *ACM Transactions on Computer-Human Interaction* 20, no. 1: 3:1–3:30. http://dx.doi.org/10.1145/2442106.2442109.

Klevjer, Rune. 2012. "Enter the Avatar. The Phenomenology of Prosthetic Telepresence in Computer Games." In *The Philosophy of Computer Games (Philosophy of Engineering and Technology)*, edited by John Richard Sageng, Hallvard Fossheim, and Tarjei Mandt Larsen. London and New York: Springer: pp. 17–38.

Langeslag, Sandra J. E., Peter Muris, and Ingmar H. A. Franken. 2012. "Measuring Romantic Love: Psychometric Properties of the Infatuation and Attachment Scales." *Journal of Sex Research*. doi:10.1080/00224499.2012.714011.

Leino, Olli Tapio. 2015. "I Know Your Type, You Are a Player: Suspended Fulfillment in Fallout: New Vegas." In *Game Love: Essays on Play and Affection*, edited by Jessica Enevold and Esther Maccallum-Stewart. Jefferson, NC: McFarland & Company. Kindle edition.

Maxis. 2000–2019. *The Sims*. Electronic Arts. Microsoft Windows et al.

McBride-Charpentier, Michel. 2011. "Affordance Design in Half-Life 2." *Gamasutra* (blog). www.gamasutra.com/blogs/MichelMcBrideCharpentier/20110102/88710/Affordance_Design_in_HalfLife_2.php.

McLuhan, Marshall. 2011. *The Gutenberg Galaxy: The Making of Typographic Man*. Toronto, Canada: University of Toronto Press.

Mediatonic. 2014. *Hatoful Boyfriend*. Devolver Digital. Microsoft Windows et al.

Merleau-Ponty, Maurice. 1962. *Phenomenology of Perception*. Translated by Colin Smith. London and New York: Routledge.

Meyer, Meghan L., Elliot T. Berkman, Johan C. Karremans, and Matthew D. Lieberman. 2011. "Incidental Regulation of Attraction: The Neural Basis of the Derogation of Attractive Alternatives in Romantic Relationships." *Cognition and Emotion* 25, no. 3: 490–505. doi:10.1080/02699931.2010.527494.

Morrison, India and Tom Ziemke. 2005. "Empathy with Computer Game Characters: A Cognitive Neuroscience Perspective." In *Proceedings of the Joint Symposium on Virtual Social Agents*. Hatfield, UK: The University of Hertfordshire, 73–79.

Newman, James. 2002. "The Myth of the Ergodic Videogame." *Game Studies* 2, no. 1.

Paz, Octavio. 1995. *The Double Flame: Love and Eroticism*. Translated by Helen Lane. New York, San Diego, and London: Harcourt Brace & Company.

Platek, Steven M. and Todd K. Shackelford, eds. 2006. *Female Infidelity and Paternal Uncertainty: Evolutionary Perspectives on Male Anti-cuckoldry Tactics*. Cambridge, UK: Cambridge University Press.

PlatinumGames. 2017. *Nier: Automata*. Square Enix. Microsoft Windows et al.

Plato. 2018. *Phaedrus*. Translated by Panagiotis Doikos. Thessaloniki: Romi.

Praz, Mario. 1951. *The Romantic Agony*. Translated by Angus Davidson. London, New York, and Toronto: Oxford University Press.

Price, A. W. 1981. "Loving Persons Platonically." *Phronesis* 26, no. 1: 25–34.

Quantic Dream. 2010. *Heavy Rain*. Sony Computer Entertainment. PlayStation 3 et al.

Ravenet, Brian, Florian Pecune, Mathieu Chollet, and Catherine Pelachaud. 2016. "Emotion and Attitude Modeling for Non-player Characters." In *Emotion in Games: Theory and Praxis*, edited by Kostas Karpouzis and Georgios N. Yannakakis. Switzerland: Springer, 139–154.

Roffe, Jon and Hannah Stark eds. 2015. *Deleuze and the Non/Human*. London, UK: Palgrave Macmillan.

Rotobee. 2003. *Singles: Flirt Up Your Life*. Deep Silver. Microsoft Windows.

Rotobee. 2005. *Singles: Triple Trouble*. Deep Silver. Microsoft Windows.

Sartre, Jean-Paul. 1956. *Being and Nothingness*. Translated by Hazel E. Barnes. New York: University of Colorado.

Secomb, Linnell. 2007. *Philosophy and Love: From Plato to Popular Culture*. Edinburgh: Edinburgh University Press.

Sicart, Miguel. 2008. "Defining Game Mechanics." *Game Studies* 8, no. 2.

The Sims Studio. 2000–2019. *The Sims*. Electronic Arts. Microsoft Windows et al.

Stang, Sarah. 2019. "This Action Will Have Consequences: Interactivity and Player Agency." *Game Studies* 19, no. 1.

Sternberg, Robert J. and Karis Weis, eds. 2006. *The New Psychology of Love*. New Haven & London: Yale University Press.

Telltale Games. 2016. *Batman: The Telltale Series*. Telltale Games. Microsoft Windows et al.

Tinwell, Angela. 2015. *The Uncanny Valley in Games and Animation*. Boca Raton, FL: CRC Press.

Turner, Phil. 2017. *A Psychology of User Experience: Involvement, Affect and Aesthetics*. Switzerland: Springer.

Varela, J. Fransisco, Evan Thompson, and Eleanor Rosch. 2016. *The Embodied Mind: Cognitive Science and Human Experience*. Cambridge, MA: The MIT Press.

Vella, Daniel. 2014. "Player and Figure: An Analysis of a Scene in Kentucky Route Zero." *Proceedings of Nordic DiGRA 2014* 11. http://www.digra.org/wp-content/uploads/digital-library/nordicdigra2014_submission_2.pdf.

Vella, Daniel and Stefano Gualeni. 2019. "Virtual Subjectivity: Existence and Projectuality in Virtual Worlds." *Techne: Research in Philosophy of Technology* 23, no. 2.

Waern, Annika. 2015. "I'm in love with someone that doesn't exist! Bleed in the Context of a Computer Game." In *Game Love: Essays on Play and Affection*, edited by Jessica Enevold and Esther Maccallum-Stewart. Jefferson, NC: McFarland & Company. Kindle edition.

Wiener, Norbert. 1948. *Cybernetics or Control and Communication in the Animal and the Machine*. Cambridge, MA: The MIT Press.

Zahavi, Dan. 2002. "First-Person Thoughts and Embodied Self-Awareness: Some Reflections on the Relation between Recent Analytical Philosophy and Phenomenology." *Phenomenology and the Cognitive Sciences* 1: 7–26.

Zahavi, Dan. 2007. "Subjectivity and the First-Person Perspective." *The Southern Journal of Philosophy* 45: 66–84.

CHAPTER 5

Would You Kindly Parent?

Parenting, Caretaking, and Love in Games

Karen Schrier

CONTENTS

INTRODUCTION

How do games express and represent parental love, affection, and caretaking through their goals, game mechanics, and other design elements? How is parental love both exalted and problematized? This chapter discusses how these tensions play out in two different games (*That Dragon, Cancer* and *Life Is Strange 2*), building off a previous analysis conducted with *BioShock*.

To do this, this chapter will provide a close "reading" of the game as a text, as well as analyze its gameplay. Ainsworth's attachment theory is used as a framework for evaluating these games. In brief, this theory explains that parent and child form a bond based on how the parent responds to the child's needs. The child develops an attachment style (typically one of four different styles), which can be secure, ambivalent, avoidant, and disorganized-insecure.

This chapter argues that the games, *That Dragon, Cancer* and *Life Is Strange 2*, enable players to build relationships with other characters and/or practice affection and caretaking in various ways, such as through routine support of other characters in their care. These games express the tensions of parenting in their storyline, themes, and the player's activities. Moreover, the game itself also acts as a type of authority figure, who parents the player through a system of rules and boundaries, which can be enforced or transgressed. Thus, this paper also seeks to answer: how does a game (or game designer) seem to also build a "parental" type of relationship with the player, and in turn, how can the player respond?

This chapter, will not clinically evaluate the players' attachment to games, or the types of attachments in the game, but rather will use this framework to think more broadly about authority, bond-making, caretaking, and affection. How do designers and players themselves build "attachments" or affective engagement through games? Do some games foster a "secure and trusting attachment" for the game player, through clearly defined goals, feedback, and responsiveness to the player? Or, are some games fostering a more insecure bond and feeling of helplessness? How might these differences relate to the player's connection to the game, as well as to the game's story, themes, and game play? More broadly, how might answers to these questions show how designers can better support or parent their players through the game experience?

OVERVIEW: ATTACHMENT THEORY

To further unpack the affectional relationship among parent/caretaker figures and children in games, this chapter will use attachment theory as a framework for interpreting games (Ainsworth 1982; Ainsworth & Bowlby 1991; Bowlby 1969). It will discuss how love and caretaking gets operationalized between parent and child through the game's play. Moreover, it will explore how games themselves may mediate a parenting and affectional relationship between design and player.

For one, parenting does not just happen to a person or a child, but it emerges through a developing relationship between them over time. Likewise, games, game design, and game play are not just thrust upon the player, but they unfold as a relationship among the game developers, the game, and the players (Schrier 2018).

Attachment theory relates to the bonding that is formed between the parent or caregiver and a child, which can result in different types of secure (or insecure) attachment. This theory explains that the caregiver tries to meet the needs of their child, and the child teaches the caregiver what their needs are (Seifer & Schiller 1995). In turn, the parent teaches the child to trust them and understand that they will try to respond to their needs and take care of them.

According to Seifer and Schiller (1995, 146–174), there are five different elements that relate to the formation of this attachment:

1. The attachment behavior, or the "specific behaviors related to increasing infants' proximity and contact with a caregiver,"
2. Exploration, or the "specific behaviors that decrease proximity to the attachment figure, but promote infants" interaction with the environment,"
3. Attachment system, or the "theoretical organization and control of proximity and exploration behavior,"
4. Attachment strategy, or the "organizational structure of behaviors observed in context from which a strategy for maintaining attachment relationships is inferred"
5. The bonds that form, "between infants and their caregivers attachment."

Caregivers and infants cultivate a relationship with each other that (hopefully) involves the caregiver as a "secure base" where an infant can find protection. From this base, the infant can also leave briefly to explore and return. The infant relies on the caregiver for nourishment, care, safety, and protection, as they are still dependent on others for survival (Seifer & Schiller 1995). Ainsworth used the "strange situation" to investigate different types of attachment. In this procedure, she looked at the nature of the attachment to that home base, with the assumption that the infant is attached to the primary caregiver (she used mothers in her initial procedures) (Ainsworth, Blehar, Waters & Wall 1978; Ainsworth & Bell 1970). Her question was whether the "secure base" was a place that the infant could explore, while returning for safety and comfort, or whether they were less trusting that the caregiver would respond and be available to them (Ainsworth, Blehar, Waters & Wall 1978; Ainsworth, Bell, & Stayton 1971; Ainsworth & Wittig 1969; Vaughn & Waters 1990). In the strange situation studies, the infant is in a room and the mother leaves temporarily.

While away, another person (a stranger) comes in. The mother returns and comforts the child (Ainsworth, Blehar, Waters & Wall 1978; Ainswoth & Bell 1970).

Based on the responses to the strange situation, Ainsworth et al. (1978) named four main types or patterns of attachment that get developed and observed:

1. ***Secure attachment***. These infants have a secure attachment relationship with their primary caregiver. They may cry when they are away from their caregiver, but they are comforted when the mother returns, rather than angry, uncomfortable, or withdrawn. Ainsworth found that 65%–75% of the middle class one-year-olds tested with secure attachment.

2. ***Insecure-avoidant attachment***. These infants may or may not cry when they are away from their parent, but upon return, they are not as confident that their caregiver will give them comfort and respond to them. They may not even notice the mother has returned and may play or ignore her, or begin to approach but then turn away.

3. ***Insecure-resistant (or anxious) attachment***. These infants are also not as confident that their caregiver will comfort them, but they cry a lot during separation and may continue to cry or struggle when held after the caregiver returns. They may also be angry and not return to playing as they had before.

4. ***Insecure-disorganized***. In this classification, the infants do not behave predictably. They don't follow a set pattern and seem to act under a different type of motivational system. They found that though this was less than 5% of the infants that they studied, it appeared that they made up 50%–75% of the high-risk infants who end up having social and emotional struggles later on.

It is important to note, again, that the formation of the relationship between caregiver and child, and the attachment style that gets developed is a dynamic and complex interaction that relies on many factors beyond just responding to needs, such as temperament of the child, medical needs, social context and community, and parental sensitivity to cues (Seifer & Schiller 1995). Just as the formation of the bond is a complex interaction, so is the system of "letting go" of each other, and enabling increasing independence between caregiver and infant. Over time, the two units start to allow greater and greater exploration of the world apart from the other. No caregiver-child relationship is the same, and types and timing of interactions that are encouraged adapt and evolve depending on their complex understanding of each other and their world.

While these patterns have been primarily focused on parent-infant attachment, these patterns can continue with other relationships throughout one's life. According to the theory, one's relationship with their primary caretaker develops a mental model of attachment that then influences all future relationships (Hazan & Shaver 1987).

Moreover, this model of attachment has been critiqued for being centered on white, middle class, North American modes of parenting and care, rather than being universally relatable. It also focuses on the mother as being the primary caregiver, though in many situations a primary caregiver is not the mother. And, it does not necessarily take into account different developmental challenges (such as kids with special needs, like autism and/or prematurity). For instance, Keller (2018) critiques the universality of attachment theory, arguing that it ignores non-Western style parenting and the cultural diversity of caregiving systems. However, emotional expression and stranger interactions vary in different cultures. Children and peers may be the primary caregivers in some communities. The concept of children needing to be "responded to" in terms of their needs, rather than directed or guided to meet the needs of others, is a value and view in middle class, Western communities but may not be in rural or non-Western communities, for example (Keller 2018).

PREVIOUS CASE STUDY ON *BioShock* AND PARENTING

A previous paper argued that the *BioShock* series "reflects familial tensions and questions, allowing us to play through some of the most crucial challenges confronting contemporary parents," and serves as a type of model or thought experiment for different parenting styles and attachment types (Schrier 2018). This current chapter extends the author's previous work and considers games and parental attachment more deeply by looking at two additional games.

In the original *BioShock*, players play as Jack Ryan, a genetically modified human being who needs to explore an underwater, post-apocalyptic world called Rapture. Schrier's previous paper, *BioShock as the Infinite Parent* (2017) argued that parenting and parenting styles were thematically and ludically addressed through the game, and also that the game itself served as a model for how game design is like parenting. For instance, the paper discussed how the player in *BioShock* is first dropped into an unfamiliar scenario; it is a disorienting type of "birth" where they need to swim ashore and get grounded. The game scaffolds this interaction by giving instructions on what to pick up (e.g., the first weapon, a wrench), where to go, how to move, and what to press, while keeping the player bounded and safe from enemies while they practice and experiment with their new abilities. When the player first encounters an enemy (a splicer), the player is instructed on how to fight with a weapon or how to use the EVE (or "mana," for magic-like interactions, in the form of plasmid modifications) to defeat enemies. The game gives the gentle nudges and just-in-time information so that a player can reach each sub-goal, leading ultimately to the main goal. Throughout the game, the player learns how to cope with greater challenges. "The game designer must 'let go' of and 'trust' the player (and the game itself), and allow the player to explore the new world they have created" (Schrier 2018). By earning this trust, the player can continue to progress in the game (by completing missions or checkpoints) and the game rewards the player with more challenges, more freedom, and eventually, victory. The paper notes that throughout the series, the game "parents" the player in a number of ways, such as through:

1. ***Boundaries, constraints, and rules*** that govern and restrict play, for instance, being able to respawn in a vita-chamber or the subtle design of walls, paths, and the gardens that compel the player to continue to move forward in a particular way.

2. ***Giving feedback or consequences*** to the player when they make a choice or do something "right or wrong," such as by earning more EVE (replenishes their plasmids) or ADAM (helps them earn more plasmids) (rewards) or by lowering their meters (punishments).

3. ***Dynamically and meaningfully changing*** depending on the player's decisions and actions in the game, and gameplay emerges from those interactions. The game is a mini-world where players can exercise control over not just a series of challenges, but over an evolving world where their choices and actions matter and have gameful and emotional resonance.

While many games express these three features, *BioShock* also thematically explores parenting and in some ways, both upholds and subverts the notion of a "supportive and kind" parent, who is gently nudging the player along.

BioShock provides a litany of references to family in nomenclature and situation. It features game characters with familiar connections in their names and interactions—the Big Daddies (genetically enhanced human beings who are protectors of Little Sisters) or Little Sisters (genetically altered girls who collect ADAM) (see more at Stang 2018; Vanderhoef & Payne 2018). Many of the rules or instructions in *BioShock* are prefaced by the words, "Would you kindly," narrated by Atlas (a character who stands in for the game designer or "parental authority" of the game). However, the player later finds out that Atlas is Frank Fontaine, an enemy of the Ryan family, who orders Jack to kill his actual father. Moreover, the player gets acclimated to this type of overriding authority, where "Would you kindly" becomes such an embedded part of their environment that they may not even realize they are being parented and told what to do. This reflects the themes of *BioShock*, and the tension between thinking one has free will versus the realization that nothing is under our control.

One of the key questions in this chapter is the balance between freedom and constraints in *BioShock*—just as Jack Ryan did not realize he was being "compelled" to behave in a certain way, did the game also overparent (intensively parent) the player while making them think they were free? Does the game help us better understand what it means to be a "good parent" both through its design and gameplay, as well as its themes, character, and story?

The exploration of parenting themes is supported by an analysis of two additional games that explore themes of parenting through the game's story, as well as its design: *That Dragon, Cancer* and *Life Is Strange 2*.

THAT DRAGON, CANCER

That Dragon, Cancer (Numinous Games 2016) is an indie game made by Ryan and Amy Green, two parents who were faced with the real cancer illness of their son, Joel. They started to make the game while he was in remission from cancer, but then while making the game, the cancer returned and he died. The game features scenes from their life, sometimes expressed from the perspective of the parents or the child.

As in *BioShock*, the players begins birthed in a new world, and they are immediately oriented to its gameplay and emotional contours. For example, the player is taught some simple controls through interactions and instructions (e.g., feeding ducks, rocking on a toy rocking horse). The authentic voices of Joel's parents (recordings of Ryan and Amy Green actually talking to their son and family) are used to help teach and encourage the player in the game to feed ducks. We hear Ryan say, "Don't touch the birds" to Joel, and simultaneously the player is also told this, as they practice lifting Joel's arm and throwing the pieces of bread at the duck. Likewise, Amy says "Ready, set, go," while Joel sits on a rocking horse, and the game instructs the player what controls to press or tap to make Joel rock. The recordings of the Green family also provide the narrative exposition that sets up the real-world story of this family and game: that Joel got sick right after turning one year old and is developmentally delayed as a result. These voices, as well as the muted colors and simple character shapes, also immediately orients and inscribes the player emotionally into the authentic world of this family—their real struggles and concerns, as well as their joys and humor. Notably, Joel is faceless, possibly helping players to more easily inscribe their own child or imagined cared-for individual (McCloud 1993/2004; Noddings 1984).

Many games reduce the amount of scaffolding throughout the game as the player progresses, by not continuing to give hints or messaging once the player has mastered the game. However, *That Dragon, Cancer* continues to provide this type of supportive messaging throughout the entire game. Part of this may be because the game continually changes in the types of actions the player needs to take. For instance, in one scenario, a player needs to move a stethoscope on a dog, and in the next, they need to race around a hospital hallway in a red wagon. The goals and actions keep changing from scene to scene, but the player feels continually protected by the game designer. The designer seems to have affection and care for the player, making sure to continually lead them down a path to the end of the game. Although there is no "win" condition in the game (and in fact, the player experiences the loss of Joel no matter what they do or how they play), the "parenting" game designer stays on the journey with the player. This is not surprising given that the developers of this game were relatively new to game design, and may have been more protective of their players, similar to first-time parents and their newborn child. Moreover, like parenting, this particular game is not about winning, losing, or achieving a particular goal, but staying safe, recognized, and cared for.

Players are not just being parented by the game; they are actually practicing parenting and caretaking activities through their game play. In many of the scenarios, the player acts as the parent or caretaker of Joel (by taking on the role of Amy or Ryan), such as rocking him as a baby in a hospital chair, giving him a beverage, or going to meetings with doctors. Throughout, we also hear the perspectives from the parents during these caretaking activities, such as through authentic voice mail messages or recordings made by the family. These elements often relate to those described by Seifer & Schiller (1995), such as behaviors that increase proximity and contact with the parent (holding and rocking the baby), and ones that decrease it, such as exploration or experimentation (racing in a wagon, playing with a toy). While taking on the role of the parent, we are constantly navigating between these two rhythms—proximity, care, and closeness, versus letting go, exploration, and distance—often within the same scenario. The player shows love in this game through the rhythms of caretaking: the continual ebb and flow of closeness and release.

Likewise, the pace and tone of the game also continually changes throughout, reflecting the varied pace of parenting, from the mundane routines of caretaking to the chaos of change. Like a parent, sometimes the player just needs to wait, listen, and attend, while other times the player needs to suddenly act and respond, reflecting the tedium of waiting and wanting time to pass, as well as the sudden rush and feeling that time is too quickly gone. This is particularly acutely felt, as we see with the Greens, when parenting a sick child with only a few weeks to live.

In *That Dragon, Cancer*, sometimes the player is forced to fail (Chen 2016) at what they are supposed to do in a scene, and this also serves a purpose gameplay-wise, thematically, and narratively. Some examples of instances of forced failure and lack of agency in the game: the player is step removed from the direct parenting, such as by watching the mother holding and singing to him (while the player looks through get well cards), or seeing the parents sit and listen at a meeting with doctors when they explain there are no more treatment options for Joel. The player cannot interact or do anything but listen to the interaction, which sometimes repeats, reflecting the hopelessness that the parents are feeling. Eventually the scene fills with water and the couple is swept away by the waves, and the player is not able to take any actions. In another scene, the player plays as Ryan and is trying to give a drink to a crying Joel, but there is nothing the player (or Ryan) can do to ease his thirst or take away his pain. The player (like Joel) is helpless and cannot soothe the cries, which continue for a painfully long, and slow time, no matter what Ryan says or does. "I can't hold you, I can't make you feel better…okay buddy, I'll hold you," says Ryan, to his son, and we feel his despair, as well as his tension between wanting to help and loving his son, but being overwhelmed by a lack of agency over his son's experience. Often a lack of agency is deleterious for a game's design, but Farber and Schrier discuss how this scene shows a lack of agency, or control, for the player resonates because of the themes of parenting, grief, helplessness, and loss in the game (Farber & Schrier 2017; Schrier & Farber 2019). Despite trying to do everything we can (as a player, or in the role of a parent in the game) we still may not be able to console the child, respond to him, and form a secure attachment. This inability to soothe the child may reflect Ainsworth's insecure or disorganized attachment, where the child continues to cry, no matter what we do to show support.

This paper argues earlier that the game sticks with the player, bringing them on the journey as a teacher and trainer, never fully letting go but watching from a distance. In this way, we feel the designer's affection and care for our ability to progress in the game. On the other hand, we are not always rewarded or given the responses we need in this relationship. While we sometimes know what to expect from these game designers (that they will support us through our journey and continue to teach us what to do in each scenario), we also learn that we may not be soothed or rewarded when meeting our goals or doing what was asked of us. The game seems to have a disorganized, chaotic response to our gameplay (constantly changing scenarios, tone, and rhythms, with no clear rewards, progression, or goals, and the scaffolding of actions without the real possibility of success). This underscores the anxious, insecure, and grief-stricken feeling we have while playing the game and while imagining ourselves in the shoes of these parents. The possibility of loss is always looming (whether the loss of Joel or the loss of the game). The complex and insecure attachment that is enacted reflects the themes of parenting in this game, and the real-world anxieties about parenting, love, and loss.

Life Is Strange 2

Life Is Strange 2 (Dontnod 2018–2019) is not as obviously about parenting—thematically and narratively—as *That Dragon, Cancer* or *BioShock*. The game begins in Seattle, Washington and follows a teenage boy,

Sean Diaz, and his younger brother, Daniel, reeling over the sudden death of their father, Esteban, who had been their sole caretaker. Sean and Daniel had already been managing being abandoned suddenly by their mother, who has been mysteriously away during the first three episodes of the game. As a result of being involved in a problematic interaction with the police, the two boys need to run away to safety, and Sean becomes a de facto caretaker or "parent" of his brother. At the writing of this chapter, only the first three episodes had been released, therefore, this chapter will only focus on what these three episodes reveal.

Like in the other two games, the players have the opportunity in the beginning to get oriented to the world of the game (the controls, themes, character backgrounds) before the real danger begins. Players need to interact with a friend, Lyla Park, and decide which objects to bring for a party that night (e.g., soda or beer, chips, condom), they need to negotiate choices with their family (such as to whom to give the last piece of candy) or whether to ask for or steal money. The game play consists of doing actions (such as picking up a can of soda, or moving to a room) as well as making dialogue and other types of situational choices, such as choosing whom to give the candy to (father, brother, or self), or deciding how to respond to a friend who wants to go to a party. The game's story unfolds through dialogues with other players, as well as through actions with objects or explorations of the spaces of the game.

After this brief orientation to the family's history, their relationships, and their context, the rest of the game centers on the two boys evading police and other dangers. In the first episode, the player controls Sean, who needs to teach and protect his brother in the woods. Although Daniel is not an infant, the player establishes an attachment relationship with Sean, as he becomes his primary caretaker. We explore the area, but we also need to parent him: we need to make sure Daniel is nearby, and that he eats the appropriate foods and stays safe. For instance, we need to test whether the berries we find are poisonous or not and deter or encourage him to eat them. We look for shelter and make a fire. Throughout these exchanges, we also need to continually negotiate whether to just focus on survival and protection, or whether to also encourage Daniel to be silly, imaginative, and have fun. For instance, do we encourage him to create an imaginative "barrier" (out of sticks and stones) for the shelter to protect them at night, and do we decide to teach him how to skip stones in the lake? How patient are we as we try to teach him? The game, for instance, first asks us whether we want to teach him at all about skipping stones, and then we have to decide whether to keep encouraging him to try again, or to spend time doing other essential tasks (such as our main goal of building a fire). The game invites us to encourage (or not encourage) this behavior four times before Daniel is finally successful in skipping the stones (and the game gives us a reward for encouraging perseverance).

Likewise, later in the episode, we have to make choices about how to spend our minimal money on food and beverages at a gas station. Do we only spend money on what is necessary (e.g., bread, meat, drinks) to keep us surviving another day, or do we also spend on the candy that we know our brother wants? Throughout these exchanges, the game continually has us navigate the tension between wanting to meet our goals (the game goals of protecting our family, but also reaching new checkpoints in the game), while deciding whether to veer off the path and support our family's other social and emotional needs: to express joy, tell stories, or to feel trusted and empowered. Our choices in these navigations have consequences for the relationship that we build with our brother. Do we earn his trust by keeping him physically safe and emotionally cared for, as well as by enabling his imagination and encouraging his pursuits? These tensions serve to underscore the ways we show affection to and love for our brother in the game—we can take actions to keep him safe, and we can also actively encourage and teach him. The tensions also serve to enhance the anxieties of playing the game and being "a parent." As we navigate the park, for instance, we see signs of dangerous wildlife everywhere. There are teeth marks and poisonous berries, and "danger: wild animal" signs. The dark toned art style of the park, and ominous sounds and animal noises underscore these dangers. The park is empty of people except for the two boys. While we navigate the park, we are also trying to stay close to our brother. However, at one point, he seems to disappear and we have a momentary feeling of panic—further emphasized by Sean's pleas for Daniel in the game. Suddenly Daniel reappears as a surprise (he was hiding from us), further suggesting the dichotomy between parental authority and childhood freedom and leisure.

As a result, depending on the players choices and actions in *Life Is Strange 2*, relationships with characters in later scenes or episodes may be impacted. In-game consequences and feedback may suggest that your brother has a secure and trusting relationship with you, or perhaps, less secure, resistant, or even angry interactions with you. The game limits choices and interactions as it progresses, sometimes based on previous choices, which may lead to less and less secure bonds between the two characters. For instance, in my game, in episode three, Sean and Daniel's relationship becomes particularly strained, and Daniel begins to spend more time with Finn, another character at a campsite they are staying near. It's possible that the game has constrained the choices such that no matter what the player does, this tension between Sean and Daniel emerges, as the game designers need to tell a particular story, and this strain progresses the story. Thus, while the first episode may enable the player to build a secure attachment with their brother, later episodes may enable other types of attachments due to circumstances and other factors, further suggesting the need to understand the dynamic system among all parties and their context, rather than just a one-to-one relationship when building attachment.

Furthermore, although we cannot clinically map the four different attachment types to the in-game relationships that form throughout the game—the types of actions and strategies that the player needs to make throughout the game are similar to those described earlier (attachment behaviors, exploration behaviors, the system surrounding these, and the bond that is formed) (Seifer & Schiller 1995). Throughout the entire game, we are continually enabling support and protection for our brother, whether to stay close and be careful, or to explore and expand one's imagination. We take the actions we believe will keep him safe, happy, secure, and protected, even though he may not like it. Though we are still a teenager in the game, we are thrust into a role that requires us to be the authority, the parent, and the moral decision maker. And in tandem, we, as the player, are also navigating this for ourselves. We are carefully following the rules and goals and being rewarded for this, and we are also deciding when and how to break rules or explore new situations, such as when to take time to draw in our notebook and observe our world, give money to a stranger who is playing an instrument, use a phone or computer when we are reminded not to do so, or steal an item to give to our brother for the holiday.

Thus, the game is also parenting us, as players, while we are also parenting another character. The game shows affection for us by guiding us through rules and goals, while also allowing us to experiment and explore, and even transgress those boundaries. The game teaches us what is "right and wrong" in this world, but then lets us go and allows us to be moral arbiters and decide how we will negotiate the system's morality (Schrier 2014, 2017; Sicart 2009). The game's system then serves up the consequences to our decisions in the form of punishments and rewards.

Likewise, the player, as Sean, can do the same for his brother, Daniel. As Sean, we show affection for our brother through the rhythm of keeping him close and letting him go, and sometimes allowing him to make his own moral decisions, and serving him feedback for those decisions.

Finally, the game also suggests the tension between being a parent (responsibility) and leisurely pursuits. Sean can no longer just be a carefree child—he needs to now be responsible as an authority figure and caretaker for someone else. The game also continually teases the player as to this responsibility—do we continue to follow its authority and rules and goals, or do we allow ourselves to be leisurely and carefree? The game, thus, also represents the tension between games and reality itself—the freedom and experimentation that a game allows, which reality does not always afford. The game is both a parental authority, teaching and training us, while also being itself an escape from those quotidian and routine responsibilities of parenting and life.

CONCLUSION

This chapter reprised a review of *BioShock* and investigated two new examples (*That Dragon, Cancer* and *Life Is Strange 2*) in relation to parenting and parental love and attachment. This chapter explored how parenting was expressed thematically and narratively, as well as through game play goals, mechanics (actions and activities), and the mood, tone, and environment of the game. The games showed the tensions that underscore parenting and how to take care of others: whether to reinforce boundaries or enable freedom, whether to keep family close or let them explore, and how to express care and protect another while also trying to protect oneself.

In *That Dragon, Cancer,* players feel the tension between wanting to help your child and being frustrated that you cannot help your child, as well as trying to meet goals and follow instructions, while being frustrated that you cannot ultimately meet the goals of the game. Furthermore, the game persists in prodding and parenting the player throughout the experience, almost hopelessly, since Joel succumbs to cancer in the game (as in real life) no matter what the player does.

In *Life Is Strange 2*, players navigate tensions between authority and freedom, boundaries and exploration, and responsibility and leisure. Players are continually torn between upholding rules or breaking them, or protecting others or encouraging experimentation.

In both games, the system continues to reinforce the overriding anxiety—whether the possibility of loss and grief, or the possibility of never being able to fully escape one's responsibilities. Likewise, in both games, the game play reinforces these parenting themes and narratives. The game play serves to further enhance how the player (sometimes awkwardly) handles their role and responsibility as a game player, but also as a parent or caretaker in the game. In *That Dragon Cancer*, the player learns that parenting is always changing, chaotic, and lacking in control and predictability. Despite this, routines remain, and players need to keep trying to maintain stability in an unstable time. They are often helpless in the game to meet goals and keep their in-game child soothed, and likewise, they feel the helplessness of the parents represented in the game, who cannot cure their son of cancer.

Thus, while all different strategies for attachment and caretaking may be taken by the player—from the routine (e.g., feeding a child) to the fantastical (e.g., pretending to slay a dragon or build a fort)—the result may not be a secure attachment between parent and child, game and player. In fact, an insecure or disorganized attachment may further reveal the challenges and difficulties of parenting, and particularly, parenting under dire circumstances, as both games feature. The context and system of parenting, these games seem to suggest, matter just as much as what we can (or cannot) do within those systems. The game designer (and our real worlds) ultimately dictate what we can do. And, likewise, so much of parenting is ultimately beyond our control and reliant on a system we did not design. These games show us that even parents may have limited authority over the relationships they can build with their children, and how they can respond or connect to them.

Finally, what are the broader implications for how to design games and how to parent a player through its experience? It could be argued that all well-designed experiences place appropriate boundaries and need to teach its users how to interact with its system. However, these games suggest that designers can intensively parent their players (or overparent them), and provide too many boundaries, constraints, or prodding, possibly because they are afraid to release their designed experience to the players, and relinquish their control over it. Designers need to trust their players to learn and grow appropriately throughout their system. On the other hand, these games also suggest that the designers' constant scaffolding or overparenting of a player can further emphasize a game's themes of parenting, attachment, and loss, and in particular, parenting during dire circumstances, furthering the effectiveness of the game overall.

REFERENCES

Ainsworth, M. D. S. (1982). Attachment: Retrospect and prospect. In C. M. Parkes & J. Stevenson-Hinde (Eds.), *The Place of Attachment in Human Behavior* (pp. 3–30). New York: Basic Books.

Ainsworth, M. D. S., & Bell, S. M. (1970). Attachment, exploration, and separation: Illustrated by the behavior of one-year-olds in a strange situation. *Child Development*, 41, 49–67.

Ainsworth, M. D. S., Bell, S. M., & Stayton, D. J. (1971). Individual differences in strange-situation behaviour of one-year-olds. In H. R. Schaffer (Ed.), *The Origins of Human Social Relations*. Academic Press.

Ainsworth, M. D. S., & Bowlby, J. (1991). An ethological approach to personality development. *American Psychologist*, 46, 331–341.

Ainsworth, M. D. S., Blehar, M. C., Waters, E., & Wall, S. N. (1978). *Patterns of Attachment: A Psychological Study of the Strange Situation*. Hillsdale, NJ: Erlbaum.

Ainsworth, M. D. S., & Wittig, B. A. (1969). Attachment and the exploratory behaviour of one-year-olds in a strange situation. In B. M. Foss (Ed.), *Determinants of Infant Behaviour* (Vol. 4, pp. 113–136). London, UK: Methuen.

Bowlby, J. (1969). *Attachment and Loss*. New York: Basic Books, Vol. 1.

Chen, S. (2016). "Forced Failure in *Spent*," *Gamasutra*, https://www.gamasutra.com/blogs/SandeChen/20160629/276106/Forced_Failure_in_SPENT.php.

Farber, M., & Schrier, K. (2017). The strengths and limitations of using digital games as "empathy machines," working paper for the UNESCO MGIEP (Mahatma Gandhi Institute of Education for Peace and Sustainable Development, https://s3-us-west-2.amazonaws.com/lms-chi/pdfs/MeNzjYmpqKKNzPgtt_empathy-and-compassion-through-games-the-limits-and-strengths-of-using-digital-games-as-empathy-machines-farber-schrier.pdf.

Hazan, C., & Shaver, P. (1987). Romantic love conceptualized as an attachment process. *Journal of Personality and Social Psychology*, 52(3), 511–524. doi:10.1037/0022-3514.52.3.511.

Keller, H. (2018). Universality claim of attachment theory: Children's socioemotional development across cultures. *PNAS*, 115, 45.

McCloud, S. (1993/2004). *Understanding Comics: The Invisible Art*. New York: Harper Perennial.

Noddings, N. (1984). *Caring: A Feminine Approach to Ethics and Moral Education*. Berkeley, CA: University of California Press.

Schrier, K. (2018). *BioShock* as the infinite parent: Parenting and play in the *BioShock* series. In J. Aldred & F. Parker (Eds.), *New Perspectives on BioShock*. Montreal, Canada: McGill-Queen's University Press.

Schrier, K. (2017). Designing role-playing video games for ethical thinking. *Educational Technology Research and Development*, 65(4), 831–868.

Schrier, K. (2014). Designing and using games to teach ethics and ethical thinking. In K. Schrier (Ed.), *Learning, Education and Games vol. 1: Curricular and Design Considerations*. Pittsburgh, PA: ETC Press.

Schrier, K. & Farber, M. (2019). Open questions for empathy and games. *Proceedings of Connected Learning Conference'18*. Boston, MA: ETC Press.

Seifer, R. & Schiller, M. (1995). The role of parenting sensitivity, infant temperament, and dyadic interaction in attachment theory and assessment. *Monographs of the Society for Research in Child Development*, 60(2–3), 146–174.

Sicart, M. (2009). *Ethics and Computer Games*. Cambridge, UK: MIT Press.

Stang, S. (2018). Big Daddies and their little sisters: Postfeminist fatherhood in bioshock series. In J. Aldred & F. Parker (Eds.), *New Perspectives on BioShock*. Montreal, Canada: McGill-Queen's University Press.

Vanderhoef, J. & Payne, M. T. (2018). Big daddies and monstrous mommies: BioShock's maternal abjection, absence, and annihilation. In J. Aldred & F. Parker (Eds.), *New Perspectives on BioShock*. Montreal, Canada: McGill-Queen's University Press.

Vaughn, B. E. & Waters, E. (1990). Attachment behavior at home and in the laboratory: Q-sort observations and strange situation classifications of one-year-olds, *Child Development*, 61(6), 1965–1973.

II

Case Studies

CHAPTER 6

The Restoration of Female Friendship in *Life is Strange* and *Night in the Woods*

Stephanie Harkin

CONTENTS

INTRODUCTION

A recent movement in video games toward the inclusion of adolescent girls as primary subjects is a significant development given the mainstream image, financial viability, and critically-valued status attached to those games. Studies of girlhood have been relatively unexplored within feminist video game analysis, while media critics often devalue "women's" genres (Bode 2010). Twenty years ago, game narratives formulated around female friendships were mostly confined within the girls' game genre of the 1990s in games like *Chop Suey* (Magnet Interactive Studios 1995) and *Secret Paths in the Forest* (Purple Moon 1997). Such games represented an attempt to attract young girls to computer games, although they unfortunately reinscribed feminine stereotypes while continuing to isolate girls from mainstream gaming. Despite their shortcomings, these games began to experiment with emotional bonds and female connectedness among their adolescent characters, meeting the desires communicated by the market research groups comprised of young girls (Cassell and Jenkins 1998; Ochsner 2015). This chapter examines the complicated affections between female friends and how the re-emergence of this theme (and its improved handling) is interwoven within the ludic and narrative elements of two video games that explore reunions between estranged friends: *Life is Strange* (Dontnod Entertainment 2015) and *Night in the Woods* (Infinite Fall 2017).[1]

Female friendships are traditionally an undervalued form of love in comparison to the social value and academic attention granted to women's romantic and maternal relationships (see O'Connor 1992; Schaefer 2018). Friendships between adolescent girls have likewise been culturally dismissed and often regarded as a temporary phase in preparation for later heterosexual relationships (as noted by Aapola, Gonick and Harris 2005; Berridge 2016; Hatch 2011; see also Rich 1980). Despite this, Sally Theran's (2010) study on young girls' self-esteem found that girls' adolescent friendships are crucial sites for identity construction and psychological health. As Sinikka Aapola, Marnina Gonick and Anita Harris (2005, 111) write, female friendships are "a powerful cultural force, representing sites of collective meaning-making, and a necessary requirement in the multilayered process of making gendered identities." Media texts that feature relationships between women therefore meaningfully permit the visibility of a feminine identity that is informed separately from women's relationships to men (Hollinger 1998).

Troubling these optimistic observations, Alison Winch (2012, 5) proposes that female friendships (at the encouragement of friendship films and lifestyle blogs) rather frequently contain an assemblage of "ugly feelings" that include jealousy, competition, and the policing of normative feminine behavior. Prior to Winch, Pat O'Connor (1992) similarly cautioned against a theorization of friendship between women as unequivocally joyous, productive, and liberating. She cites class difference, oppositional social politics, and limited time and emotional commitment as common barriers. Driven by the views of Winch and O'Connor, I propose that the estranged female friendships in *Life is Strange* and *Night in the Woods* attest to the complexities and imperfections of friendships, while simultaneously highlighting their resilience in the face of these conditions. The two games offer a digital space for exploring raw coming-of-age complexities between female friends that crucially remain unobstructed by heterosexual pursuits.[2]

Set in a bayside town's high school, *Life is Strange* is a narrative-adventure game, released episodically in five parts. Its action is primarily driven by its choices and dialogue options that have various effects on the plot's outcomes. The ability to rewind time to alter decisions and to solve puzzles operates as its defining mechanic. The remaining player actions meanwhile consist of taking photos or interacting with objects and characters in limited explorable areas like the school's hallways and dormitories. Most of those interactions are optional and non-integral to the storyline's outcome although they develop greater nuance toward the game's world-building, particularly in drawing attention to the school's bullying problem and leaning more about its broader cast of students, teachers, and parents.

The protagonist is Max Caulfield, a quiet eighteen-year-old student with a passion for photography. She has returned to her former hometown of Arcadia Bay after being accepted for a scholarship at the prestigious Blackwell Academy. Each of the five episode's key narrative moments and player decisions are summarized from Max's perspective within the written entries of her diary, accessible at any time within the menu interface (Figure 6.1). The game's events begin from the discovery of Max's power to rewind time and progresses as she utilizes those powers to help her friend

FIGURE 6.1 Max's diary is frequently updated throughout the game, offering a summary of events and further insight into her thoughts and feelings.

Chloe Price investigate the truth behind the disappearance of Blackwell student, Rachel Amber. Their investigation mostly involves searching and retrieving evidence and navigating sensitive dialogue puzzles with the rewind feature accessible to amend unsuccessful or disastrous consequences. The rewind feature, however, is limited to its immediate use, that is, once a player progresses to the next sequence in the game they are unable to undo their previous actions. The effects of many decisions are therefore not made apparent until later in the game.

Night in the Woods is a 2D narrative-and-exploration–adventure game. It is set in the economically declining rural town of Possum Springs and features an eccentric cast of anthropomorphic animals. Players will likely spend most of their time wandering the open town, balancing along telephone wires to access rooftops or concealed areas, or initiating casual and humorous dialogue with its various residents. The repetition of exploring the town each day and being rewarded with subtly new experiences—like new characters, areas, or mini-games—effectively captures a sense of living in a small rural community.

The protagonist is Mae Borowski, a college dropout, queer, anti-authoritarian cat.[3] Having abruptly withdrawn from college, Mae's return, intended to be comfortably familiar, is simultaneously disorienting The town's general appearance and residents are the same, although several businesses have been replaced by large corporate franchises, her friends have unfulfilling full-time jobs and her parents are struggling to keep their house, prompting Mae to gradually learn of the crippling effects of a fading economy subjected upon her hometown's residents. *Night in the Woods'* storyline is not as central as the events that unfold in *Life is Strange*, where despite Mae's investigation into what she believes to be a ghost, the game is ultimately characterized by the playful act of mundane wandering. While the mystery of the ghost physically brings her friends together, Mae's realizations—born from her wandering—meaningfully strengthen their emotional connectedness.

Life is Strange's Max Caulfield and *Night in the Woods'* Mae Borowski are both late-adolescent women who have returned to their small hometowns. Upon returning, they both encounter tense reunions with their estranged childhood friends. The friendship between Max and Chloe collapsed when Max moved to Seattle for five years. She failed to maintain contact with Chloe who subsequently felt abandoned as Max's departure coincided with Chloe's father's untimely death from a motor vehicle accident. Their relationship is a key feature of the game although the nature of the relationship is dictated by the player when presented with the option to kiss Chloe. As Adrienne Shaw (2014) argues, the option itself represents a neo-liberal responsibility for accessing queer content. For the purpose of this chapter the discussion of their relationship will be limited to a reading of their friendship (for notable analyses of *Life is Strange*'s queer representation, see Knutson 2018; Alexandra 2018).

Mae likewise returns to a tense reunion with her former childhood friend Beatrice "Bea" Santello (hereafter Bea), who is one of two friendship routes the player can pursue throughout the game. Like Chloe, Bea has lost a parent (her mother to cancer) and feels anchored to her hometown due to the redistribution of her college funds toward her late mother's medical and post-mortem bills. As Mae attempts to restore their childhood friendship, Bea struggles to accept Mae's decision to drop out of college. The designs of three areas of contention between the two pairs will be elaborated in this chapter: Max and Mae's unmet expectations upon returning home, their differing levels of maturity when compared to Chloe and Bea, and the conflicting moral compasses of Max and Chloe.

The friendships are inevitably restored in both games regardless of the player's actions, driven together firstly through their shared detective work. In *Life is Strange* this is the investigation into Rachel's disappearance and in *Night in the Woods* it is Mae's mysterious ghost. Secondly, the pairs engage in rebellious appropriations of space. These moments represent an empowering use of game space as these young women assert a form of feminist anti-authoritarianism via their occupation in off-limited areas.

These complicated estranged friendships further elicit a feminist potential for they challenge the mythology of an idealized female friendship comprised of unequivocal pleasure and empowerment. They instead attest to heartache, abandonment, and misunderstanding, while eventually renewing their former intimacy after accepting their differences and (re)discovering their similarities. The portrayal of conflict between girls is then not restricted to a harmful promotion of their competition, but potentially serves, as Winch (2012, 71) writes, as "invaluable in offering the female viewer a cathartic space to explore the complexities of women's relationships." Regarding other visual media platforms, studies of female friendships continue to expand, yet scholarly attention on this subject in video games has mostly been confined to critical analyses of the girls' games movement. This is most reasonably due to the limited presence of female friendships within those games. This recent re-emergence of female friendships in video games therefore necessitates updated consideration. Mapping these video game designs deepens how the construction and presentation of female friendships are theorized and in turn encourages designers to continue to pursue productive feminine content in mainstream games.

DESIGNING FRIENDSHIP COMPLEXITIES

As *Life is Strange* and *Night in the Woods* are both narrative-centric games their portrayals of friendship complexities are primarily communicated through literary processes like dialogue. Their ludic qualities, however, evocatively support the various avenues of their tensions and differences. The first of these is the protagonist's unmet expectations upon returning to their hometowns. Their nostalgic unrealized longing subsequently leads to disappointment, breeding frustration amongst all four characters who are powerless in their inability to restore their former lives. A second major difference formulated during their time apart is their opposing willingness toward embracing adulthood. Both games frequently draw attention to their adolescent protagonists' complicated liminal status between childhood and adulthood. Max and Mae's uncertain identification signifies what anthropologist Victor Turner ([1969] 1977, 95) describes as the "necessarily ambiguous" condition of adolescent liminality. Finally, in *Life is Strange* the friendship is further tested through the various difficult choices presented to the player. Throughout the game, the player is positioned to negotiate between their personal values and what they believe Max the character would do, which will often be at odds with the decision that Chloe insists. In this way, Max's compatibility with Chloe is placed into question when players are made to decide whether to submit to her "bad" influence. These factors combine to communicate meaningful complexities specific to adolescent friendship.

EXPECTATION

Max and Chloe endure an abrupt and awkward reunion when Chloe saves Max from a violent school peer, Nathan Prescott. As they drive away a cutscene ensues where Chloe observes, "After five years you're still Max Caulfield" and angry that Max has been in Arcadia Bay for a month without contacting her she further remarks, "Don't give me the guilty face. At least pretend you're glad to see me." While Max remains familiar to Chloe,

Chloe is hardly recognizable to Max. Designed with markers of rebellion, Chloe now adorns bright blue hair and tattoos, has been expelled from Blackwell Academy, carries a firearm, and is in debt to an intimidating narcotics dealer. She also now harbors a great deal of anger and is determined to escape Arcadia Bay in pursuit of a fresh start. This contrasts to Max, who chose to return to Arcadia Bay for a promising scholarship that will support her passion for photography.

Max records her thoughts and feelings in her diary where her early entries—available to read at the beginning of episode one—reveal her unfulfilled expectations. The first line of the first entry excitedly reads, "I GOT ACCEPTED INTO BLACKWELL ACADEMY" yet this sentiment is contrasted four entries later with the opening line, "Blackwell sucks ass!" This sentiment continues to manifest as Max and Chloe increasingly uncover Arcadia Bay's secrets and corruption. Max writes, "'High school should be the best years of your life,' I've heard over and over from my parents and other experts. Fuck do they know?"

Night in the Woods likewise examines the expectations of returning home. Seeking the comfortable familiarity of Possum Springs, Mae is disoriented by its rapid economic decline, all the more apparent after spending time away. The residents are exhausted, her friends have grown up, and her favorite Italian restaurant has gone out of business. She now has little in common with her former friend Bea who had to sacrifice her college fund for her late mother's bills. Bea is now overworked from solely running her family's hardware store while managing the stress of its financial tightrope. Mae's comments to herself most explicitly express her displeasure at these changes. When approaching the closure notice on the window of the "Pastabilities" restaurant, the player's movement is abruptly halted while a dialogue bubble above Mae reads, "What the... What... No!" *Night in the Woods'* overall ludic guidelines, however, more succinctly establish the dreary impacts of Possum Springs' financial regression.

Mirroring Mae's uncertain lifestyle, the game poses few objectives or challenges to its players, encouraging them instead to freely wander the town of Possum Springs each day. Their only objective is to spend time with either Gregg or Bea (the two friendship routes) by meeting them at their workplaces. The rest of the town, however, is open for exploration and the free wandering that takes place on the way to Mae's friends is where *Night in the Woods* is most playful. Players optionally navigate along the telephone wires to access rooftops and hidden areas

FIGURE 6.2 The traversable telephone wires invite playful exploration of Possum Spring's rooftops and hidden areas.

(Figure 6.2). They may also befriend other members of Possum Springs, often leading to optional sequences and mini-activities like scavenging for junk in the tunnels or searching for dusk stars with her former high school teacher.

Wandering around the same areas of Possum Springs each day, however, eventually evolves into a repetitive routine. This format offers players an insight into the collective melancholy of the town's struggling residents.[4] The lack of objectives and directionless wandering serve as invaluable ludic representations of Mae and Bea's differences as the player's actions are simultaneously representative of Mae's illusory freedom and uncertain future and Bea's mundane routine and sense of entrapment. This meaningful design strategy recalls Ian Bogost's (2007) conception of "procedural rhetoric." *Night in the Woods* enacts what Bogost (2007, 3) theorizes as "a practice of using processes persuasively," that is, its design incorporates an argument. *Night in the Woods'* design processes operate as powerful expressions into the broader intersections of melancholia, class inequality, and rural exploitation.

Max and Mae both experience the disappointment of unmet expectations when they return to their unfamiliar hometowns and their unfamiliar former friends. Chloe and Bea are also disillusioned from their expectations of their futures, where they now feel hopelessly anchored to their insular hometowns. The disappointment and cynicism that arises from these unmet expectations lead to difficult reunions that take time over the games' progression to mend.

LIMINAL IDENTITY AND QUESTIONS OF MATURITY

Further distinguishing Max and Mae from Chloe and Bea is their inhabitance across disparate degrees of maturity. All four are positioned across an ambiguous adolescent threshold, meaning their identities are uncertainly situated between childhood and adulthood. Turner ([1969] 1977, 95) defines liminal transition as "neither here nor there" and "betwixt and between." Developing ideas of adolescent uncertainty, Catherine Driscoll (2011, 66) frames maturity as performing a central role in the teen genre, operating as an obstacle that poses a "question" and a "problem" rather than a reflection of values. She therefore conceptualizes the genre as "less about growing up than about the expectation, difficulty, and social organization of growing up" (Driscoll 2011, 66). Both video game texts under examination explore the question of maturity among its adolescent characters, framing its varying degrees as obstacles to their friendships.

At eighteen years old, Max occupies a liminal status and, representative of its ambiguity, she appears to be emotionally younger than Chloe. In Max's diary, her character profile for Chloe explains, "She's all grown up now, but it doesn't seem like she's only one year older than me." Chloe's circle of friends, for example, includes Frank Bowers, an older man who deals narcotics to the town's residents from his RV. Max's developing maturity meanwhile borders on moments of naivety. This is most evident when she discovers a swimsuit magazine in the school janitor's stock room. Upon interacting with the magazine, players would likely assume that the man derives voyeuristic pleasure from the models featured inside. Max, however, remarks that she was not aware of his interest in runway fashion. This humorous moment, while subtle, is rare amidst the game's generally serious tone, although it significantly establishes Max's underlying innocence in contrast to Chloe's cynicism.

The game's point-and-click format gestures towards Max's resistance to growing up via her comments of nostalgic longing that accompany the everyday mementos available for interaction. Interacting with Chloe's dresser, for example, prompts a recalled memory of painting it together or interacting with the backyard swing-set activates the audio of a conversation held between them as children. Max's ability to rewind time and her passion for photography further signify her grasping onto the past. In her diary Max describes a photo of herself and Chloe captured by Chloe's father on the day of his death: "The picture seemed to sum up everything we had as children and lost as adults… whatever being an 'adult' means." By focusing on the photo, Max travels back in time to the afternoon it was taken in order to prevent Chloe's father's death. She hopes this will restore Chloe's former personality as Chloe attributes his death to be the origin of her troubles. This well-intentioned act backfires and ultimately teaches Max a crucial lesson in accepting misfortune. (It should, however, be noted that Max's longing for simplicity is not narratively unreasonable given that her newly acquired rewind powers bestow an elevated sense of responsibility).

Even more prominently than *Life is Strange*, *Night in the Woods* depicts Mae and Bea's opposing levels of late-adolescent maturity to be a major source of conflict. The age of twenty is presented as a particularly troubled period of in-betweenness. Those who leave and go to college are seen as maintaining the pleasures of adolescent freedom while those left behind must participate in the adult workforce in order to get by. If players choose to chat to Mae's mother before they leave the house, she will one day explain, "A lot of adulthood is number stress." Bea is indeed familiar with "number stress" running her family's hardware store on her own. Her resentment for her obligations is made clear during an obligatory dialogue sequence (which is a sequence similar to a cutscene with a lack of player input other than pressing a button to activate each new line of text). Bea mirrors Chloe when she confesses to Mae, "When my mum died, my life ended too." In effect, she resents Mae for dropping out of college, continuing with, "I can't not hate you for that." Mae meanwhile has few responsibilities and is unsure of how she identifies.

As players navigate the town, they are able to approach and interact with various members of the community who address Mae in equally varied terms. Most of these interactions will incite short pre-written conversations with little to no dialogue options for the player. Upon interacting with a group of teenagers in the underpass, she will greet, "Hey kids!" to which they reply, "Hey adult," inciting Mae to defensively proclaim that she was their age only a few years ago. At the same time as she refutes kids calling her an adult, she resents adults addressing her as a child. Unprompted, an elderly neighbor Mr. Penderson calls out, "Hey! You kid!" Correcting him, Mae automatically responds, "Adult." A former school peer upon hearing about her situation concludes, "So you're basically a teenager again," to which Mae contests, "No, I'm just an adult living with her parents."

Bea is especially resentful of Mae's seemingly easy lifestyle, which culminates in multiple arguments between the two of them throughout the game.

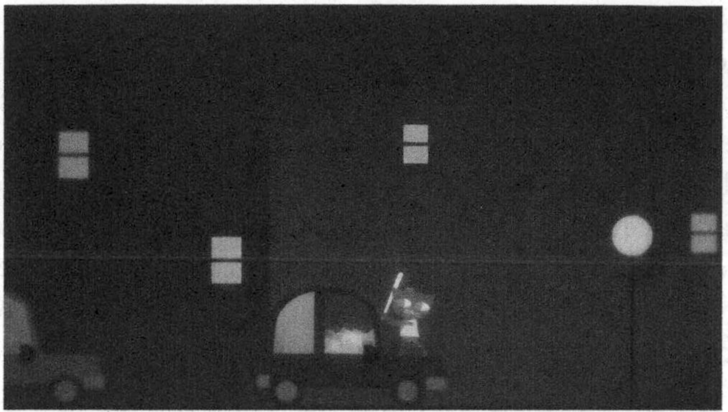

FIGURE 6.3 Mae's dream invites players to vandalize Possum Springs.

In another compulsory dialogue sequence following a party where Mae becomes intoxicated, Bea drives her home and frustratingly questions,

> What happened to you? You used to be smart!!! You used to be cool! You used to be worth talking to! Why did you even come back? Oh, did college not work out for you? Was it inconvenient? Were you not in the mood? I would have killed for that. I still would. I'd kick you out of this moving car right now if it meant I could go to college.

As she helps Mae into bed Bea says, "It's not your fault you're just a kid" and refuting Mae's protests, states, "I stayed here and got older while you went off and stayed the same." On this same evening, Mae's anger and confusion becomes projected within her dream sequence where players traverse an abstracted and obscured version of Possum Springs with a baseball bat, encouraged to break car windows and streetlights (Figure 6.3).

MORALITY AND PEER PRESSURE

The friendship in *Life is Strange* is particularly tested through its high-stakes choice mechanic. Like Max, Chloe's maturity and identity is also still in development. Unlike Max, her misfortunes have bred immense anger and have resulted in her departure from the innocence and childhood pleasures that Max is still negotiating. Chloe's cynicism and short temper contribute to her rebellious design markers, configuring her as the "bad" counterpart to Max's moral conscience.

Traditionally video game relationships are an achievement unlocked by navigating a certain path within a pre-written dialogue tree

(Khandaker-Kokoris 2015; Kelly 2015). While the friendship between Chloe and Max is inevitably restored, the game instead emphasizes the journey between them, testing players with decisions that pressure Max to choose between her friend's peer pressure and upholding her moral values. Players are presented with multiple morally grey decisions with unknown consequences later in the game, but it is often the ideas Chloe puts forth to Max that are less ambiguously right or wrong, like stealing money from Blackwell's handicapped fund in episode three. While the broader consequences remain unknown, Chloe will immediately react with her approval or disappointment. Players are therefore positioned to choose between pleasing Chloe by capitulating to her "bad" influence or to do the right thing and risk upsetting her. The player's actions may also endanger Chloe. Stealing the money, for example, will help Chloe pay back her debt to Frank, who has threatened violence if she fails to repay him. Players therefore must assess between supporting Max's personal interest in helping Chloe or the accessibility for prospective handicapped students. If players steal the money, Chloe stands up and hugs her. If persuaded to leave it, however, she will remark of its potential use and walk away from Max. In episode four, a building permit notice outside the dormitories will detail the dates of upcoming accessibility upgrades to which Max will express relief upon interaction: "Whew," or if the money was taken the sign will announce the project's delay and Max will express guilt: "We're going to hell."

Players tend to insert their own moral values into games that pose ethical decisions prompting a majority to make "good" choices on their first play-through (Busch, Consalvo and Jong 2019). Character archetypes also influence player decisions, aligning their actions with what they believe the game's "hero" would do. Busch, Consalvo, and Jong (2019, 221) found this tendency among their interviewees, who often felt that a game would "nudge them to enact certain roles." *Life is Strange* experiments with this process through its construction of Max as a character rather than an avatar; that is, according to Shaw's (2014) distinction, she upholds an established background and personality rather than operating as a digital proxy of the player. Max is previously established as morally upright, which players then consider—along with their own moral values—when making decisions. When confronted with whether to steal from the handicapped fund, Max's position is made clear when Chloe anticipates a lecture from Max before the decision is made and again when even if the player chooses to take it, Max will inform them, "I feel

FIGURE 6.4 Players are presented with two options: "Leave the money" or "Steal the money."

like shit." The language utilized—"*steal* the money" instead of "*take* the money" [emphasis added]—further "nudges" players toward the more ethical decision of leaving the money (Figure 6.4).

Shaw (2014, 101) distinguishes between "sameness identity" and "empathic identity" between players and avatars, where the former refers to the self-referencing produced by ludic-centric video games while the latter is the connection to characters constructed by narratives. *Life is Strange* utilizes a player's empathic identification to Max to produce tension between the two friends, differentiating Max as "good" and Chloe as "bad" when shaming players for submitting to her influence. Max's coding of innocence is hence further contrasted from Chloe's rebelliousness when this choice mechanic frequently tests their compatibility. This design in turn supports the complexities at play between two estranged friends whose adolescent identities and value systems have been formulated separate from one another.

RESTORING INTIMACY: SHARING PASSION, SHARING PROXIMITY

The restoration of friendship is a central theme to both *Life is Strange* and *Night in the Woods*. The majority of this chapter has explored the ways that the two video games narratively and ludically express difference and tension between estranged friends. This section now addresses how their affection is successfully reconstructed. In *Life is Strange* Max and Chloe's closeness is shared through their investigation into the disappearance of Rachel's Amber. *Night in the Woods* also features detective work although their bonding is not established through their shared dedication to justice but rather, as they admit, to the companionship that forms from proximity. The girls' rebellious occupations of space—sneaking into the gym's pool in *Life is Strange* and tampering with the mall's fountain in *Night in the Woods*—further expresses a form of playful anti-authoritarianism that bridges the gap between the girls' differences, helping Max to release her guard around others and enabling Bea to embrace forgotten childish pleasures.

DETECTIVE PLOTS

Max and Chloe initially unite after Max agrees to utilize her rewind abilities to investigate Rachel disappearance. In the second episode players must use the rewind mechanic several times in the diner and again in the junkyard in order to demonstrate its legitimacy and usefulness to Chloe for her investigation. When Chloe discovers that Max has used her rewind powers to save her life her trust in Max builds, as does her willingness to put them both in dangerous situations like breaking into Frank's RV to investigate the nature of his relationship with Rachel. The player's success in solving various puzzles with the rewind feature, like lifting Frank's keys or negotiating with him without anybody getting hurt, is rewarded with Chloe's trust and warmness towards Max. They may receive supportive text messages from Chloe or additional narrative content. Chloe shows Max her gun, for example, only if Max intervenes in Chloe's argument with her step-father. So, although their friendship is inevitably restored, players retain a degree of agency in determining the path of its restoration. Significantly they also determine its future, having to choose between saving Chloe's life or the town of Arcadia Bay in the final episode.[5]

Examining the role of genre conventions to adolescent identity, Roz Kaveney (2006, 180) posits that horror themes provide an allegory for adolescence as a "nightmare" while detective tropes correspond to painful self-discovery. *Life is Strange* incorporates these themes to produce similar ends. Max and Chloe commence their own investigation into Rachel's disappearance, uncovering horrors from Mr. Jefferson and Nathan Prescott's "dark room" to the corrupt influence asserted over the town by the wealthy Prescott family. Max increasingly adopts Chloe's anger the further they investigate, culminating in her most expressive diary entry: "FUCK YOU ARCADIA BAY" after uncovering Rachel's remains. Their shared anger and determination that drives them to achieve justice for Rachel represents the empowering potential of feminine solidarity. Female friends that perform heroic tasks additionally undermine the lone-wolf tradition, promoting a contrary notion that girls work better with the support of other girls (Ross 2004).

The restoration of Mae and Bea's friendship, however, is driven by proximity over passion. Like Max and Chloe, they also undertake detective work to investigate a ghost that Mae insists is real, although Bea makes it clear that she does not believe in ghosts, asserting at one point that she only accompanied Mae to the cemetery because she was going to visit her mother anyway. Likewise, at the library searching through newspaper records Mae, frustrated, snaps, "If you think it's so stupid why are you here?" Yet in this instance Bea replies, "Because you're my friend, you asshole!" Such interactions contrast from the passion that drives Max and Chloe to expose Mr. Jefferson and the Prescotts. Mae and Bea rather fall into a friendship again, based upon their shared sentiment of being anchored to Possum Springs. Mae voices this perception to remind Bea that she is not alone. In a compulsory dialogue sequence Mae assures, "We're both trapped. But we're trapped together."

While confessional dialogue drives Mae and Bea's relationship forward, the ludic elements of *Night in the Woods* support and enrich how the player understands their shared troubles. Their affection develops as their knowledge of each other is obtained, which is gained the more the player wanders the town, discovering sites of decay and abandon, experiencing boredom, and eavesdropping on the grievances of other residents. Mae articulates how the town's fate and her friend's lives are intertwined in the game's cutscene epilogue (when Bea's route is chosen), "None of us asked for any of this [...] You can work as hard as you want but the universe is gonna keep doing what it does and I don't think any of us deserved all this. This is all stuff that started long before we were born." The ending of *Night in the Woods* does not conform to an action-based climax, despite the ghost's identity belonging to what Mea describes as a "death cult of conservative uncles." The climactic finale is rather centered on friendship, communication and problem solving, where Mae, Bea, Gregg and his partner Angus must find a safe path out of the mines.

SPATIAL REBELLIONS

Both *Life is Strange* and *Night in the Woods* present pivotal moments of affection when their characters appropriate off-limit spaces. In doing so, they represent a "tough girl" branding, yet the texts do not mark them as vulnerable and responsible for their own problems as Aapola et al. (2005) have observed in other visual mediums. Max, Chloe, Mae, and Bea are rather coded as "resilient," expressed through their anti-authoritarian occupations of space. In episode three of *Life is Strange*, Max and Chloe sneak into Blackwell Academy's swimming pool after hours. During a cutscene, they strip to their underwear and playfully splash each other before the player is tasked to stealthily avoid security on the way out. Max recounts in her journal: "I love that Chloe brings out the 'just don't give a fuck' side of me" emanating the pleasures of rebellion and its empowering potential for teenage girls. Their playful rebellion evokes their former shared childhood memories, bridging the gap forged between them from their five years apart. Max reflects this sentiment in her diary: "Chloe smiled at me like we were in the most secret club in the world." Their time in the pool is hence a crucial moment in forwarding their friendship and affection as they promise in the cutscene to never leave each other's side.

Mae, meanwhile, upholds the anti-authoritarian influence in her friendship to Bea who does not have the luxury of time or energy to be playful or break the rules. When the two of them visit Possum Springs' derelict mall, Bea is saddened when the mall reminds her of joyful early memories. The player's objective is to then cheer her up by applying their knowledge of climbing the town's structures to reach the top of the mall's art installation. In doing so, Mae gains access to a control panel stationed above the artwork that is connected to the mall's water feature. Players must then aim and spray water at unsuspecting passersby and are rewarded by each successful hit with Bea's laughter in the corner of the screen.

Discussions regarding representations of girls and women's friendships frequently evaluate the feminist potential of inhabiting public space. Winch (2012) argues that portrayals of female friends from private to public spaces are still polarizing because most often those public spaces—shopping malls and beauty salons—are still separate from male spaces. Aapola, et al. (2005, 129) meanwhile identify two common tropes; non-threatening "sweet and fashionable" friendship groups that comply to normative feminine behavior, and unfeminine "tough girls," who "take over" public space "aiming to please themselves first and foremost, even if by ridiculing or aggravating others." Theorizing beyond the politics of their actions, Sarah Projansky (2014, 119) writes, "for girls to inhabit and take pleasure in social space, I would argue, is feminist." Each of these perspectives may be applied to these sequences in *Life is Strange* and *Night in the Woods*, although the girls' rebellious actions do not foreshadow their downfall as Aapola et al. (2005) suggest but rather meaningfully strengthen their unions via their shared appropriation of these spaces.

The pairing of friendship and female spatial occupation additionally evokes the non-violent exploration and emotional friendship narratives of the girls' games era in the 1990s. While these games failed to endure after losing the support of major developers they continued to appear in unnoticeable forms; obscured amongst the flood of Playstation 2 games or relegated to the casual mobile games industry, culturally disregarded by hardcore gamers and gaming journalists despite their profits (Chess and Paul 2018).[6] While *Life is Strange* and *Night in the Woods* would not traditionally be perceived as mainstream games, their critical and commercial success signifies a restored and significantly popular valuation of this forgotten form of affection between female friends.

CONCLUSION

The reincorporation of female friendship themes to critically and commercially successful games is politically significant to video gaming's improving representational trends. *Life is Strange* and *Night in the Woods* share thematic attributes in their exploration of the complexities of restoring estranged friendships. In doing so, they provide productive representations of adolescent girlhood, allowing alternative, rebellious femininities and their bonds with other girls to be visible, without upholding a shallow idealization of indisputable pleasure. Their bonds are primarily communicated and advanced through narrative dialogue, while their complexities are supported through the games' persuasive designs. Identifying how these narrative and ludic processes function contributes to how we may measure video gaming's industrial improvements as these contemporary designs of female friendship are indicative of representational progress.

NOTES

1 This chapter limits its discussion of *Life is Strange* to its originally released first season to the exclusion of its prequel and second season.

2 Players have the option to form a heterosexual romance with Max's Blackwell Academy peer Warren. His role in the game overall, however, is strictly supportive and the optional kiss between Max and Warren is not a critical objective or influential to the plot. See Tasker (1998), who provides an affective appraisal of women achieving their strength without the aid of (or in spite of) heterosexual romantic partners in her chapter on female friendships in melodrama and romance genres.

3 The term "queer" is used here to avoid mislabeling Mae's identity. Her statement "I don't care if they're a boy or a girl" may indicate pansexuality or bisexuality yet the game does not disclose a specific term.

4 Another powerful example of this design strategy worth citing is Porpentine's *With Those We Love Alive* (2014), a text-based game developed on Twine. The game similarly utilizes a procedural repetition to communicate to players what it is like for some who live with depression. Each day players are free to explore the mysterious palace and city although each visit to a particular

area becomes less interesting. Players are then prone to hasten the game's progression by simply remaining in bed, as going to sleep marks the beginning of a new day. For further discussion see O'Connor (2014).

5 See Butt and Dunne (2017) for a critical analysis of videogame narratives where rebel girls are sacrificed to preserve a community's patriarchal status quo.

6 The Playstation 2 remains at the time of writing to be the highest selling videogame console on record with 159 million units speculated to have been sold by early 2019 (Sirani 2019). The high volume of wide-ranging videogames is an outcome specific to this platform's particularly high sales figures.

REFERENCES

Aapola, S., Gonick, M. & Harris, A. 2005. *Young Femininity: Girlhood, Power and Social Change*. Basingstoke: Palgrave Macmillan.

Alexandra, H. 2018. Let queer characters be happy. In *Kotaku*, June 27. https://www.kotaku.com.au/2018/06/let-queer-characters-be-happy/.

Berridge, S. 2016. Cher and Dionne BFFs: Female friendship, genre, and medium specificity in the film and television versions of Amy Heckerling's *Clueless*. In *Refocus: The films of Amy Heckerling*, eds. T. Shary, and F. Smith, 17–34. Edinburgh: Edinburgh University Press.

Bode, L. 2010. Transitional tastes: Teen girls and genre in the critical reception of *Twilight*. *Continuum* 24, no. 5: 707–719.

Bogost, I. 2007. *Persuasive Games: The Expressive Power of Video Games*. Cambridge, MA: MIT Press.

Busch, T., Consalvo, M. and Jong, C. 2019. Playing a better me: How players rehearse their ethos via moral choices. *Games and Culture* 14, no. 3: 216–235.

Butt, M.-A. R., & Dunne, D. 2017. Rebel girls and consequence in *Life is Strange* and *The Walking Dead*. *Games and Culture*. Advance online publication: 1–20.

Cassell, J., & Jenkins, H. 1998. Chess for girls? Feminism and computer games. In *From Barbie to Mortal Kombat: Gender and Computer Games*, eds. J. Cassell, & H. Jenkins, 2–45. Cambridge, UK: MIT Press.

Chess, S., & Paul, C. A. 2019. The end of casual: Long live casual. *Games and Culture* 14, no. 2: 107–118.

Dontnod Entertainment. 2015. *Life is strange*. Paris, France: Square Enix.

Driscoll, C. 2011. *Teen film*. Oxford, UK: Berg.

Infinite Fall. 2017. *Night in the woods*. Grand Rapids, MI: Finji.

Hatch, K. 2011. Little butches: Tomboys in Hollywood film. In *Mediated Girlhoods: New Explorations of Girls' Media Culture*, ed. M. C. Kearney, 75–92. New York: Peter Lang.

Hollinger, K. 1998. *In the Company of Women: Contemporary Female Friendship Films*. Minneapolis, MN: University of Minnesota Press.

Kaveney, R. 2006. *Teen Dreams: Reading Teen Film and Television from Heathers to Veronica Mars*. London, UK: I. B. Tauris.

Kelly, P. 2015. Approaching the digital courting process in *Dragon Age 2*. In *Game Love: Essays on Play and Affection*, eds. J. Enevold, and E. MacCullum-Stewart, 46–62. North Carolina: McFarland and Company.

Khandaker-Kokoris, M. 2015. NPCs need love too: Simulating love and romance, from a game design perspective. In *Game Love: Essays on Play and Affection*, eds. J. Enevold, and E. MacCullum-Stewart, 82–95. North Carolina: McFarland and Company.

Knutson, M. 2018. Backtrack, pause, rewind, reset: Queering chrononormativity in gaming. *Game Studies* 18, no. 3: n.p.

Magnet Interactive Studios. 1995. *Chop Suey*. Georgetown, WA: Magnet Interactive Studios.

Ochsner, A. 2015. Lessons learned with girls, games and design. In *Proceedings of the Third Conference on Gender IT*, 24–31. New York: ACM Press.

O'Connor, A. 2014. Physically interactive fiction: *With Those We Love Alive*. In *Rock Paper Shotgun*, November 14. https://www.rockpapershotgun.com/2014/11/14/drawing-violences-mundanity-with-those-we-love-alive/.

O'Connor, P. 1992. *Friendships Between Women: A Critical Review*. Hertfordshire: Harvester Wheatsheaf.

Porpentine. 2014. *With Those We Love Alive*. Oakland, CA: Twine.

Projansky, S. 2014. *Spectacular Girls: Media Fascination & Celebrity Culture*. New York: New York University Press.

Purple Moon. 1997. *Secret Paths in the Forest*. Mountain View, CA: Purple Moon.

Rich, A. 1980. Compulsory heterosexuality and lesbian existence. *Signs* 5, no. 4: 631–660.

Ross, S. 2004. "Tough enough": Female friendship and heroism in *Xena* and *Buffy*. In *Action Chicks: New Images of Tough Women in Popular Culture*, ed. S. A. Inness, 231–255. New York: Palgrave Macmillan.

Schaefer, K. 2018. *Text Me When You Get Home: The Evolution and Triumph of Modern Female Friendship*. New York: Dutton.

Shaw, A. 2014. *Gaming at the Edge: Sexuality and Gender at the Margins of Gamer Culture*. Minneapolis, Minnesota: University of Minnesota Press.

Sirani, J. 2019. Top 15 best-selling video game consoles of all time. In *IGN*, April 17. https://au.ign.com/articles/2019/04/17/top-15-best-selling-video-game-consoles-of-all-time.

Tasker, Y. 1998. *Working Girls: Gender and Sexuality in Popular Cinema*. London, UK: Routledge.

Theran, S. A. 2010. Authenticity with authority figures and peers: Girls' friendships, self-esteem, and depressive symptomatology. *Journal of Social and Personal Relationships* 27, no. 4: 519–534.

Turner, V. 1977 [1969]. *The Ritual Process: Structure and Anti-Structure*. Ithaca, NY: Cornell University Press.

Winch, A. 2012. "We can have it all." *Feminist Media Studies* 12, no. 1: 69–82.

CHAPTER 7

Over Her Dead Body

Love and Affection in Japan Through Shadow of the Colossus

Miguel Cesar Rodo

CONTENTS

> You walk the empty stony shrine towards the central altar. There, immobile, you lay the body of your lover, lifeless, pale, but calm. You are a young warrior who has travelled to these empty forbidden lands to amend the unjust world that took her away from you. You are there to bring her back, no matter the consequences. You love her. And that is all that matters.
>
> *Shadow of the Collossus, ICO Studio, Sony PlayStation 2, 2005*

This is the introduction of the 2005 video game *Shadow of the Colossus* by ICO Studio and directed by Ueda Fumito. The game tells the story of

Wander, a warrior whose lover was sacrificed putting him in a journey to the forbidden Ancient Lands where he has heard dwells a force, a spirit that can resurrect her. The quest is forbidden by the laws that bound the mortals and by the authorities of Wander's world. But he does not care. Carrying the body of his lover, Mono, he is accompanied by his horse Argo, his sole companion in an adventure that will take them to transgress the most essential boundary of their world: the one that separates life from death. The theme, called Essential Boundary Transgression (EBT) has been a recurrent matter of exploration in Japanese history. The EBT in Japan appeared as late as the 711 C.E in the *Kojiki* (Records of Ancient Matters) where the founder god Izanagi breaks the taboos of the netherworld while trying to bring his wife back, the goddess Izanami. Since then, the EBT has journeyed through different periods and media until, recently in the Second Lost Decade (2000–2010), it was incorporated and explored through different discursive media such as manga, anime, and video games. There, in the videoludic medium, *Shadow of the Colossus* (*Shadow*) stands as one of the most relevant engagements in the EBT. First, *Shadow* uses the EBT as the main dramatic tension that structures and moves the story forward. Second, the approach to the theme of life and death intersects with worries, hopes, and anxieties of twenty-first century Japan. Third, by thoroughly addressing the relation between game and player *Shadow* challenges ethical concepts of evil, moral responsibility, and the resolution of moral dilemmas.

However, *Shadow* uses the EBT not only as its main thematic framework but also as a canvas over which it challenges and interrogates universal and contextual worries of Japan such as the relationship between individuals and the community, the morality of modern individualism, and the risks of toxic love and attachment in contemporary times. The instability and uncertainty of love in contemporary times has been thoroughly discussed by philosopher Zygmunt Bauman in his book *Liquid Love* (2003). In his book, Bauman builds on his concept of Liquid Modernity, discussing the lack of solidity of current emotional bounds, relations, and attachments. Bauman argues that in contemporary times love has become extremely unstable, lacking the firmness of previous times. This is a characteristic of what he defines as liquid modern societies in which categories that used to be stable and firm dissolve their most essential concepts by constant challenge and interrogation by their postulates. This argument is shared by sociologist Berman (1982) who argues about a general liquefication of every concept, category, or ideal in contemporary times and how these are leading to an intense feel of uncertainty and ontological insecurity (Giddens 1991). This transformation can also be seen in the 1990s Japan, with the melting of its solid categories during the 1990s. This decade saw the end of the economic miracle and the shattering of Japanese trust in their present and future. Among these existential pillars the most relevant were internal national security, faith in the traditional family and education systems, and trust in the government, the companies, and the oligarchy—an alliance known as the Iron Triangle (Arai 2000; Chiavacci 2008). Of these institutions, the crisis of family, since 1945 now in the shape of the nuclear family, was among the most relevant for its central role as the representation of Japanese middle-class stability (Ochiai 2003). The general middle-class model was, together with the family model and the Japanese economic system, a prescriptive way of life of the country (Chiavacci 2007, 40–41). That model seemed to guarantee a sense of optimism, successful future, and the prosperity of future generations (Chiavacci 2008, 16). All these institutions and prospects collapsed by the end of the century, leading the country into a deep crisis that went far beyond the economic (Kingston 2010). Nothing was sure or stable anymore. Every ideal, concept, or category was apt to be interrogated and challenged, in the words of Gavan McCormack "[t]here is a whiff of late Tokugawa (1850–1860) in the air, of institutions grinding under the weight of their many contradictions, of economic, political, and social malaise deepening, with no obvious alternatives in sight" (2007, 44). In that logic, *Shadow* proposed an exploration through the transgression of life and death of everything that seems pure, including, and especially, love and affection.

This is the central focus of this chapter, to study and discuss how the concept of love was approached, constructed, and challenged by *Shadow of the Colossus* through the videoludic medium. To do that this chapter is divided into three main sections. (1) The first deals with a brief literature review on the study of love and emotions in Japan, in video games, and, more particularly, in *Shadow*. This section also includes the theoretical and methodological approaches that guide my analysis of love and affection in *Shadow*. (2) The second section deals with the analysis of how *Shadow* proposes a triple meditation: about love, about the socio-cultural role of video games, and the possibilities and limitations of discussing such themes through this medium. (3) Finally, the last section proposes a discussion of the intertextual conversation on love that ICO studio proposed through its games *Ico* (2001) and *Shadow*. It also proposes some final remarks regarding the role the studio gives to love and affection in the Second Lost Decade of Japan.

LOVE: JAPAN AND VIDEO GAMES

This section addresses the historical conversations around love, affection, and attachment in Japan, its current state in contemporary times and how have these debates permeated the videoludic medium, in particular the video game *Shadow of the Colossus*. This historical approach aims to help a better comprehension of *Shadow*'s engagement to the wide conversation on love and affection in Japanese culture. Thus, this section argues that Japanese understandings of love have fluctuated throughout time, remaining a central interest that shifted in relation to social transformations. The section ends with an outline of the main methods to study love in *Shadow* through design theory.

Love in Japan: Cultural Fluctuations

"Love" is a difficult term to define in Japan for its elusive semiotic and semantic conditions, and how these have shifted throughout history. It has been argued that it is a modern term, one that needs to be understood together, and only together, with sex and lust (Ryang 2006). It has also maintained a varying relation to power and the state, being used, manipulated, and directed to the interest of the different rulers and forms of governance in the country (Morris 1964). It is also hard to know when exactly the concept and ideal of love started, and how was it comprehended back then. In the beginning of Japanese history, we find abundant rituals which involved sex, fertility, and affective relations (Uyeda 1991). Some of these rituals find inspiration in the cosmogenesis of Japan as stated in the mythological book within the *Kojiki* that establishes the creation of the world, the gods, and every form of life. In those mythical times we find the first tale about love and grief as Izanami, the goddess who created the world with her husband Izanagi, passes away. Izanagi, incapable of dealing with the pain journeys to the netherworld to resurrect her, for he cannot live without her. He fails, breaks the rules of the afterlife, and brings death and pollution to the world (Rubio and Tani 2013).

The myth of Izanami's death has been approached and studied by many different disciplines, from history (Rubio and Tani 2013), to history of religions (Kamstra 1967; Uyeda 1991), to psychoanalysis (Berne 1975), and to gender studies (Lai 1992). But on top of that, the myth is also the first written source for the EBT, the theme on transgressing life and death boundaries, and the foundation structure for future engagements. The myth of Izanami's death, and therefore the EBT theme, is a meditation on life and death, on their separations and connections, and on the moral consequences of isolation, loneliness, grieving, and mourning. But the transgression is always triggered by a deep, intense feeling of attachment brought up by affection and, in most cases, an emotion we can define as love. Thus, from the beginning love is presented in Japanese literature as a perilous emotion if uncontrolled and driven by attachment and obsession. As this section presents, this complex relation between love and danger appears throughout the EBT conversation and Japanese history.

Love as emotion is therefore not alien to Ancient and Classical Japan. On the contrary, early literary works in Japan were mostly occupied by stories of courtship, romance, and affection, many of those, well-documented testimonies on the life and habits of nobles (Morris 1964). One such example is *Genji Monogatari* (The Tale of Genji) written around the eleventh century by Murasaki Shikibu, a female courtesan that worked and lived in Heian (Classic period and capital) Japan (Napier 1996). *The Tale of Genji* narrates and discusses the life, customs, ceremonies and, overall the society and culture of the ruling class. It is interesting to note the central role that love, sex, romance, and courtship has in the novel, as well as the problems and conflicts love as a form of power can originate (Hughes 2000, 65). In it, as in the *Kojiki*, love is a force of obsession and suffering, a complex emotion that awakens the most negative behavior in humans.

The Tale of Genji also deals with the EBT as a consequence of love through regret, grievance, and resentment. As the first novel in Japan, it has influenced literature as well as the use of the theme of love, loss, and mourning in Japanese narrative. One example of such is the 1957 book *Yume no ukehashi* (Bridge of Dreams) (1963) by Tanizaki Jun'ichirō. In it, Tanizaki addresses the decadence and demise both materially and metaphysically of a Japanese family as the father decides to bring home a woman identical to his deceased wife. The disturbed psyche of the father goes so far as to ask his son to call the newly arrived woman his biological mother and to reproduce the same acts and behaviors he had with his mother, including breastfeeding from her. We find here a clear example of Bronfen's argument that "the double enacts that if what has been lost return, nothing is ever lost" (1992, 52). From that very moment the family starts to manifest symptoms of illness and pollution. Socially cast out by the community, they finally die (as the case of the parents) or journey in an endless exile (in the case of the protagonist and his younger brother).

The short novel uses recurrent references to *The Tale of Genji*. One explicit reference is the novel's title, *Bridge of Dreams*, as it is the same as the title of the last chapter of the Heian narrative. But the reference goes beyond that as Genji too "restlessly seeks to replace his dead mother in a series of new lovers" (Napier 1996, 43). Thereby, Tanizaki's *Bridge of Dreams* not only presents the first most explicit example of EBT in postwar literature in Japan, but also makes a clear reference to traditional ancient Japanese texts. As in the foundational work, love is a source of conflict, decadence, and boldness. This repeating trope stresses the unsureness and mistrust within Japanese discourses on love, its origins, and consequences.

Later, in 1983, the theme was mentioned in Murakami Haruki's short story "Tony Takitani" and in the film adaptation of that story (2004). As Tony loses his wife in an accident, he decides to hire a woman physically resembling her, just to ask her to wear his wife's clothes and stay at home. Both finally understand how wrong what they were about to do is and refrain from such behavior. As in Tanizaki's story, we find multiple themes such as the relations between life and death, loss, isolation and intersecting them, love and attachment. In Tanizaki's story love is an overarching theme shared with the motif of incest while Murakami's includes a wide number of debates and motives that connect his work to the frenetic 1980s in Japan—the consumerist frenzy and the emptiness of existence in late modern Japan. Murakami is, however, the first author to represent love as a force of redemption from loneliness and solitude, a way to solve Japan's issues with isolation and pain. But love can also turn into a destructive influence that leads humans to the most atrocious acts. In conclusion, these texts show the enduring interest in the theme of love and its negative manifestations, a trend that will continue, affected and shaped by the shocks of the lost decade (1990).

Love in a Vanishing World

The transformation of Japanese categories as agreed ideals and concepts that organise and give meaning to the life of communities and individuals included unsureness on individual agency, collective responsibility and, increasingly, love and affection (Ryang 2006, Ogihara 2017). This social and cultural trend can be traced to the end of the Imperial project with the defeat in World War II, but it increased during the 1990s. There are three main events that shook the country, diminishing the Japanese existential security and optimism in the future. By the mid-1990s the country was in a deep state of disarray. The economic crisis shattered the frenetic optimism on the Japanese system, the pride of the nation, and the security of the nuclear family (McCormack 2005). The frenzy of the 1980s turned everything into a disposable good—into a commodity that mattered only as it produced immediate satisfaction and pleasure. This general feeling permeated the country's literature linking consumerism to love and loneliness, and a general sense of malaise that would implode in the following decade. A major example is Murakami's "Toni Takitani." In this story Murakami foresaw the grim consequences of a society emphasizing materialistic values over human connections (Thornbury 2011). These concerns about the viability of Japanese capitalism increased after the Kobe earthquake and the subsequent inoperant response by the government. In 1995, a 7.2 on the Richter scale earthquake devastated the city of Kobe causing 6,200 deaths. Almost a third of the city was destroyed leaving thousands of families homeless (Iida 2000). The situation was aggravated by the slow and inept response of both municipal and central governments (Kingston 2010, 29).

The response and aid came from the non-governmental sector of society, more than a million students turned up from all over the country while the yakuza (the Japanese organized crime syndicates) opened the first kitchens for the survivors (Kingston 2010, 29). This reinforced the sense of community as non-profit organizations helped to coordinate the volunteers, playing a crucial role supporting desolated communities. But the earthquake had an unexpected consequence, fostering an attack by the terrorist group *Aum Shinrikyō* in Tokyo, fueled perhaps by their guru's schizophrenic paranoia (Iida 2000, 440).

Aum Shinrikyō was a major religious cult established in 1984 obsessed with apocalyptic narratives. After the Kobe Earthquake the group's "science minister" suggested the seismic activity had been caused by U.S. experiments (Iida 2005, 440). Shōkō Asahara then called to take up arms in a war directed against the Japanese government and the United States. Some members of *Aum Shinrikyō* under direct orders of its messianic and supreme leader committed a series of indiscriminate attacks in Tokyo's underground train using sarin gas, killing and injuring more than five thousand people (Iida 2000, 426; Kingston 2010, 29). The news spread across the country deeply harming the myth of Japan's internal security. The mission of *Aum* was to purify the spiritual decay spread around the world inaugurating a new era lead by "psychically-gifted" individuals (Iida 2005, 239).

An anxious feeling about the failure of the government to secure the safety of the people spread around the country. The Japanese citizenry could not understand the ineffectiveness of its government, the police, and the institutions that guaranteed the internal security of the country. This unsureness and disbelief led many to accuse the government of dereliction of duty (Kingston 2010, 30) making it the target of many angry, scared, anxious, and frustrated citizens. But the situation got even worse with the "Young A" murders, the most violent manifestation of loneliness, lack of affection, attachment, and isolation that evidenced the frictions of the Japanese system (Arai 2000).

The "Young A" of Kobe was a case in which a 14-year-old boy from an ordinary family was arrested for committing a series of attempted murders and two successful murders (Iida 2000). The boy carefully planned the murders in advance and committed them cruelly and calmly (Iida 2005, 234). A decapitated victim's head was mutilated and left in front of the school gate with a note declaring the beginning of a "game" with the "foolish police" as "a revenge against the school system" that has transformed him into a "transparent being" (ibid, 234). Eventually the boy turned himself in to the authorities. During the investigation, he explained his motivation as a "sacred experiment" testing "the fragility of humanity" (Iida 2005, 234). The event shocked Japan not only for the ordinary origins of the boy but also for his uncanny motivations and his defeat of the police as a synecdoche of the "adult world" (ibid, 235).

The murder, however, was not lacking a "true cause" but one so uncanny, complex, and sophisticated that it still attracts attention from Japanese literature. Part of the bewilderment of Japanese society with the case was due to the murderer's confession letter. In it he wrote his motivations in verse, showing a high level of sophistication that emphasized his intelligence and cunning. Some have read in it a sharp sense of doubt about life as a self-evident fact and death as less evident (Ōsawa 1997, 226). That doubtful second category is what attracted the boy, troubling and fascinating him into a state of extreme anxiety (Iida 2005, 236). In this logic Iida has argued that the "Young A" shows the manifestation of a mind split between a need to experience reality, to make the world tangible and solid, and a consciousness obsessed with the enigma of human existence and the fear of nothingness, of emptiness, and meaninglessness. From that tension, the Young A's need to experience the materiality of death led him to commit horrible crimes to alleviate his existential void, his anxious feeling of non-existence.

Overall, the "Young A" case manifested the deep problems affecting the pillars that have maintained the image of Japan as a peaceful crimeless society. This also raised questions about the family system, the relations between parents and their children, the school-system, and even more abstract concepts. Among these, perhaps the questioning of finite and infinite categories, the stretching and questioning of boundaries and the aim to answer them is what bears most relevance for this study. Socially, the "Young A" case led Japan into an uneasy feeling of deep uncertainty. The general state of the country was that nothing was solid, stable, and sure anymore. Then, in that socio-cultural landscape, different media discourses started to question every topic, challenging the most essential values, concepts, and boundaries.

It is in that context that *Shadow* challenges one of the most basic and pure emotions, interrogating its possibly obscure, dangerous, or fluid dimensions: love. In this regard, Óliver Pérez Latorre has argued that *Shadow*, as well as its prequel *Ico*, are both stories of love, suffering, and pain (2012). Pérez-Latorre stresses the depiction of love as a problematic force. He argues that the game can be read literally (a story of the suffering for a lost love), a less literal reading (a story about a difficult love, the suffering from keeping it alive, scarifying yourself to save it), and one much general reading (love as a monotonous relationship, the hardships of the different sacrifices of every relationship). Thus, Ueda's meditations on love in *Shadow* is an exploration on pain, loneliness, and loss that, in turn, it is revealed as a pure obsession. The quest is a heroic act for saving Wander's lover but it is also darkened by the rightness of the consequences of his mission.

Pérez-Latorre's argument, however interesting, does not gives much relevance to the ethics of *Shadow* and the experience it proposes. If, indeed the game is about love, it does not revolve around the relationship between Wander and Mono, ambiguous and obscure for the lack of information. Love is the central force of the game, nevertheless, it is taken as a synecdoche for something bigger: isolation, individualism, and, more specifically, male possession over the female body, soul, life, and death. That is where Miguel Sicart's work on the ethics of computer games and his approach to *Shadow* offers some helpful insight into the game's moral dilemmas and challenges. One of Sicart's concepts while discussing the game is "closed ethic" design, that he defines as:

> an ethical experience in which the player cannot implement her values beyond the constraints of the game. The game is designed to create a set of possible actions with different moral weights [...] without the possibility of contributing her values to the game itself. (2009, 214)

This is a useful concept as we can build from it the mechanics and narrative elements of the game that restrain the players' ethical experience and interpretation of it. In this chapter I look into the closed design on love, what it is, how the game constructs this experience and engagement on this emotion, and what it says about it in the wider polyphonic conversation within its context. To do so, there is a second term coined by Sicart that guides my approach, that is "subtracting ethics":

> the process of creating a game that has ethical choices made by an ethical agent at the core of its fictional universe by means of gameplay mechanics. Subtracting ethics creates a moral experience, but leaves the ethical reasoning to the player, thus respecting their presence as moral agents in the networked ethical system of computer games. (215–6)

This is key to the understanding of how *Shadow* is experienced, how its mechanics work, and the narrative features that are subtracted from these relations. *Shadow* is not a game that forces a story upon the player, it does, as well as with the ethics it challenges, suggest them to the player as s/he plays the game. There are no clear messages, everything is obscured, ambiguous, and challenged from the mechanics to its aesthetics and story. It is a complex game, one that plays with the player, challenges her/his expectations, and proposes a world of unsureness, fluidity, and insecurities (a perfect reflection of twenty-first century Japan). But if the game is so complex, how to approach it? How can we study it? In the next section, I propose an interdisciplinary eclectic theoretical-methodological apparatus for the study of love and transgression in the ethical system of *Shadow*.

Studying Love, Death, and Transgression in Video Games

When studying the representation of love in *Shadow*, one of the main issues to discuss is the active involvement and necessary performance of the player. In opposition to other media forms, *Shadow* demands the player transgress the boundaries of life and death if they want to play and experiences the kind of love the game constructs. There, the necessity (or opportunity) to commit a transgression raises questions about the responsibility of the player, but also raises emotions such as guilt and trauma from loss and separation (Suttner 2015). This section presents and proposes a set of methods and approaches for studying *Shadow*—its engagement in the interrogations of love and its contribution to the videoludic medium.

First, this section approaches *Shadow* from game design theory which focuses on the game as an object to be experienced (Sicart 2009). Design theory focuses on the creation of successful ludic experiences with the use of different arts and technologies, it considers how game designers think about their practice, what techniques they use in the process of creating rules and game worlds (ibid, 37–38). In that endeavor, game designers try to predict and map the way their product will be experienced. In this discussion I will draw on a variety of different sources, from the gameplay and artbook ICO Studio released in Japan discussing the creative process and the way they expect *Shadow* to be experienced, to different interviews and comments from Ueda.

Thus, to study the design of *Shadow*, I refer to what James Ash (2012) defines as "affective design," a term related to the production and construction of computer games. This concept comes from Stiegler's (2010) "retentional economy," which studies the transmission of human knowledge through the relationship between affect and attention of human memory. This, when applied to computer games, helps us to understand the techniques designers use to captivate and manipulate attention. The aim of this focus is, therefore, to understand how designers modulate affect to ensure a successful gameplay experience—one that is not only fun to play but also meaningful to interact with. Ash proposes three concepts to understand how affective design works to transmit "the potential for affect through a range of technical systems and environments" (Ash 2012, 3).

Developing on that, attention is relevant for the construction of computer games as it focuses on how they are designed to be experienced. This comes from the understanding that games are consumed based on the manipulation of players' passions and enthusiasms—on the capture and management of their emotions through sensory design (Thrift 2006, 286). Computer games, as with any product, are designed to appeal to the enses in different ways (Berlant 2008; Featherstone 2010). They are, as Shaviros (2010) argues, machines for generating affect, to extract value from the affective relation created between player and game. Attention, therefore, becomes a central point for the design of computer games, and consequently, to comprehend how a computer game is designed and how it works, we need to study how attention is captured and modulated to generate particular forms of affect (Ash 2012, 5).

These concepts for studying attention and the construction of emotional reactions and experiences in the game guide the analysis of *Shadow*, structured following the methodology designed by Wolf (2007) that focuses on graphics, interface, algorithm, and interactivity, and Schmierbach's (2009) content analysis approach. Wolf's book defines "graphics" as the changeable visual display on screen, the "interface" as the boundary between player and game (including the screen, speakers, controller), the "algorithm" as the program that controls the game, and "interactivity" as what the player does in the game and the game's response to the player (Wolf 2007, 24). Schmierbach's content analysis approach argues that one challenge in analyzing computer games is their length, which makes it necessary to structure and cut the gameplay into different stages to be studied later. This necessity comes as an essential prerequisite to the study of many products where gameplay might last for days. *Shadow*, however, provides a clear and differentiated episodic pattern and organization. The game is composed of sixteen encounters with the colossi plus a final battle where the player's avatar is turned into a colossus. Each of these encounters is organized in two stages: the finding of and killing of the enemy. These well-differentiated stages aid the fragmentation of the game as this internal organization guides the analysis of *Shadow*. This decision is, however, not based solely on the structure of the game but on its construction and manipulation of the gameplay experience. That is, the feeling of progression is marked by the different cutscenes and the increase in power that allows Wander to succeed in his encounters with the colossi. This sequential development constructs an impression of moving forward while it punctuates the episodic nature of the quest, since the end of every encounter implies a restart from the shrine and a reproduction of the pattern: find-kill-repeat.

Last, considering the central role the interrogation of love has in *Shadow* and the way the game approaches it, I consider it relevant to engage *Shadow* as an ethical system. I thus focus on *Shadow*'s exploration on the capacities of the medium to create ethical experiences and meditations on our ontology, existence, and the consumption of computer games. The whole ludic experience of *Shadow* is structured around a core ethical conflict based on its protagonist's (Wander) non-acceptance of the death of his love and his rebellion against the rules of the community, the authority, and the cosmos. Wander is aware of the possible disastrous consequences of his actions, but he does not care. *Shadow*'s experience is therefore based on the player's involvement in the conflict, to distance her/him from the negative consequences of toxic and possessive love while, at the same time, it maintains the interest of completing the transgression. The following section explores the experiencing of love and its challenges through *Shadow*'s ludic and narrative organization.

LOVE AFTER DEATH: VIOLENCE AND TRANSGRESSION IN SHADOW

The study of *Shadow*'s construction of love and affection is marked by the simultaneity of its gameplay and narrative. In other words, it is by playing the game that we discover more information about the story, the world, the characters, and the quest. Therefore, to analyze love in *Shadow*, I first focus on the experience it aims to construct and the meanings it aims to communicate through playing the game. To do that, as mentioned in the previous section, I refer to a study of its content, its organization through its patterned progression, and the construction of affective attention through the game mechanics. For clarity and feasibility, this account of *Shadow* studies the game focusing on the separated patterns it presents of exploration and confrontation—their relation and repetition. Once this structure is analyzed, I discuss the phases combined and how its mechanics tell a story and propose an ethical experience. Thus, I begin with a ludological approach that focuses on the mechanics of the game design and, second, how and what is the story that is subtracted from them (Pérez-Latorre 2012).

The Structural Pattern of Shadow

Every quest to defeat a new colossus is organized in two interconnected phases: first, the exploration of the Ancient Lands and, second, the battle against the colossus. Both are part of every encounter, but for clarity I propose a chronological study of the experience they propose.

Exploring the Land of Obsession

Exploration in *Shadow* is a necessary part of the mission for the resurrection of Mono. It leads to the battles and defeat of the colossi and finding the colossi constitutes part of the puzzle. To solve it the player is aided by the information from the Head-up Display (HUD)—textual information that forms part of the player's interface. Through this display the player is informed about her/his strength, stamina, weapon, and health. This is the only information communicated to the player.

This scarcity of information was defined by the director of the game, Ueda, as "subtractive design," and it aims to maintain a mimetic relation between the game and its representation of reality (Sony 2006). HUD's are an artificial tool to facilitate gameplay, but they are not available in our world outside the game. Thus, Ueda aims to keep the visual display to a minimum, focusing the player on the straightforwardness of the quest, eliciting Wander's obsession.

Added to the limited resources, *Shadow* proposes a deserted world that emphasizes the loneliness and isolation of the player. There is nothing else to do in the Ancient Lands except for riding and finding the next colossus. Consequently, *Shadow* lacks any secondary missions, side quests, or the presence of Non-Playable Characters (NPC's). This design choice has an effect that connects mechanics and narrative. As the Ancient Lands are deserted of any living creatures to interact with, the feeling of isolation increases. Moreover, it stirs Wander to kill the colossi to revive his lover as soon as possible. This obsession and rush are aided by constant revisiting of the shrine where Mono's body rests. The feeling of repetition is therefore maintained and stressed throughout the whole gameplay. The spatial center is constantly revisited while time starts all over again in a cyclical structure as the body of our lover becomes the core of our world, our journey, our obsession.

Consequently, Mono's presence reinforces the emptiness of the land—the lack of choices in our cyclical experience—to stress the fixation of Wander on his mission. Every time we succeed, we are transported back in front of Mono as Dormin, the uncanny spiritual force that aids us, tells us about our next foe and how to defeat it. Thus, as Pérez-Latorre (2012) argues, the space (and I will add time) of *Shadow* is of obsession beyond solitude (286). In a land of wide expanses, in a game that allows us to travel wherever we want from the start and to disengage from combat anytime, the avatar—and through him the player—only seeks one thing: the next colossus.

So then, what do we do during these long and empty rides? There is only one thing to do: to lead our horse to the next battle and to think. We attend to our doubts and internal struggles; this is the only moment that we are allowed to respond reflectively to the story. As Ciccoricco (2007) argues, "the player not only inherits the task of [Wander] but also (potentially and ideally) the psychological baggage that his ordeal entails." This does not imply that both player and Wander are in psychological harmony as we cannot know if Wander is himself questioning his quest and actions.

Thus, by giving time for self-reflection, *Shadow* increases the player's uncertainty about the morality of her/his acts and the disruption and destruction of an alienating world that constantly rejects you. This intense moral interrogation contrasts with the resolution of Wander who straightforwardly commits to his only objective: to satisfy his loss and to alleviate his pain (Suttner 2015). Only by killing can you progress, and every time you are haunted by the guilt of murder you are placed in front of your lover. There is no room for questioning your quest. There is only haste. Love is our justification, our reason to kill, to destroy and to risk the whole world to cease the horrible pain we suffer from losing the only thing that keeps us alive. Love in *Shadow* is our only solid foundation. The ontological and bedrock sustaining our existence. Without it we are nothing. And so, we will blindly sacrifice everything to get it back.

Here, however, arises a dichotomy, a tension between player and avatar caused by the closed ethic game design. We know Wander wants to destroy the colossi, but the player may choose to stop this transgression, to reconcile with nature and its flow instead of interrupting it. Nevertheless, s/he will then be trapped in a land of isolation and obsession. In fact, if the player decides to cross the bridge and leave the Ancient Lands, a gale will fix him in the spot not allowing him to advance. Therefore, regardless of the player's decision to perform the EBT or not there are no options left to advance in the game. Once in the Ancient Lands, all you need to care about is how to kill the colossi.

Disruption and Violence

The violent battles between Wander and the colossi are the central climactic encounters necessary to the success of the quest. Their first characteristic is the asymmetry of the fight. While Wander stands as a minuscule figure with scarce resources, the colossi are enormous armed beings, solid as rocks. However, during the first moments of each encounter most of the colossi behave reactively, that is, it is the player who must provoke the fight.

Thus, the only way to succeed is to climb on them, find the colossi's weak spots and how to reach them to stab the enemy repeatedly until it is killed. The hero must then get into close contact, climb up and down and confront the face of the colossus as he draws its life out. The violence of these encounters stresses the negative consequences of obsessive toxic love. This main mechanic also forces the player to confront and attach herself/himself physically to the being s/he is murdering. Thus, the heroism of the quest is nuanced by the brutality and violence of the battles. While the player stabs the monster, it tries to throw him off by shaking its head or body, which stresses the condition of the colossi as sentient, suffering beings. There the player acknowledges by himself the only clear characteristic of these monsters: that they suffer.

As we emerge victorious, we witness the collapsing of our foe as black tendrils coming from his corpse reach us and leave us unconscious. This moment of victory is key to understanding how the quest is designed by Ueda. Contrary to epic adventure games, there is no celebration of the killing of our enemy. The music turns to a sad melody Ueda places deliberately to stress the feeling of wrongness and defilement while it mourns the dead creature (Suttner 2015, 83). There is no celebratory music or winning messages, no rewards for our victory, which emphasizes the ambiguity and defilement of our acts (ibid, 35). The player is then deprived of agency and is given it back just to be chased by the dark tendrils that leave the colossus' body and enter his body no matter how much s/he tries to escape from them. It is, then, by manipulating the conventional rules and mechanics of games that Ueda forces the player to interpret his actions (Sicart 2009, 216).

This mechanic, narratively impactful, works using a concept defined as "futile interactivity" (Fortugno 2009). The term refers to scenes in which the player is given agency with a task that seems accomplishable despite being designed to be mechanically impossible (Fortugno 2009, 176). In the case of *Shadow* "the game uses multiple moments of futile interaction to give the tragedy its emotional power" (ibid, 185). Fortugno's first example is the moment a colossus is defeated, and the player is given agency back; then, trying to escape from the black tendrils he is, inevitably caught and penetrated by them. The reason behind this design has to do with the way the player would experience the moment. Using futile interactivity designers can create dramatic necessity as they play with the player to believe there is something to do there, a way to dodge the tendrils as this allows the player to take control back. But *Shadow* uses the player's agency and its manipulation to increase the sense of entrapment by his quest.

Futile interactivity is a central mechanic in *Shadow*'s meditation on the medium and what attachment, toxic love, and affection can lead us to. It also relates directly to Wander's quest and the player involvement and experiencing of it. From the beginning of the quest, the player's agency is futile, there is no power over Wander's obsessed love. The capacity to choose and decide on the transgression is an illusion—a deception constructed through the possibilities and limitations of the medium. Furthermore, we are not forced to commit the transgression, we can choose to leave the game, or simply not to progress. But the attraction of the possibility to do something impossible outside the game world and yet forbidden is too captivating. This tension, our futile attempts to escape the temptation of the transgression, the obsession of our avatar and our irreversible fate structures the story and the gameplay synecdochally represented by the black tendrils—a sign of our pollution—as the only reward for our actions.

This aftermath is a moment of reflection, of bewilderment, and insecurity about the meaning and consequences of our quest. Moreover, after each killing our possible victory over death draws near. If in the beginning our quest seemed desperate but heroic, its performance and its close conclusion make us face the once distant possibility of the dimensions and forms of the resurrection of Dormin, a force of violence and mystery that has promised us it can resurrect Mono but at a great loss. Consequently, *Shadow* is a game that warns about love turning as violence, obsession, and individualism over community. Nevertheless, to better understand how these tensions are represented in *Shadow*, I now study their narrativization through the videoludic medium and the subsequent EBT engagement it constructs.

Immoral Mechanics of Immoral Quest

Shadow's main narrative features are discussed and experienced while framed within intertextual debates on moral philosophy. As such, the game uses concepts such as moral dilemma, deontological and consequentialist ethics, and the concept of evil to express and engage the main debates of contemporary Japan, debates that are originated and permeate how the game and player define, understand, and experience love.

The whole experience *Shadow* proposes is based on turning what a priori seems like a moral dilemma into a complete unethical mission. A moral dilemma is a situation in which the agent is required to do each of two (or more) actions but where s/he cannot do both (McConnell 1986). The agent is therefore condemned to moral failure as none of the options overrides the other. This is not the case of *Shadow*. Wander's conundrum is a moral conflict, as one of the options, abandoning his transgression, clearly overrides his obsession over resurrecting his lover. This difference, apparently a merely conceptual issue, is key to comprehending the ethical representation of our quest. There is where other concepts help us understand how Ueda turns a moral dilemma into an evil act.

To do so, *Shadow* shows how two opposing ethical systems are, in fact, compatible, simultaneous, and related. Deontologically, the transgression breaks the laws of the mortals. It is forbidden to enter the Ancient Lands, and it is forbidden to aid Dormin as well as resurrecting the dead. But if rebelling against these norms was not enough to frame the mission as unethical, *Shadow* increases the negativity of the quest by warning about its consequences. Not only do we murder peaceful, suffering beings, but we also bring the world to its coming destruction. Our quest turns from a heroic desperation to a selfish obsession. Thus, although we may struggle to justify the unfairness of a world that has killed our young lover, it is in the repetition of our constant violence and murders that the defilement of our quest is stressed. This is done through the combined use of mechanics, aesthetics, and narrative of the gameplay.

I have already mentioned the term subtractive ethic and closed ethical design (Sicart 2009). These concepts are key to understand what *Shadow* is proposing and how. By constraining the ethical decisions and the moral agency to the game, to the avatar Wander, the player is forced to perform and experience the designed ethical choices of the game. The player can react and reflect on them. The game respects the player as a moral agent, it does not force him to play but he is attracted, engaged on the uncomfortable ethical position that *Shadow* proposes, acknowledging the moral capacities of the player, which maximises the experience. The exploration of ethical boundaries and the challenge of every category is at the core of *Shadow*'s philosophical stance through mechanics such as "futile interactivity," which strips agency out of the player but increases the dramatic and ethical impact of the game. This is achieved through the dichotomous and complex phenomenological relation between player and avatar (Klevjer 2012, 17). This is a symbolic but intangible connection, the avatar being an extension of our agency and body, but one restricted and pre-designed by the developers. In *Shadow*, this mimetic relation with our avatar, amplified by its subtractive design, is altered through our constant dialogue, questioning, and fluid connections with Wander. In a game that liquefies everything, Shadow asks the player about her/his own control over the game, moral responsibility, and overall agency. Who is being played here?

But there is a last, but central and key interrogation and challenge by *Shadow* to the player, a question on the ontology and phenomenology of being evil. This is Ueda's main approach to computer games, a medium not only to tell stories but to create and explore experiences, to wander through our human condition and to test the limits of our own existence. Our quest is part of the debate on the understanding of evil beings and actions. How does doing evil make you feel and what it means to do evil is a central feature of the significance and form of love and affect in the game.

Performing the EBT in *Shadow* is sanctioned as an immoral selfish act. The killing, the risking of the world and the non-acceptance of the rules established by the community are represented from the beginning as unethical choices. But is Wander an evil character? And if so, how does it feel for the player to be and do evil? In *Shadow*, Wander is not treated by others, not even those whom he threatens, as an evil being. When Lord Emon finds out about what he has performed he expresses only mercy and pity. Even after Wander, transformed into a demon, tries to kill him, Lord Emon wishes for Wander's redemption, and even anticipates his part in the future, resolved in the game *Ico*. This external judgment is also repeatedly manifested throughout the game. Wander is not killing the colossi because he enjoys it, he is not jeopardizing the whole world because he despises its existence, but because he is incapable of detaching himself from his love—to let go and accept her death.

Consequently, Wander is the example of the moral imbecile, of a mind so troubled that he cannot think of anything else but the resurrection of Mono (Scarre 2010). As the mechanics and the structure of the game reinforce that there is no distraction, no time to stop and think. Wander is aware that some fatal consequences will befall after he breaches the boundaries of life and death, but he does not care. However, that he is not portrayed as an evil being does not mean his actions are not evil. Wander is a deeply selfish and obsessed individual who disregards others for his own satisfaction. His individualism leads him towards his egoistic quest.

However, if we are defined by our actions, Wander is not alone in this evil quest. The player is always present from the moment the transgression starts. *Shadow* uses recurrent indications of the immorality of the quest. In the prologue we are told that the trespassing to the Ancient Lands is forbidden. Then Dormin warns the player about the dangerous consequences of the quest. Mechanically and narratively he stresses the defilement of the quest. Thus, from the beginning *Shadow* ensures the player will have doubts about the morality of his actions while it does not discourage him from finishing the game. But if moral evil and ethics is central to *Shadow* what is then their relation to love—the original and ever-present motivation for our quest? To answer this question, it is necessary to look at the cosmos created by ICO Studio both in *Shadow* and its prequel *Ico*—a game where love, affection, and friendship become not only its central theme but also its vectorizing mechanic.

LOVE IN A LAND OF LONELINESS

Shadow is a game that can be experienced on its own, it stands alone as a coherent and complete unit. Nevertheless, to fully understand the complex cosmos it proposes and, furthermore, ICO Studio's intake in love, affection, and loneliness, it is necessary to consider *Shadow*'s prequel, *Ico* and their *possible* connections. I say *possible* since there is no exact explanation from Ueda about how both game's link, although we know *Ico*'s story comes centuries after Wander's quest. But let's explain first what is *Ico* about.

Ico starts with a horned child being imprisoned in a metal container within a castle by some riders. Apparently, being born with horns is a sign of doom and pollution and the rite rules that such kids should be shut down in the fortress. Ico, the protagonist, manages to escape and to free a female child held in a cage. Together they fight the impossible architecture of the castle, the horned shadows that try to capture Yorda (our female friend) and the immortal queen (Yorda's mother). After much struggle we manage to recover the magic sword and kill the queen, freeing Yorda of her imprisonment, although it is her who puts us in a boat as the castle collapses. Finally, we witness the total destruction of the impossible architecture and wake up on a deserted beach. We keep walking and, eventually, we find Yorda lying unconscious. We wake her up. She smiles at us and the game ends.

There is much speculation over the links between both games, worlds, and characters. This is further problematized by Ueda's ambiguity and the fact that *Ico* is a consequence of *Shadow*, although the players experienced both game in the opposite order. I argue, however, that many clues and elements connect both stories. The most evident one is the horned baby in *Shadow*'s ending that links to *Ico*'s story, in which horned children, reincarnations of the polluted Wander, are sacrificed and sealed away before they reach adulthood. It is the quest for Ico, Wander reincarnated, to kill the evil queen, to free the world from the state in which he has submersed the world. But playing *Ico* first brings back memories and remembrance of the killing and defeat of the mad queen while experiencing *Shadow*. The apparent success of reviving Mono spoils our only moment of victory as we acknowledge what she will turn into, our foe and sole enemy in *Ico*. This increases the transgression as a defiled quest for we know the consequences of our action and the eventual decline of Mono into insanity, a fate created by our own obstinacy. If the work of Ueda is extensively ambiguous and paradoxical, the connection between *Ico* and *Shadow* increases it: reviving Mono means turning her into our foe but having killed her signifies the murder of our lover, for whom we have sacrificed everything. That is the consequence of our defiled, toxic, and obsessed love. What is then, Ueda's warning and challenge about the concept of love through the videoludic medium?

Ueda started making video games during the turn of the century, releasing *Ico* in 2001. Therefore, it is no surprise his games are a reflection, a meditation, and exploration of the convulsed Lost Decades. As everything was being liquefied, Ueda's games not only challenged the concept of love, but also the challenged those that questioned it. Both *Ico* and *Shadow* are warnings about our belief systems, our worldviews, and the structures that create and maintain them. But Ueda is not very optimistic on the possible challenges to these concepts, ideals, or beliefs. He is concerned about humanity's capacity and motivation on the melting of these solid categories. If humans challenge the beliefs made by them, these interrogations would only produce new monsters, new problems, and crises. And love, no matter how pure we see it, is experienced and manifested through human-made nets and webs of behavior, that is, it does not exist away from us.

But love, in these dire times, is the last frontier to hold up, to save us from a total existential and ontological meltdown. Love has turned into the only category, together with death, that remains pure, unchallengeable. Not so much for Ueda. Love, Burkitt warned us, becomes idealized, unreal, and a vessel to our expectations (2014). We essentialize it, as our last resort to alleviate our existential anxiety—a fear Anthony Giddens calls ontological insecurity—a lack of sense of order and continuity according to the individual's experiences (1991). Love, therefore, essentialized and pure, is beyond criticism, turning into an ever-unchallenged justification for our actions and our decisions, no matter the ethical transgressions and consequences. It is that premise that Ueda's games challenge. Let's see how.

Ico is a game about the benefits of love, friendship, affection, and belonging in a world that secludes and isolates us. Ico is us, but so is Yorda. Two children, cast away by the world of the adults, being objectified as dangerous or useful as an object to obtain immortality. The castle in *Ico* is a perfect representation of our liquid society. Empty and abandoned, seemingly peaceful but inhabited by shadows that haunt us and harm us as soon as we try to escape. It is a world ruled by an obscure authority that only wants to exploit us, to make us comply with the biopower and the cosmology of the castle. In that dim world, only friendship, love, and solidarity can save us and, eventually, destroy the oppressing system. *Ico* is, therefore, an optimistic proposal by Ueda. Trust, help, and sacrifice yourself for those who, like you, live outside the margins of society and are exploited by it. *Shadow* is, however, the opposite approach. It is a challenge to love and a warning on individualistic rebellious transgressions and absolute freedom (Elliot et al., 2012). But *Shadow*, nevertheless, is not attacking love as a whole, but a form (a particular understanding) of love. It is that obsession, that reification of romantic love that worries Ueda. Love (given its power) should not become the force that allows possession of our lover, of apocalypses, or of disregard for the consequences of our actions. That is what Ueda warns us about: the idealization of love and the dangerous form we might give that feeling by obsessing over it.

This is a constant in liquid Japan. The liquefication of every value, even love, is fought back by a paradoxical irony: while relationships and bounds disappear in the country, young people fantasize with a form of love that only exists in their imagination. Love is only acceptable when there is no responsibility, no ups and downs, no crises and troubles. The kind of love young Japanese dream about can only exist in fiction by essentializing their partner and stripping away any agency from her/him. To think that your lover can disagree with you (displease you) is denied, turning that relationship upside down and searching for that true love that only exists in fiction. That is what Ueda's work warns about. Love is frustration, it is hardships and loneliness. But it is also friendship and solidarity. And only once we understand the ambivalences and incoherencies of something made by humans can we really construct a new world, solid, peaceful, and free of our own obsessions. Love in the form of friendship, sacrifice, and empathy is the only thing that can defeat death. Love as a toxic obsession, possession, and selfishness only perpetuates and expands it. Love can be pollution, or purification.

CONCLUSION

In his book *Liquid Love* (2003) Zygmunt Bauman argues about the difficulty to love and to learn how to love in our liquid modernity. Love is another commodity, he says, something to be consumed, used, and thrown away. He, and others before him, have worried about our capacity to be humble and brave enough to sacrifice our egocentrism, to see love for what it should be and not what we have come to think it is. Possession, power, and disenchantment are the main reasons why love fails, the very same traits of the kind of love Ueda challenges in *Shadow*, an experience to explore how not to love.

This has been the aim of this chapter, to argue and explain what Ueda tries to teach and to express through *Shadow*, how does the game do it, and how do we as players experience it. That *Shadow* remains as a central piece of Japanese contemporary culture, being remastered and continuously discussed shows the relevancy of its premise. *Shadow*'s importance remains, for its questions have not reached a definitive answer, its challenges are still valuable, and its postulates still worthy of being experienced. Some of *Shadow* values may linger, as it discusses universal ontological and existential questions regarding death, afterlife, love, and humanity. Ueda and his team foresaw and witnessed the crisis of liquid modern Japan, the melting of values such as friendship and love and the dangers it will bring for a boundless society, one prone to, if not disintegration, at least perpetual crises and eventual collapse. A new form of love must rise to create a new world that supersedes a decadent dying old world. It is in these liminal times that *Shadow*, through the videoludic medium proposes an original and complex answer to that challenge: to learn how to love, to learn how to live. Apparently, we still have to learn it.

REFERENCES

Allison, A. 2015. Precarity and Hope: Social Connectedness in Postcapitalist Japan. In *Japan: The Precarious Future*, eds. F. Baldwin and A. Allison, 36–57. New York: New York University Press.

Arai, A. G. 2000. The "Wild Child" of 1990s Japan. In *Japan After Japan Social and Cultural Life from the Recessionary 1990s to the Present*, eds. T. Yoda and H. Harootunian, 216–238. Durham, NC: Duke University Press.

Ash, J. 2012. Attention, Videogames and the Retentional Economies of Affective Amplification. *Theory, Culture and Society* 29(6): 3–26.

Bauman, Z. 2000. *Liquid Modernity*. Cambridge, UK: Polite Press.

Bauman, Z. 2003. *Liquid Love: On the Frailty of Human Bonds*. Cambridge, UK: Polite Press.

Beck, U. and E. Beck-Gernsheim. 2001. *Individualization: Institutionalized Individualism and its Social and Political Consequences*. London: Sage.

Berlant, L. 2008. Thinking about Feeling Historical. *Emotion and Society* 1(1): 4–9.

Berman, M. 1982. *All That is Solid Melts into Air: The Experience of Modernity*. London, UK: Verso.

Berne, J. H. 1975. *Two Essays in the Mythology of Conflict*. Ann Arbor, MI: Xerox University Microfilms.

Bronfen, E. 1992. *Over Her Dead Body: Death, Femininity and the Aesthetic*. Manchester, UK: Manchester University Press.

Burkitt, I. 2014. *Emotions and Social Relations*. London, UK: SAGE Publications.

Chiavacci, D. 2007. The Social Basis of Developmental Capitalism in Japan: From Postwar Mobilization to Current Stress Symptoms and Future Disintegration. *Asian Business & Management* 6(1): 35–55.

Chiavacci, D. 2008. From Class Struggle to General Middle-Class Society to Divided Society: Societal Models of Inequality in Postwar Japan. *Social Science Japan Journal* 11(1): 5–27.

Ciccoricco, D. 2007. Play, Memory: Shadow of the Colossus and Cognitive Workouts. www.dichtung-digital.org/2007/ciccoricco.htm.

Elliott, A. Katagiri, M., and Sawai, A. 2012. The New Individualism and Contemporary Japan: Theoretical Avenues and the Japanese New Individualist Path. *Journal for the Theory of Social Behaviour* 4(1): 425–443.

Featherstone, M. 2010. Body, Image and Affect in Consumer Culture. *Body & Society* 16(1): 193–221.

Fortugno, N. 2009. Losing your Grip: Futility and Dramatic Necessity in Shadow of the Colossus. In *Well Played 1.0. Videogames, Value and Meaning*, ed. D. Davidson, 171–186. Pitsburgh, PA: ETC Press.

Giddens, A. 1991. *Modernity and Self-Identity*. Cambridge: Polity.

Hughes, H. 2000. Familiarity of the Strange: Japan Gothic Tradition. *Criticism* 42(1): 59–89.

Iida, Y. 2000. Between the Technique of Living and Endless Routine and the Madness of Absolute Degree Zero: Japanese Identity and the Crisis of Modernity in the 1990s. *Positions* 8(2): 423–464.

Iida, Y. 2005. *Rethinking Identity in Modern Japan: Nationalism as Aesthetics*. London, UK: Routledge.

Kamstra, J. H. 1969. Encounter or Syncretism: The Initial Growth of Japanese Buddhism. *Archives de Sociologie Des Religions* 28: 214–215.

Kingston, J. 2010. *Critical Issues in Contemporary Japan*. Oxford, UK: Blackwell.

Klevjer, P. 2012. Enter the Avatar: The Phenomenology of Prosthetic Telepresence in Computer Games. In *The Philosophy of Computer Games*, eds. J. R. Sageng, H. Fossheim, and T. Larsen, 17–38. Dordrecht, the Netherlands: Springer.

Lai, S. 1992. Patriarchal Fallacies East and West: A Comparative Study of Gender Imposition in the Writings of Hell. PhD Dissertation, Urbana Champaign, IL: University of Illinois.

McConnell. 1986. More on Moral Dilemmas. *The Journal of Philosophy*, 82: 345–351.

McCormack, G. 2005. Disputed Bones Fracture Japan-North Korea Relations. *OhmyNews* Available http://english.ohmynews.com/articleview/article_view.asp?menu=c10400&no=221670&rel_no=1

Morris, I. 1964. *The World of the Shining Prince, Court Life in Ancient Japan.* Oxford, UK: Oxford University Press.

Napier, S. 1996. *The Fantastic in Modern Japanese Literature: The Subversion of Modernity.* London, UK: Routledge.

Ochiai, E. 2003. PostWar Transition in the Japanese Family. In *Women in Japan and Sweden: Work and Family in Two Welfare Regimes*, eds. C. Grand and T. Tsukaguchi, 137–166. Stockholm, Sweden: Almqvist & Wiksell International.

Ogihara, Y. 2017. Temporal Changes in Individualism and Their Ramification in Japan: Rising Individualism and Conflicts with Persisting Collectivism. *Frontiers in Psychology*, 8. https://www.frontiersin.org/articles/10.3389/fpsyg.2017.00695/full

Ōsawa, M. 1997. Bamoidooki-shin no kao. *Gunzō*: 224–36.

Pérez-Latorre, O. 2012. *El lenguaje Videolúdico: Análisis de la Significación del Videojuego.* Barcelona, Spain: Laertes.

Rubio, C. and R. Tani. 2013. *Kojiki: Crónicas de Antiguos Hechos de Japón.* Madrid, Spain: Trotta.

Ryang, S. 2006. *Love in Modern Japan: Its Estrangement from Self, Sex, and Society.* London, UK: Routledge.

Scarre, G. 2010. Evil. In *The Routledge Companion to Ethics*, ed. J. Skorpuski, 582–595. London, UK: Routledge.

Schmierbach, M. 2009. Content Analysis of Video Games: Challenges and Potential Solutions. *Communication Methods and Measures* 3(3): 147–172.

Shaviro, S. 2010. *Post-Cinematic Affect.* Ropley, UK: Zero Books.

Sicart, M. 2009. *The Ethics of Computer Games.* Cambridge, MA: MIT Press.

Sony. 2006. *Wanda to Kyozō.* Sony: Tokyo.

Stiegler, B. 2010. *For a New Critique of Political Economy.* Cambridge, UK: Polity.

Suttner, N. 2015. *Shadow of the Colossus.* Los Angeles, CA: Boss Fight Books.

Thornbury, B. 2011. History, Adaptation, Japan: Haruki Murakami's 'Tony Takitany and Jun Ichikawa's 'Tony Takitani'. *Journal of Adaptation in Film & Performance* 4: 159–171.

Thrift, N. 2006. Re-inventing Invention: New Tendencies in Capitalist Commodification. *Economy and Society* 35(2): 279–306.

Uyeda, I. 1991. Rites of Passage and Purification in Japanese Society: A Study of Shinto Rituals. *Self-transformation and Their Impact upon Japanese Culture* ProQuest Dissertations. University of Oregon.

Wolf, J. P. 2007. *The Video Game Explosion: A History from Pong to Playstation and Beyond.* Westport, CT: Greenwood Press.

CHAPTER 8

Love Without Consequences

Ideology of Romance Representation in Video Games. Case Study of Dragon Age: Inquisition

Moyzhes Leonid

CONTENTS

THIS IS A CASE STUDY of the ideology behind the representation of love in the video game *Dragon Age: Inquisition* by Bioware, which it shares with many other video games, both made by the same studio and by other developers. It proposes that throughout the industry, love and romantic relationships are depicted as a retreat from conflicts, dangers, and the stresses of the wider world. To this end, developers often depict love as something which does not influence anything aside from the personal feelings of the partners involved, stripping it of any potential political, philosophical, religious, or other context.

But this "ghettoization of love" is often at odds with cultural inspiration behind particular love stories, as is the case of the *Dragon Age* series. This text is inspired by an attempt to role-play a romance between main character and non-player character (NPC) Cassandra Pentaghast as a story of love between a religious person and a non-believer who is gradually converted as their relationship progresses. But, despite the fact that Cassandra is one of the most interesting religious characters among a multitude of different NPCs present in fantasy video games, her romantic lines painstakingly exclude any possibility of romantic conflict, making a story of conversion through love something that players can imagine for themselves without any narrative support from the game. This, in turn, hints at a deeper ideological problem in an approach of AAA-studios to the depiction of romance in video games.

DRAGON AGE ROMANCE

Dragon Age: Inquisition is a roleplaying video game developed by Bioware Studio in 2014. It is the third game of the *Dragon Age* franchise, started in 2009 with *Dragon Age: Origins*. The events of all *Dragon Age* games happen in the universe of Thedas, a classic fantasy world populated with races familiar to any fan of the genre—humans, dwarves, elves—and the giant Qunari, designed by Bioware themselves. All games of the franchise were commercially successful, praised by critics, and gained a cult following among gamers. The fourth game of the franchise, *Dragon Age: The Dread Wolf Rises*, is in progress as of the publication of this writing.

Due to its popularity, many authors have analyzed this franchise, and the way it deals with the themes of romantic relationships, love, and sex in particular. From the early 2000s BioWare earned a reputation as a developer that payed attention to these areas with such games as *Baldur's Gate 2*, *Jade Empire*, and *Knights of the Old Republic*. Their games formed and improved on the model of relationships between the main character and their companions that had become a standard for the entire genre, even in games from other studios, such as *Neverwinter Nights 2* or *Pathfinder: Kingmaker*.

In the *Dragon Age* franchise, much like in the synchronously released *Mass Effect*, the developers attempted to provide the player with as many options as possible in the realm of romantic relationships. They sought to produce more romanceable companions, more races, more LGBT+ characters designed to show the studio's dedication to inclusion. The quantity of these options rose from game to game, with *Dragon Age: Origins* allowing the player to romance 4 out of 9 companions, *Dragon Age II* with 5 out of 9, and *Dragon Age: Inquisition* with 8 out of 12 secondary characters (9 companions and 3 advisors).

The abundance of potential partners willing to enter a relationship with a character of any gender, or those presented as openly LGBT+, attracted the attention of not only gamers and journalists, but also academics (Kelly 2015; Bennis 2019, Frick 2019). Some researchers focused on the queer-potential presented in the game (Navarro-Remesal 2018), in particular between two of the player's companions—the qunari Iron Bull and the mage Dorian Parvus (Pelurson 2018). At the same time, the romantic lines in the franchise romances were often criticized as heteronormative or as caricaturizing and distorting images of LGBT+ people (Dym 2019).

Peter Kelly's article *Approaching the Digital Courting Process in Dragon Age 2* (2015) is of particular importance. While he explores romantic relationships in *Dragon Age II*, many of his observations can be applied to *Dragon Age: Inquisition*. Kelly suggested that the romantic plotlines in the franchise procedurally follow the logic of so-called pick-up guides. In both cases the relationships are reduced to a simple opposition of "correct" and "incorrect" responses, where choosing "correct" responses in a certain order helps to develop a relationship. This development, in turn, invariably follows a progression with clear stages: a kiss, physical intimacy, and life together.

Sex here does not appear as a part of the relationship, but rather as a "reward" for saying the right words, a characteristic which brings together video games and pick-up ideology in depersonalizing the partner and mechanizing the relationship. Kelly suggested that this approach toward relationships reveals the developers' desires to please, first and foremost, the male and heterosexual part of their auditory, perhaps because of outdated notions of the domination of young white heterosexual men among gamers, noted, for example, by Janine (2007).

While acknowledging the merits of Kelly's work, it is possible to present a different perspective on one small, yet important, detail. In his article, Kelly focuses on the fact that the approach presented in *Dragon Age II* (as well as in pick-up manuals) depersonalizes partners, turning them into simple "machines" for exchanging correct words and actions for sex. And while this observation is generally just, it seems important to highlight the fact that unlike pick-up manuals, developers of the *Dragon Age* franchise put in significant effort to force the player to pay attention not only to the general attributes of all the available partners, but also their individual differences. While the ideology behind pick-up manuals—male-oriented texts that promise a reader an easy and practical guide for starting romantic and sexual relationship with any person of another gender—implies the existence of some universal words able to please any person *Dragon Age* franchise, albeit clumsily, attempts to present a different approach wherein relationships serve as a reward for attention payed to the feelings, thoughts, and priorities of the partner. Correct answers are based on assumptions about the companions' character and knowledge of their biography. This attempt to present companions not only as a tactical resource, but also as characters with their own personalities, may seem naïve, and is practically negated by the ability to instantly reload a save in case of a mistake. But still, it should not be ignored.

Considering this, it seems that the main problem with the pick-up approach is not the depersonalization of the partner as such, but rather the ease with which the player is able to choose the correct dialogue option to progress the relationship. In his analysis of pick-up ideology, Kelly brings up the example of the book *How to Become a Women's Puppet Master* (Swingcat 2011), concentrating on the depiction of love as something quantifiable and consisting of predictable logical steps. But even the title of the book suggests that the central premise of the text is not the solution of love to simple and understandable steps, but rather the depiction of romantic relationships as inextricably connected with control over the partner and avoidance of the necessary loss of control by the pick-up artist.

It is this pursuit of control, in which the main character "conquering" others with strategically assured responses while avoiding personal risks, that creates the sense of similarity between romances in *Dragon Age* franchise and romantic pick-up artistry or play. This, in turn, is connected to the problem mentioned at the beginning of this article: the lack of romantic conflicts in *Dragon Age: Inquisition*.

In my opinion, that is the main problem with the representation of love in this game, as well as in many other projects. But this article focuses on one game, which will be analyzed using the concepts of "simulation" proposed by Frasca (2003), and "resonance" proposed by Adam Chapman. Chapman, in turn, relies upon the works of Thomas Apperley and texts in ecopsychology.

VIDEO GAMES AND REPRESENTATIONS

Game studies have a tradition of analyzing representation of phenomena in the bounds of video games. This venue of research is tightly connected with the polemics of ludologists and narratologists that unfolded at the dawn of the entire discipline. An example of research dedicated to the analysis of representation in a video game can be found in Ian Bogost's book *Persuasive Games: The Expressive Power of Videogames* (Bogost 2007) which focuses on video game representations of war, politics, and religious life.

Is it possible or appropriate to discuss video games as reflecting objects in real world? Perhaps it is more correct to speak of video games as demonstrating an already existing tradition of representing phenomena in culture, using their own creative resources.

In general, this refers back to the tradition of the semiotic school and the works of authors such as Roland Barthes (Barthes 1972). From his point of view, our perception is always culturally structured, even in cases where a desire to see an *object as such* could be rewarded. Here we can turn to Bruno Latour's assertions that our scientific knowledge is conditioned by cultural constructs (Latour 1986). In this context, to assert that the entertainment industry represents not objects as such, but rather popular cultural narratives is to acknowledge the obvious.

This refers back to Gonzalo Frasca's proposal that video games essentially act as simulations. According to him, "to simulate is to model a (source) system through a different system which maintains to somebody some of the behaviors of the original system" (Frasca 2003).

Inside the bounds of the game we are faced with representations of objects and phenomena that exist outside of said bounds, with a number of simplifications. The necessity of these simplifications is dictated, at a minimum, by material limitations—modern technologies do not allow for the representation even of simple phenomena with perfect accuracy; much less representations of complex systems, such as "government" or "romantic relationships."

Frasca claims that the decision of which elements of the simulated system make it into the final products is determined by the ideology and culture of the developer. For instance, in a representation of war some may find important to represent large numbers of assorted weaponry, while others focus on the suffering of non-combatants. But either of these approaches refers not to the real world, but to an established narrative of events in the real world which determines the logic of inclusion and exclusion from the simulation of some objects or others, dedicated to insuring that observers can recognize the original in the simulated system.

But even if we assume that video games are theoretically capable of simulating real phenomena and not cultural constructs, most large projects don't even try to do this. Instead, they prefer to rely on the fact that players can and will recognize at least some of their parts and narrative structures. In *Digital Games as History*, Adam Chapman, writing about historical video games, duly notices that "by presenting historical representation related to histories that many players are likely to have some kind of narrative understanding of, those games may find it easier to establish and maintain historical resonance" (Chapman 2016: 36).

However, for the theme of romantic relationships, a more relevant text is Sebastian Möring's article dedicated to the game *Marriage* (Möring 2015). It introduces another important concept that describes how video games represent known phenomena—"metaphor." The distinction between metaphors and simulations was introduced even earlier, for example in Bogost's works in which he separated "simulations" as detailed, realistic, and visually understandable representations of objects in a game, and "metaphors" as abstract and non-realistic treatment of ideas (Bogost 2011). *Marriage*, which depicts two partners in a relationship as multicolored squares and problems and opportunities as circles, undoubtably belongs to the second category. Möring, however, describes *Marriage* not as a metaphor of a relationship, but rather as a simulation of a metaphor, where the traditional metaphors often used to describe love in Western culture is taken as the simulated original system and is represented by abstract symbols that reveal how the system functions.

While the game's developer insists that *Marriage* represents personal experience, Möring shows how this game can be seen as a simulation of the concept of love familiar to most people of Western culture. At the same time, he notes that even for games that traditionally belong to the genre of simulation, i.e., *The Sims*, the simulated system is more correctly understood as a cultural concept and not a real-world phenomenon.

In this way, we see that representations of romantic relationships invariably simulate not the relationships as such, but rather the cultural constructs that describe how said relationships should look. These constructs can be abstract or realistic, but they are in any case conditioned by the totality of texts dedicated to the particular subject.

ABSTRACT PLAYER

This article positions *Dragon Age: Inquisition* as part of Western, and primarily American, culture, as the culture that contains most texts describing systems of romantic relationships simulated in the game. Obviously, this is not the only possible reading, but it seems justified in light of the fact that the majority of the developer team and target audience belong to Western culture.

This assertion in itself brings up additional issues. It is possible to recall the song by the German band Rammstein, "We're All Living in America," and ask ourselves where in the modern global and postcolonial world can we draw the borders between belonging to Western culture in the American variety, familiarity with it, and exclusion from that cultural space. As a researcher from Russia, I face this issue on everyday basis. But this is too complex question to be covered in this article. For now, it is sufficient to say that the simulated cultural systems used in the game belong to the tradition of representation of love introduced in Western European literature and later rethought as part of American mass culture.

It is necessary to introduce here the figure of an *abstract player*, similar to that of an *abstract reader* from Wolf Schmid's *Narratology*. Schmid's *abstract reader* is the "author's concept of the receiver which is marked in the text by means of some [indicial] symbols" (2010). Schmid distinguished two forms of an abstract reader: the *supposed recipient*, which is the ideal carrier of factual codes and norms required for the understanding of the text, and the *ideal recipient*, which perceives the text in ideal way, implied by its structure, and, most importantly, assumes the point of view that the text is suggesting.

In the case of *Dragon Age: Inquisition* we see a conflict between these two forms. Perhaps, it happens because Western cultural models of representing love that are simulated in the game cause the *supposed recipient* to perceive romantic stories in a different fashion than the *ideal recipient* that shares the game's ideology. To explain how this contradiction forms, it is necessary to refer to the theory of resonance proposed by Thomas Appeley and developed by Adam Chapman.

RESONANCE

Chapman, following the work of Apperley (2010) defines "resonance" as the following: "resonance describes the sensation of interpreting a representation of the game as relating to something other than only the game's rules, as referring to something not entirely contained within the game itself and of the everyday world in which we live" (Chapman 2016, 35). For instance, the figure of a person in a recognizable headwear with an assault rifle in hand resonates with the image of an Islamic terrorist depicted by mass media and mass culture.

Chapman analyzed the ability of video games to depict history and focused on the resonance between games and real events. But resonance can also appear in relation to something that is not real. For instance, in the bounds of the fantasy genre, players will recognize the depictions of popular races, placing the game in a wider cultural context. It is also important to note that resonance is not limited to a visual level. The player can recognize situations, plotlines, audio elements, text, terms, and theoretical concepts. Even the genres of the video games can be described through resonance, following Paweł Frelik proposition of conceptualizing genres as optics, dependent on the viewer's ability to recognize them (Frelik 2016). It is enough to recall that for a long time games that are now called RPGs were called "DnD-like," and shooters—"Doom clones."

In a general sense, resonance is another way to discuss the importance of recognition described by Barthes in his own time. But Chapman, citing Apperley, distinguishes a form of resonance unique to video games: "configurative resonance." He defined it as follows: "configurative resonance or dissonance involves the player deliberately configuring and/or performing actions in the game—out of all possible potential configurations and performances—in order to create a specific resonance" (Apperley 2010, 135).

Chapman himself brought up the example of the game *Sleeping Dogs*, in which he received a quest to escort the main character's friend to a wedding, and arrived to pick him up in an undamaged vehicle, despite the fact that it required additional time and effort and was unnecessary to progress through the game. In this example the configurative resonance resides in something that has meaning only for the player. The game does not distinguish the outer appearance of the main character's car. But often developers put in effort to reward players acting according to similar logic. For instance, global strategies such as the *Europa Universalis* franchise offer specific rewards for closely following the events of real history, or vice versa "fixing" mistakes of the past.

In this article, the ingame availability of configurative potential for a particular configuration, following Linderoth's lead (2011), will be called "affordances." This term entered game studies through ecopsychology, in particular, from works by Gibson (1986). And the totality of meaningful affordances in a game concerning a certain resonance can be named the configurative potential.

Configurative potential and resonance are linked. The game demonstrates to the player recognizable objects, causing resonance and creating certain expectations. For example, seeing a zombie in a game, a player will most likely assume that the game contains the ability to kill zombies. That assumption would be based not only upon ludical suggestion that the game can be won, but also on resonance with knowledge of zombie apocalypse trope in movies and zombie shooters in video games. If the affordances of the game coincide with corresponding affordances created by the resonance, the player perceives the game world as complete. Inability to meet such expectations with expectations, on the other hand, leads to frustration which then leads to perceived lack of realism or sense of constraint.

It is important to understand that resonance implies a manifold of linked affordances. For instance, the appearance of zombies is associated not only with violence, but also with running away. The absence of expected affordances, in turn, can be seen not only as a restriction, but also as a unique feature of the game. However, this is only possible with the condition that the very absence of affordances itself causes resonance. This logic can be seen in many horror games like *Slender* or *Amnesia*, in which the lack of mechanics for fighting the monsters recreates the helplessness of characters in a horror movie.

If we correlate the idea of Chapman and his predecessors with Schmid's conception, the supposed recipient would be a player that reads all of the game's elements as resonating with something beyond the game according to the game's own logic. And the ideal recipient, in turn, would make the ethical and ideological conclusions suggested by the game when faced with the game's content, resonance created by it, and affordances contained within it.

The conflict between these two aspects of abstract player appears if the suggested ideology (which in turn resonates with something beyond the game) comes into conflict with phenomena that resonate with individual game elements. Theoretically, according to Schmid, the abstract player in this situation will read the suggested hierarchy of opinions and integrate into it. But in cases where such hierarchy is unclear, for example, because of lack of a consistent ideology, the perception of the game becomes problematic.

SIMULATION OF ROMANTIC LOVE

This article views Romanticism as an intellectual movement which forms the base of Western culture's understanding of love, affecting, among other things, the representation of this feeling in video games and among players. Romanticists paid significant attention to the inner world, creating approaches to its conceptualization that still affect mass culture today. It was based, of course, upon previous traditions, going as deep as Middle Ages and Antiquity. That allowed the romanticists to create an understanding of love that not only affected later texts, but also included previous stories, rethinking them and giving them new meaning. This is especially important in the context of *Dragon Age: Inquisition*, as many of the romance plotlines in the game resonate with plotlines that chronologically precede romanticism, such as chivalric romance.

The important theme of the romantic conceptualization of love is conflict. One of the clichés in discussions of romanticism is the opposition between a romantic hero and the world, with the conflict taking the form of love. The hero is ready to sacrifice social standing, sanity, friendship, and life itself for love. Love became something that did not belong to the "mundane" world, doomed to be tested by conflict between people, social norms, or mystical forces. The conflation of love and conflict and the understanding of conflict as a sign of true love is one of the fundamental legacies of romanticism.

It is necessary to distinguish two main forms of such conflict. First is the internal conflict, or emotional conflict, that happens inside the hero's mind and forces him to face his/her own prejudices, fears, or beliefs that stand in the way of their love. In the last decades, this conflict has become popular, perhaps because it suits psychological discourse requiring any person to be ready to change for a loved one.

The second form is the external or material conflict, which threatens a hero with a loss of social standing, a confrontation with other characters or society in general, a risk of death or with death itself, etc. It is worth noting that in romantic depictions of love the second form of conflict always includes the first. It is never just about overcoming an obstacle, but about making an emotional decision, overcoming fear, relinquishing ambitions, etc.

This differs with the conception of love as conquest that can be seen in folktales and epics. The later suggests that a hero receives the object of their passion as a "reward" for victory or possession of certain qualities, bypassing the moment of emotional decision or leaving it obscured.

The other alternative worth mentioning depicts love as something opposite to conflict, a sudden miracle that affords a hero a safe haven from the troubles of everyday life.

All of these approaches to representing love differ not in form, but in ideology. Different authors and readers perceive same stories as having different meanings. For instance, Robin Hood's relationship with Maid Marian (Child 1888) can be understood as love that pushes Robin toward confrontation with the rest of the world, and demands Marian to reject her social standing. But it can also be understood in terms of love as a reward, where Marian becomes the "trophy" that Robin wins from his enemies, or even as love as a shelter. The last approach suggests that heroes' relationship serves as the only simple and peaceful part of their lives, giving them strength to face new challenges and adventures.

But the possibility of various interpretations of the same archetypal story does not change the fact that inside a specific work, a suitable plotline signals to the abstract reader to which type it belongs. One of the signs that show the affiliation of a work to the logic of romantic love is the presence of emotionally conditioned conflicts that occur because of characters' feelings, which from now on would be called romantic conflicts.

The romantic plotlines of *Dragon Age: Inquisition* are structured according to Bioware's established scheme, initially introduced in *Baldur's Gate II: Shadows of Amn* and later developed in *Knights of the Old Republic*. The main character, known as Inquisitor or Herald of Andraste, has a base, where they can interact with their companions, and attempt to enter into a relationship with them by choosing a special dialogue option marked with a heart icon. In such dialogues, and during missions, the player makes choices that increase or decrease companion's approval of the main character.

Certain values of that parameter in turn allow access to extra dialogue options, including those related to romance. Depending on the race and gender of the character, and in some cases on a choice between several dialogue options that serves as a "test" of how well the player knows the character, the romance plotline progresses. Reaching certain thresholds in the romance plotlines is marked with special dialogues, cutscenes, reactions of other companions, and side missions that the player must complete to take further steps in the relationship.

But what is particularly striking is that this system does not suppose romantic conflicts. It does not imply any emotional change for the protagonist: choosing dialogue options motivates the player to better understand romanceable character, but does not require compliance with their values (for example, their religious views). The game "punishes" the player for disrespecting the religion of their chosen partner, but does not require conversion. Basically, it follows the third above-mentioned approach to love, considering it a safe haven from ills of the bigger world, with lovers striving to be as emotionally safe for each other as possible.

Of course, for some people (for instance, those who decided to play a militant atheist), the necessity to respect religion can work as a source of emotional conflict. So for an analysis of the game itself, and not a fan reaction to it, we must turn to the figure of the abstract player. The abstract player has a measure of freedom—they are free to hold on to any interpretation of the work that the work itself can suggest. However, this range has well defined limits, which in our case include the ability to see multiple faiths as true, but do not support proselytization from the player or the NPC's.

This approach to romance also excludes "external" romantic conflict, which is especially visible in *Dragon Age: Inquisition*. Unlike many main characters from other RPG's, the Inquisitor is not a solitary adventurer traveling with a group of companions. They are an important political figure in Thedas, the leader of an organization working toward reforming the largest church of the fictional universe, and responsible for upholding peace in a number of countries. The Inquisitor is constantly making political decisions: forming alliances, distributing resources, deciding the fates of nations and peoples.

But the romances stand apart from these events. The fact that the Inquisitor is in a relationship with some character does not add any extra options of resolving a conflict to suit their partner's wishes. And the dialogues that appear in the romance plotlines contain no mention of the decisions made. Politics, and in a general sense social life, are strictly separated from romance, to the degree where the two areas have no influence over one another.

This approach is not unique to *Dragon Age: Inquisition*. Jameson noted (2006) that the image of love as a refuge from politics is typical to colonialist nations. But in the context of this game, it creates a conflict between the resonance and affordances. Many potential partners resonate with a type of character that are, in turn, associated with the Western notion of romantic love that requires partners to make sacrifices and face conflicts.

Cassandra Pentagast, as a romantic partner, causes resonances with stories of relationships between members of different confessions or between clerics and lay people. Sara resonates with the problem of different class standing, Cullen—with chivalric romance, Josephina—with Picaresque novel, Solas—with love as an obstacle for other plans. Lastly, Dorian Parvus obviously touches upon the issue of LGBT+ relationships, which are still subject to loss of social status or even criminal prosecution in many nations around the world. All of these types of romances differ significantly from the "love as refuge" that is offered by *Dragon Age: Inquisition*.

The desire to shield the player from romantic conflicts permeates the entire logic of representing love in the game. This manifests, for instance, in the lack of romances initiated by the main character's companions. It also affects the hierarchical nature of romances within the party, in which case the relationship between the protagonist and a companion "suppressing" the relationship between two companions, specifically Dorian and Iron Bull. The connection between these two characters simply does not appear if the Inquisitor pursues either of them as potential partner. In both cases we see a manifestation of the same logic—a desire to protect the player from the necessity of making a decision that mixes emotional considerations (do I like this character?) and pragmatic ones (do I want to ruin my relationship with a companion?).

The developers even adapted the fictional universe itself to bring romantic relationships outside the bounds of politics. Like many fantasy worlds, Thedas follows the canon of *neomedievalism*, a pastiche style that heavily uses popular imagery and story tropes commonly associated with European Medieval Ages (Eco 1986). *Dragon Age*'s aesthetics, terminology, and many other elements resonate with the traditional elements of this genre: conflict between Church and magic, oppression of minorities, romanticized knight culture.

But in *Inquisition*'s romances, Thedas is quite modern and even idealized. In the part of the world which appears in the game, there is no homophobia, the Inquisitor is not pressured into arranged marriages, the theme of celibacy among clerical figures is deftly avoided, and a romance between the head of the largest religious organization and a member of a different faith, such as a qunari, does not cause any scandals.

This is worth notice, that the game's strategic component would have allowed a representation of the following conflicts without much effort. For instance, the player could lose part of the *Inquisition*'s resource by entering into a scandalous relationship, which would reflect the disappointment of Thedas' more conservative circles. And the fact that the game lacks even these surface level romantic conflicts leads me to believe that it was a conscious, or, at least, semi-conscious, decision on the part of the developers. In conjunction with Frasca's ideas, they simulate love, rejecting those elements of the simulated system that seem insignificant. And the choice of said elements reflects the ideology installed into the game: the idea that love serves as a refuge for the main character where they can rest from politics. In the present article this ideology of exclusion of romantic relationships from the rest of the game world will be called the "ghettoization of love."

MASKING STRATEGIES

Dragon Age: Inquisition uses three strategies to mask both the fact that all romantic plotlines in the game follow a single ideology and the inconsistency of some elements of the ideology with the resonance caused by certain companions.

The first strategy is built around the fact that the progression of the romance stories requires time and effort from the player. They must pay attention in dialogues, complete missions, spend time watching cutscenes. This maintains the resonance between the romantic plotlines in the game and their prototypes in mass culture. The player feels invested in the Inquisitor's relationships, completing companions' requests, and holding personal conversations with them.

However, from the point of view of the abstract player, the feeling of "sacrifice" in this case is false, since while the necessity of spending more time on the game can lead to emotionally conditioned conflicts in real life, inside the game the Inquisitor's time and resources are unlimited. Dialogues and mission that occur as part of the romances do not require the Inquisitor to spend resources that could have been required in other situations.

The second strategy is based on the fact that the romantic storylines serve as add-ons to the non-romantic ones. The most obvious example is the "approval" parameter. For the romance to progress it is necessary for the player to reach a certain value of approval. The increase in approval, in turn, is made through dialogues at the base camp and through making the decisions that match companion's views both during missions and while managing the Inquisition. This can create a likeness of romantic conflicts, as these decisions imply real consequences, including problems, in the main part of the game.

But it is significant that this rather detailed system does not react to the main character's romantic relationships. The player makes decisions based on a desire to see the Inquisitor in a relationship with a specific character, but the game does not contain any reflection of this fact. Moreover, the majority of such decisions are not presented as a choice between emotions and pragmaticism, but rather between two pragmatic courses of action and the companion's assessment them is of secondary concern.

Of course, a specific player can make decisions based on a desire to please a certain companion; however, the game itself does not contain elements that would reflect such a motive. For instance, the player can perceive their decision to make Cassandra Pentagast the new head of the Church in terms of their feelings toward her, but the game will not present any details or dialogues representing that perception.

Finally, the third strategy is tied to the asymmetry in the relationships between the Inquisitor and their potential partners. At the same time as the Inquisitor avoids romantic conflicts, many of their potential partners find themselves involved in one. For example, the advisor Josephina breaks off an engagement for a relationship with the main character. For Cassandra, the very fact of a stable relationship creates internal conflict. And in the case of the mage Solas, who ends up leaving the main character, the scene before that reflects a romantic conflict, where Solas' desire to complete his plans outweighs love.

But even these sacrifices don't contradict the ghettoization—they do not affect the personalities or social standing of the characters to a point where it can't be ignored, not do they affect their ludic characteristics. Even more interesting is the fact that game presents affordances for emotional changes in companions though their character quests, but they exist parallel to romantic storylines. This asymmetry, in my opinion, is what contributes to the pick-up feeling described by Kelly. The main character forces others to change within the bound of their relationships, remaining unchanged themselves. This allows us to recollect the concept of "playersexuality" (Cole 2017), which in this case affect not only the NPCs' sexuality as such, but also reflects their readiness to enter into an asymmetrical relationship with the main character.

POINT OF ORIGIN

At this point it is worth remembering the circumstances in which Bioware games developed their approach to romances. Their mechanic of interparty relationships has a specific point of origin—the game *Planescape:*

Torment released by BlackIsle in 1999, which used the Infinity Engine, created a year earlier by Bioware for the game *Baldur's Gate.*

Like *Baldur's Gate, Planescape: Torment* is an RPG in the *Dungeons and Dragons* universe, using similar mechanics, camera position, and the approach to transferring tabletop rulesets into a computer game. However, the difference between *Baldur's Gate* and *Planescape: Torment* is that the latter told a personal story.

The narrative of *Planescape: Torment* focused on a specific character—an immortal known as The Nameless One and a small group of companions. The Nameless One was trying to find out how exactly he became immortal and what to do with it, at the same time building relationships with people around him. In terms of plotlines, *Planescape: Torment* was almost linear, with the variety of different playthrough achieved by different ways of developing The Nameless One, and personality and abilities the player had given him through interaction with NPCs and companions. The story maintains this strictly personal approach until the very end, in which The Nameless One faces his own mortality and forces it to merge with him so he can die.

This attention to the personality of the main character resulted in the attention to his social connection, including romantic ones. Key characters in the game were former lovers of the Nameless One, one of them, a ghost, meets him at the very beginning of the game. At the same time, the developers allowed the main character to enter new romances, introducing a system of relationships between the protagonist and his companions based on choices in dialogues, a system which later became the foundation for similar mechanics in other RPGs.

The game offered only two potential partners: the thief Annah and the succubus-cleric Fall-From-Grace. But both romances included romantic conflicts—like other characters, the partners could leave the party after several unfortunate dialogue choices, enter into a conflict with one another, or attack the protagonist. In the story, which for a large part revolved around a conflict between the main character and his former lover, new romance could not be ghettoized.

A good example of the lack of borders between romantic relationships and the rest of the game is the kiss with Fall-From-Grace, which leads to the death of The Nameless One. Being immortal, he is instantly resurrected, but the very presence of this scene, and most importantly, the reflection of the related choices and mechanics in dialogues allows to perceive it as a manifestation of romantic conflict, in this case an internal one, the protagonist's wiliness to face death for a kiss with his lover.

Bioware borrowed many ideas from *Planescape: Torment* for their *Baldur's Gate II: Shadows of Amn*, in particular the complex relationships between the main character and the party, and among the other party members. The game also included romantic conflicts, the most striking of which was the love triangle that could occur between the protagonist, the bard Haer'Dalis, and the elf Aerie. The contest for the attention of the latter in most cases ended in a duel with lethal consequences between the main character and his former brother in arms.

But unlike *Planescape: Torment*, the main story of *Baldur' Gate II* was an epic one, not a personal one. The protagonist stood against the mage Irenicus, who was trying to destroy the city of Suldanesselar. And the romances appeared as something important, but still secondary. Borrowing romantic lines from *Planescape: Torment*, as a way to make the main character more interesting and to increase the variety of playthroughs, the developers switched accents, moving this mechanic to the area of side missions. And this led to the necessity of controlling its level of influence on the main story and gameplay.

In the following decades the situation was complicated by market and technology. Developments in graphics (like switching from 2D to 3D) and increased aspirations from consumers made companions in RPGs more expensive for development. Each companion now required much more work to create and voice, and consequently their numbers were reduced.

The introduction of conflicts that could lead to a character leaving the party became too risky—the abundance of companions in *Baldur's Gate II* implied that a player, who didn't decide to play the game subversively, could always put together a balanced party, even after antagonizing some potential comrades. But in the *KotOR* or *Dragon Age* franchises the loss of even a single companion is a serious problem that creates, among other things, practical issues with completing the game, and signifies that the huge effort in animation and voicing was for naught.

In these circumstances developers could not risk adding to the game the most natural result of a failed relationship—parting. Companions stayed in the party no matter what, and only the player's conscious decision could make them leave. But this, in turn, required the simulation of the party dynamic not as friends, emotionally tied to the protagonist, but around more abstract ideas such as the necessity to face the Reapers, the

Blight, or other cataclysms. It led to the separation of romantic relationships into a sphere that exists parallel to the main activities and motives of the characters.

At the same time, it is important to note that in many games outside of the RPG genre, where story is based around romantic or emotional conflict involving the main character, the abstract player itself is presented as a rational and ethical actor, in need of moral, and not emotional, justification for any acts of violence. Love, friendship, and the desire to avenge the death of a loved one serve as the protagonist's motivation in many games, such as *Dead Space*, *Watch_Dogs*, and *Bioshock: Infinite*. But for the abstract player it is obvious that the opponents deserve death not because they stand in the way of love, but because they are bad people or dehumanized monsters. These kinds of stories avoid situations of real choice between the protagonist's attachments and an ethically correct decision. Love still stays in the "ghetto," serving not as a part of the story, but as a way of making the main character more interesting and sympathetic to the player.

This approach is, at least partly, based on the continuing identification of games with male audiences, and the widespread stereotype that men in general are afraid to express, and even experience, strong feelings. One can recall Ursula Le Guin's essay *Why Are Americans Afraid of Dragons?* (Le Guin 1982), where she supposed that Americans' aversion to fantasy was based upon the fear that they would appear "infantile" or "feminine." One can suppose that modern developers are still following stereotypes that link interest in emotional stories with the female gender, and interest in games with the male, as discussed by authors like Yasmin Kafai (Kafai 2008).

But many real gamers hold a different opinion on the matter. In her article *I'm in love with someone who doesn't exist*, Annika Waern researches forum posts dedicated to romances in *Dragon Age: Origins* (Waern 2015). She points out that the most popular romantic options are Alistair and Morrigan, which leaves the "ghetto" more than others, even if only in the final chapter of the game. Waern supposes that the two other romantic interests are less popular for the exact reason that they stand alone from the main story.

An even more striking and convincing evidence that players are ready to be guided by emotions is the willingness to created "romantic" mods that allow romantic pursuit of a desired character. It is important to note that these are no sexual mods, but rather fully-fledged love stories that players create for themselves. It becomes obvious that at least a part of those who play video games are ready to spend time, effort, and energy to "play love." And developers that enforce the unbreakable borders of the "ghetto" risk disappointing their fans more and more.

CONCLUSION

The "ghettoization of love" can be described in the following way: the exclusion of romantic storylines of the game into a separate sphere, excluded from other game narratives, the boundaries of which are completely controlled by the player. This process reflects the very particular, though hidden, ideology of representation of love, which obviously contradicts the ideologies of texts that affect the images of specific companions and their romantic plotlines, thus creating certain narrative tensions.

Western culture traditionally doesn't depict love as something comfortable, controllable, and secure, hence romantic relationships that combine images based in older texts with the ideology of ghettoization often create negative impressions. It can be perceived as objectification, disrespectful representation, or, on the contrary, artificial imposition of romantic storylines that require significant time and effort from the player but practically do not affect the gameplay and fictional universe.

The three strategies of concealment, and most importantly, the mastery of the people responsible for the looks, speech, and voicing of the characters allow them to hide this problem, while at the same time underlying the necessity to solve it completely. Players are ready to "fall in love" with video game characters. And the success of games that reject the "ghettoization" of love, such as the *Witcher* franchise (Majkowski 2018), or outside the RPG genre, *Life is Strange*, confirms this.

But most importantly, as Aki Järvinen demonstrates in his article (Järvinen 2008), video games always provide players with an emotional experience. And developers must learn to interact with this experience, control it, and use it to enrich their works.

LUDOGRAPHY

Baldur's Gate 2 (2000) BioWare/Interplay Entertainment
Bioshock: Infinite (2013) Irrational Games/2K Games
Dead Space (2008) EA Redwood Shores/Electronic Arts
Dragon Age: Origins (2009) BioWare/Electronic Arts
Dragon Age II (2011) BioWare/Electronic Arts
Dragon Age: Inquisition (2014) BioWare/Electronic Arts

Jade Empire (2005) BioWare/Microsoft Game Studios and 2K Games
Knights of the Old Republic (2003) BioWare/LucasArts
Life is Strange (2015) Dontnod Entertainment/Square Enix
Marriage (2007) Rod Humble
Planescape: Torment (1999). BlackIsle Studios/Interplay Entertainment
Sleeping Dogs (2012) United Front Games/Square Enix
Sims (2000) Maxis/Electronic Arts
Watch_Dogs (2014) Ubisoft Montreal/Ubisoft
The Witcher 3: Wild Hunt (2015) CD Project Red/CD Project

REFERENCES

Apperley, Tom. 2010. Gaming Rhythms: Play and Counterplay from Situated to the Global. *Theory on Demand* 6: 1–170.

Barthes, Roland. 1972. *Mythologies*. New York: Farrar, Straus and Giroux.

Bennis, Shauna Ashley. 2019. When All You Can Be Is about Who You Already Are: Dragon Age: Inquisition and the Uncovering of Real-Life Behaviour Patterns. In *Levelling Up: The Cultural Impact of Contemporary Videogames*, ed. by Brittany Kuhn and Alexia Bhéreur-Lagounaris, 63–72. Leiden, the Netherlands: Brill.

Bogost, Ian. 2007. *Persuasive Games: The Expressive Power of Videogames*. Cambridge, MA: MIT Press.

Bogost, Ian. 2011. *How to do Things with Videogames*. Minneapolis, MN: University of Minnesota Press.

Chapman, Adam. 2016. *Digital Games as History: How Videogames Represent the Past and Give Access to Historical Practice*. New York: Routledge.

Child, Francis James. 1888. *The English and Scottish Popular Ballads, 5 Volume Set* [2003]. Mineola, NY: Dover Publications.

Cole, Alayne. 2017. *Playersexuality and Plurisexuality in Videogames*. https://alaynamcole.com/academic/playersexuality-alterconf (accessed April 14, 2019).

Dym, Brianna. 2019. The Burden of Queer Love. *Press Start* 5, no. 1 (March). https://press-start.gla.ac.uk/index.php/press-start/article/view/119/76

Eco, Umberto. 1986. Dreaming of the Middle Ages. In *Travels in Hyperreality*, 61–72. New York: Harcourt Brace.

Frasca, Gonzalo. 2003. Simulation Versus Narrative: Introduction to Ludology. *The Video game Theory Reader* 2: 221–236.

Frelik, Paweł. 2016. Gazing (Back) in Wonder: Visual Megatext and Forgotten Ocularies of Science Fiction. *Science Fiction Studies* 43(2): 226–236.

Frick, Veit. 2019. Romance Is Difficult: Choice, Agency and the Sexual Identity of NPCs in BioWare's Dragon Age: Inquisition. In *Levelling Up: The Cultural Impact of Contemporary Videogames*, ed. by Brittany Kuhn and Alexia Bhéreur-Lagounaris, 85–92. Leiden, the Netherlands: Brill.

Gibson, James. 1986. *The Ecological Approach to Visual Perception*. Hillsdale, NJ: Lawrence Erlbaum Associated Publishers.

Järvinen, Aki. 2008. Understanding Video Games as Emotional Experiences. In *Video Game Theory Reader 2*, ed. by Mark J.P. Wolf and Bernard Perron, 85–108. New York: Routledge.

Jameson, Fredric. 2006. Businessman in Love. In: *The Novel: Forms and Themes*, ed. by Franco Moretti, 436–448. Princeton, NJ: Princeton University Press.

Janine, Fron, & Tracy, Fullerton &, Jacquelyn, Morie & Celia, Pearce. 2007. The Hegemony of Play. In *DiGRA'07: Proceedings of the 2007 DiGRA International Conference: Situated Play*, 309–318. Tokyo, Japan: The University of Tokyo.

Kafai, Y. B., C. Heeter, J. Denner, and J. Y. Sun. *Beyond Barbie and Mortal Kombat: New Perspectives on Gender and Computer Games*. Cambridge: The MIT Press, 2008. 398 p.

Kelly, Peter. 2015. Approaching the Digital Courting Process in Dragon Age 2. In *Game Love: Essay on Play and Affection*, ed. by Jessica Enevold and Esther MacCallum-Stewart, 46–62. Jefferson, NC: McFarland.

Latour, Bruno. 1986. *Laboratory Life: The Construction of Scientific Facts*. Princeton, NJ: Princeton University Press.

Le Guin, Ursula. 1982. Why Are Americans Afraid of Dragons? [1979]. In *Language of the Night: Essays on Fantasy and Science Fiction*, ed. Susan Wood, 31–40. New York: Berkley.

Linderoth, Jonas. 2011. Beyond the digital divide: An ecological approach to gameplay. In *DiGRA'11: Proceedings of the 2011 DiGRA International Conference: Think Design Play.* http://todigra.org/index.php/todigra/article/view/9/7

Majkowski, Tomasz. 2018. Geralt of Poland: The Witcher 3 Between Epistemic Disobedience and Imperial Nostalgia. *Open Library of Humanities* 4(1). http://doi.org/10.16995/olh.216.

Möring, Sebastian. 2015. Simulated Metaphors of Love. How *The Marriage* Applies Metaphors to Simulate a Love Relationship. In *Game Love: Essay on Play and Affection*, ed. by Jessica Enevold and Esther MacCallum-Stewart, 196–215. Jefferson, NC: McFarland.

Navarro-Remesal, Victor. 2018. Gender, Sex and Romance in Role Playing Video games: Dragon's Dogma, Fable III and Dragon Age: Inquisition. *Catalan Journal of Communication & Cultural Studies* 10(2): 177–191. https://doi.org/10.1386/cjcs.10.2.177_1.

Pelurson, Gaspard. 2018. Mustaches, Blood Magic and Interspecies Sex: Navigating the Non-Heterosexuality of Dorian Pavus. *Game Studies* 18(1). http://gamestudies.org/1801/articles/gaspard_pelurson

Schmid, Wolf. 2010. *Narratology: An Introduction.* Walter de Gruyter.

Swingcat. 2011. How to Become a Women's Puppet Master. http://becomeaplayer.com/articles/puppetmaster.htm (accessed March 1, 2012).

Waern, Annika. 2015. I'm in Love with Someone Who Doesn't Exist!: Bleed in the Context of a Computer Game. In *Game Love: Essays on Play and Affection*, ed. by Jessica Enevold and Esther MacCallum-Stewart, 25–46. Jefferson, IA: McFarland.

CHAPTER 9

Innovative Origins, Playersexuality, & Complex Inquisition

The Evolution of Relationship Mechanics in Dragon Age

Alexandra M. Lucas

CONTENTS

FROM THE RELEASE OF *Dragon Age: Origins* in 2009 to 2011's *Dragon Age 2* through to the third and most recent major installment, 2014's *Dragon Age: Inquisition*, BioWare's medieval fantasy *Dragon Age* series has set a high standard for romance and affection in digital roleplaying games (RPGs). Focusing on cultivating character depth, providing a variety of romance options, and replicating realistic friendships, *Dragon Age* helped establish expansive expectations for modern relationship-focused RPG players. Through BioWare developers' experimentation, iteration, and willingness to leave less effective mechanics behind, in-game relationships in the *Dragon Age* series evolved across the three main games to better mirror reality, promote diversity, and offer more compelling rewards for getting to know party companions, both romantically and platonically. Not only have these changes often enhanced relationship authenticity and promoted the engagement of many different types of players with the *Dragon Age* series, but they also have established a precedent for the expected romance options and social impact of future RPGs.

THE EVOLUTION OF REWARDS AND APPROVAL EFFECTS

In order to communicate relationship progression, all installments in the *Dragon Age* series provide rewards of varying types, including bonuses to non-player character (NPC) attributes, unique conversation options, and intimate cutscenes. To earn such rewards, the player can give gifts to party members in all three main *Dragon Age* games, although gifts function differently in each game in notable ways. In *Dragon Age: Origins* (Bioware, 2009), the player must simply guess which gifts each NPC would like, with NPC gift preferences only becoming truly apparent after some trial and error and after unlocking character codex entries. The first "correct" gift is worth maximum approval points (+10), with diminishing returns with each successive correct gift (e.g., +9, +8…+1). Some special gifts award +15 approval and can only be given to specific NPCs. Negative approval also reduces the effect of gifts, so less friendly players often still need to garner NPC approval through their actions and dialogue choices. The player can also sell gifts in *Origins* to merchants, a marked difference from future installments.

The gifts in *Dragon Age 2 (DA2)* and *Dragon Age: Inquisition (Inquisition)* are far less flexible than the inventory fillers in *Origins*. Instead, in *DA2*, the acquisition of a gift adds a related quest associated with a specific NPC to the player's journal. In order to give the gift, the player must go to the NPC's "home" to present it to them, which advances the associated quest as well as enhances whichever relationship type the player has already begun with that NPC (in *DA2*, friendship or rivalry). By removing monetary value and the possibility of giving gifts to the wrong NPC, *DA2* the sometimes-tedious guesswork of gift-giving and instead attaches clear, direct meaning to each gift. The gifts in *DA2* are perhaps more memorable and emotionally resonant because they are immediately associated with a specific companion and their personal quest, such as Varric Tethras' "Tethras Signet Ring" and Isabela of Rivain's "Rivaini Talisman" (*Dragon Age* [Gift Origins], 2019).

Inquisition reduces gift-giving to a purely romantic endeavor; generally, gifts only materialize once the player has progressed in a romance with an NPC and are only sometimes tied to personal quests (Gifts Inquisition, 2019). In some cases, as with Cullen, the NPC actually gives the player the gift themselves, removing player error and agency. Instead, players must earn companion approval (particularly platonic approval) almost exclusively by getting to know each individual, making choices with which the NPC agrees, and selecting dialogue options that best correspond to each NPC's personality.

Often in the *Dragon Age* series, NPCs are at odds with one another, so to maximize approval, players also are sometimes tasked with picking sides as well as anticipating the quests in which each NPC would most enjoy or dislike taking part. For example, the mage v. templar conflict is central throughout all three games, and in *DA2*, anti-mage NPC Fenris will outright leave the party if the player sides with mages a few times too many while Fenris is present in the party (in addition to a few other special circumstances). *DA2* also reflects an understanding that some players prefer antagonistic relationships with their companions, as evidenced by *DA2*'s unique concept of "rivalry." To gain rivalry with a party companion, a player must make choices of which the NPC disapproves, and doing so unlocks unique ability options, offers different dialogue choices, and creates discord within the relationship. However, an NPC at full "rivalry" (that is, maximum disapproval of the player) will not necessarily leave the party, unlike in *Origins*, and the player can even still romance some full-rivalry NPCs.

Unlike in the previous two games, the player cannot view a literal approval meter in *Inquisition*; the player only receives pop-up notifications noting an NPC's approval or disapproval after the player makes a key decision or concludes a notable conversation. Approval becomes hidden information that the player must gauge based on either meticulous extra calculation or social instinct, by way of interpreting the changing tones of NPC greetings and their reactions to different situations. This obfuscation potentially supports deeper immersion and escapism; as *Dragon Age* series executive producer Mark Darrah said in an interview about *Inquisition*, "I think it's important for people to play the characters that they want to play, that we give choice and that we try to allow escapism" (Clark, 2014). Either way, *Inquisition* forces the player to interact with NPCs more like real people who are changeable, fluid, and do not usually come with their own approval meter, rather than characters who can easily be manipulated across a visual, quantitative slider.

In addition to gifts, conversations, and the friendship-rivalry meter, sex scenes have played a pivotal role in the evolution of relationship mechanics in the *Dragon Age* series, illustrating different kinds of possible sexual relationships as well as emotional relationships that are generally positive and healthy. As former BioWare senior writer David Gaider stated in his 2013 Game Developers Conference lecture, "Sex in Games," "[e]ver since *Mass Effect*, we've included a sex scene to one degree or another...And we're not alone. The industry has entered the place where video games don't only have the technical ability to show sex scenes, but the willingness to include them" (Plante, 2013). Sex scenes in the *Dragon Age* series range from the implied to the racy, although character genitals are generally not visible, and sex doesn't mark "...the end of your relationship with the people in *Inquisition*...it makes romance and sex seem less like it's a reward for getting to know the characters" (Hernandez, 2014). By giving the sex scenes meaning, variety, and different tones—ranging from the sweet innocence of Josephine's leg-lifting kiss to the relatable silliness of being walked-in on while having sex with the BDSM-friendly Iron Bull—BioWare provides a mix from which different types of players can choose.

PROMOTING DIVERSITY, INCLUSION, AND REPRESENTATION

When it comes to representation in and diversity of romance options, BioWare displays unique evolution, exploration, and expansion during the progression of the *Dragon Age* series. In *Origins*, regardless of gender selection, the player has three romance options: two opposite-gender NPCs and one same-gender NPC. While all four romanceable characters appear Caucasian, they each showcase different approaches to romance and sexuality. Alistair, who is only available to a female player character, is loyal, funny, capable, and willing to step aside and let the player lead; additionally, he's honest and upbeat about being a virgin, providing a positive example of male vulnerability and healthy masculinity. On the other hand, Morrigan, who is only available to a male player character, is sarcastic, reserved, and focused on power and longevity rather than beauty and ephemeral emotions. Both Leliana and Zevran are available to male and female player characters, and they are generally more playful, cunning, and easygoing about romance than Alistair and Morrigan. While Leliana still prefers exclusivity, Zevran is open to a more casual sexual relationship. Providing two bisexual love interests was a unique offering in digital roleplaying games in 2009, when *Origins* was released, and their inclusion enables players to explore romantic and platonic relationships that they may not be able to safely experience in real life. The 2018 General Social Survey found that 3.3% of Americans identify as bisexual (Burkholder, 2019)—a notable rise from 1.1% in 2008—so *Origins* additionally gave a rising number of bisexual people—in America, at least—the chance to see themselves represented in a mainstream, triple-A video game.

DA2 provides a notable contrast with both *Origins* and *Inquisition* in that all non-DLC romanceable characters are "playersexual"; that is, "non-player characters in an otherwise heteronormative video game are romantically interested in the player regardless of the characters' genders" (SJW Wiki contributors, 2019). In *DA2*, a player character of either gender can pursue a romance with any of four different party members: two male NPCs (Anders, Fenris) and two female NPCs (Merrill, Isabela). A fifth romance option, Sebastian, is available via DLC, although he is only amenable to a female player character. In some ways, playersexuality simplifies romance for both players and developers; players do not have to discuss relationship preferences with NPCs before pursuing them romantically, and developers can write more general NPC relationship dialogue that is not necessarily customized based on player character gender. However, this structure does not accurately reflect real life, as people tend to have a variety of preferences beyond sexual attraction that influence their relationship choices. If the narrative goal is for the *Dragon Age* series to showcase people and relationships with the same depth as their counterparts in real life, playersexuality misses the mark.

The eight more complex and individualized romanceable characters in *Inquisition* reflect BioWare's awareness of the shortcomings of the playersexuality in *DA2*. Some companions and some advisors are available for romance, and they each have at least a few personal preferences when it comes to relationships, including gender, sexual orientation, sexual personality, and fantasy race. *Inquisition* offers players the greatest number of *Dragon Age* romance choices to date, maximizing the number of players who can see themselves and their ideal romantic partners in the game. Harkening back to *Dragon Age* series executive producer Mark Darrah's *PC Gamer* interview, Darrah highlighted BioWare's dedication to improving player representation and providing more expansive options in the *Dragon Age* series: "I think it's important for people to play the characters that they want to play, that we give choice…for as broad of an audience as possible. A lot of this comes down to choice as opposed to forcing something upon the player" (Clark, 2014). Additionally, BioWare demonstrates marked sensitivity to and research into the lived experiences of people of different gender identities and sexualities. While bisexual love interests have existed in the *Dragon Age* series since *Origins*, *Inquisition*'s hijinks-loving Sera is the first romanceable party member across the three main games who is only available to a female player character. BioWare writers also worked tirelessly to ensure that the series' first in-game openly trans character, Cremisius "Krem" Aclassi, was represented as accurately and sensitively as possible, sharing drafts of the character and his dialogue with "friends in the genderqueer community for feedback" (Makuch, 2014). For another example, regarding the importance of including Dorian as an NPC and an exclusively homosexual romance option in *Inquisition*, openly-gay former BioWare lead writer David Gaider remarked: "No character ever has to justify why they're straight, white, and male. The moment you make them anything else, you suddenly need reasons why that's okay…or do you? A certain amount of deliberateness is required to challenge the idea of a default, and while it feels a bit unnatural to do so, it's absolutely necessary" (Karmali, 2015).

According to a survey conducted by Quantic Foundry that was taken by more than 270,000 players worldwide, 48% of *Inquisition* players identify as female, which is substantially higher than the "open world" genre average of 26% (Yee, 2017). There are many factors that likely contributed to this interesting statistic, but in creating the romanceable NPCs in the *Dragon Age* series, BioWare's writing team looked beyond the "the straight male gamer," as Gaider put it, and sought to reflect the lived experiences of a variety of people, thereby enabling a variety of players to both connect with them and see themselves represented.

Video games—particularly those that can be saved and reloaded—can provide a safe, controlled environment to ask challenging questions and learn about new concepts without peer judgment or real-world social consequences. Particularly, *Inquisition*'s Cremisius "Krem" Aclassi may be the first openly transgender person that some players have encountered, in or outside of real life. While the player cannot play as Krem, they can ask Krem a variety of questions about his journey in casual, calm environments (e.g., outside Krem's tent, inside a tavern). In an interview with GameSpot about creating Krem, *Inquisition* writer Patrick Weekes stated that "any conversation about the subject [being transgender] had to come up naturally in-game" and "the character had to serve a purpose beyond 'being there to be a genderqueer person'….Krem's status as a trans man… [emphasized] Bull's character by opening up discussions of Qunari gender roles" (Makuch, 2014). In short, Krem not only supports gameplay by serving as party member Iron Bull's capable lieutenant, but he also supports the narrative by organically discussing gender roles that are relevant to both *Dragon Age*'s world of Thedas and to real life. As long as developers do their good-faith research, consult with people who have relevant lived experience, and ensure that the diverse character serves a purpose beyond "ticking a box," they can contribute to the encouraging trend of improved representation and diversity in games.

REFLECTING REALITY TO HELP BUILD SOCIAL SKILLS, EMPATHY, AND RESILIENCE

In addition to mirroring real life so as to resonate with more players, the relationship mechanics in the *Dragon Age* series also task players with utilizing real-life social skills, empathy, and inclusion to deepen NPC relationships. In *Origins*, both Leliana and Alistair are happy to chat about nearly any available topic, to the point that most positive dialogue options garner their approval. On the other hand, also in *Origins*, the stoic Qunari Sten does not respond well to personal questions or optimism that he perceives as naïve; if the player wants to earn Sten's friendship, they must slowly chip away at Sten's emotional defenses with consistent displays of competence, strategy, and intelligence. Players must decode different types of social cues, from laughter to sarcasm to silence, to understand how an NPC feels about them and about a given subject. Starting in *Origins*, each party member in the series, whether romanceable or not, requires certain types of dialogue selections and in-game actions in order for a player to earn their approval.

The relationship system in *Inquisition* tackles some more challenging topics related to diversity and inclusion compared to the previous two installments, showcasing a more transparent commitment to furthering empathy and social justice through the game's narrative. In *Inquisition*, NPC Dorian's side quest revolves around his father's disapproval of his sexuality, so if a player hopes to deepen their friendship or romance with Dorian, they must select dialogue options that demonstrate understanding and tolerance. Also, in an article he wrote about Gaider's contributions to Dorian's character, IGN journalist Luke Karmali could not help but note that Dorian is "an exquisitely well-written character" (Karmali, 2015). In the same article, according to Gaider, developers must be wary of including hastily added diverse characters merely to "tick a box," but notes that "[w]hat constitutes a gay stereotype is a difficult subject." Drawing from good-faith research and lived experience, such as Gaider's, can help steer diverse characters in games towards complex actualization and away from being reduced to disappointing one-dimensional stereotypes.

Finally, while scientific studies have found, time and again, that there is no link between video games and violence (Anderson, 2019), some studies have also found that roleplaying games can potentially improve players' ability to manage adversity in real life. Regarding the element of roleplaying games that tasks players with embracing different roles, some researchers have found that this persona-switching can actually improve real-life coping skills: "Many players switch among these avatars, forcing themselves to fluidly adjust to unique social and emotional goals. Game playing may promote the ability to flexibly and efficiently reappraise emotional experiences, teaching players the benefits of dealing with frustration and anxiety in adaptive ways" (Granic et al., 2014). By confronting players with difficult situations—both via combat and dialogue—and allowing them to save and replay those situations if they misstep, the *Dragon Age* series provides a safe testing ground for relatable, real-life challenges.

THE FUTURE OF RPGs AT BIOWARE AND BEYOND

While there has been press speculation that the upcoming *Dragon Age 4* (*DA4*) will take place in mage-ruled Tevinter (Morton, 2019), further stoking the mage v. templar conflict, BioWare has been largely tight-lipped about the game's relationship mechanics. Despite some recent high-profile departures (Khan, 2019) of lead developers on *Anthem* and *DA4*, BioWare has established such a noteworthy track record of experimentation with its relationship mechanics that there are many possible new features *DA4* developers could explore. *Dragon Age* has yet to tackle polyamory and asexuality in full force, and it would be a marked improvement in the realm of inclusion to feature more love interests who are people of color, experience different degrees of ableness, have different gender identities, span a mix of ages, and feature a variety of body types in future games. It would also be a notable advancement for BioWare to consistently hire LGBTQ+ voice actors to voice LGBTQ+ characters, voice actors of color to voice POC characters, and so on. Other relationship-minded developers have likely been taking note of BioWare's advances, as evidenced by the popularity of games like multi-award-winning interactive visual novel *Florence* (Wikipedia 2019) and inclusive dating simulator *Dream Daddy*, which was Steam's globally top-selling video game for most of July 2017

(Bartlett, 2019). Time will tell what BioWare chooses to deliver in *DA4*, but hopefully the series will continue to echo former senior writer David Gaider's erudite response to a Redditor's frustration with the relationships in *Dragon Age 2*: "The romances in the game are not for 'the straight male gamer.' They're for everyone" (Davison, 2011).

REFERENCES

Anderson, Mae. (2019, August 6). "No, there's still no link between video games and violence." APNews.com. Retrieved from https://www.apnews.com/45309e99d09e438a8b5f329f73ac7850

Bartlett, Amanda. (2019, August 15). "Forget dating apps: Play 'Dream Daddy,' a video game about dating hot, single dads." SFGate.com. Retrieved from https://www.sfgate.com/game/article/Dream-Daddy-Nintendo-Switch-Mac-PC-Game-14304480.php

Burkholder, Katie. (2019, April 25). "Percentage of Bisexual Americans on the Rise, Survey Finds." *The GA Voice*. Retrieved from https://thegavoice.com/news/percentage-of-bisexual-americans-on-the-rise-survey-finds/

Clark, Tim. (2014, November 3). "Dragon Age: Inquisition: An epic interview." Retrieved from https://www.pcgamer.com/dragon-age-inquisition-an-epic-interview/2/

Davison, Pete. (2011, March 25). "BioWare on romance demographics." PC World. Retrieved from https://www.pcworld.idg.com.au/article/380930/bioware_romance_demographics/

Dragon Age. (2019, November 4). "Gifts (Dragon Age II)." DragonAge. Fandom.com. Retrieved from https://dragonage.fandom.com/wiki/Gifts_(Dragon_-Age_II)

Dragon Age. (2019, November 4). "Gifts (Inquisition)." DragonAge. Fandom.com. Retrieved from https://dragonage.fandom.com/wiki/Gifts_(Inquisition)

Dragon Age. (2019, November 4). "Gifts (Origins)." DragonAge. Fandom.com. Retrieved from https://dragonage.fandom.com/wiki/Gifts_(Origins)

Granic, Isabela, Lobel, Adam, & Engels, Rutger CME (2014). "The benefits of playing video games." *American Psychologist*, *69*(1), 72.

Hernandez, Patricia. (2014, December 1). "The New *Dragon Age* Has Some Pretty Good Sex Scenes." Kotaku. Retrieved from https://kotaku.com/ten-sex-scenes-found-in-dragon-age-inquisition-1665184846

Karmali, Luke. (2015, July 9). "How Gaming's Breakout Gay Character Came to be." IGN. Retrieved from https://www.ign.com/articles/2015/07/09/how-gamings-breakout-gay-character-came-to-be

Khan, Imran. (2019, August 17). "Dragon Age 4's Lead Producer Leaves BioWare." GameInformer.com. Retrieved from https://www.gameinformer.com/2019/08/17/dragon-age-4s-lead-producer-leaves-bioware

Makuch, Eddie. (2014, December 5). "How BioWare Created Dragon Age: Inquisition's Trans Character." Retrieved from https://www.gamespot.com/articles/how-bioware-created-dragon-age-inquisition-s-trans/1100-6424014/

Morton, Lauren. (2019, July 22). "Dragon Age 4 setting all but confirmed by upcoming short story collection." PCGamer.com. Retrieved from https://www.pcgamer.com/dragon-age-4-setting-all-but-confirmed-by-upcoming-short-story-collection/

Plante, Chris. (2013, March 30). "'They don't set the tone': Dragon Age lead writer on the men who don't want women in games." Polygon. Retrieved from https://www.polygon.com/2013/3/30/4158724/dragons-age-writer-on-sex-and-gender

SJW Wiki contributors. (2019, November 4). "Playersexuality." SJWwiki.org. Retrieved from http://sjwiki.org/wiki/Playersexuality

Yee, Nick. (2017, January 19). "Beyond 50/50: Breaking Down the Percentage of Female Gamers by Genre." Quantic Foundry. Retrieved from https://quanticfoundry.com/2017/01/19/female-gamers-by-genre/

Wikipedia contributors. (2019, July 20). Florence (video game). Retrieved from https://en.wikipedia.org/wiki/Florence_(video_game)#Accolades. Last modified date: March 15, 2020.

CHAPTER 10

Designing Dating Games

(Re)Designing the "Oldest Game"

Casey O'Donnell and Hermione Banger

CONTENTS

BACKGROUND

In November 2017, the authors began making a "Dating Game" based on their experiences with online dating websites/apps. Both agreed, and it was generally felt by those they discussed it with, that the experience of "online dating" was less than optimal. Thus, they began exploring what kind of game might be made that enables romantic and sexual connections with others while not falling into the typical trap of treating dating as a kind of numbers game or even something that could be "won" or "gamed" in any traditional sense of the word.

The authors also wanted to expose players to modes of romantic, sexual, and friendship connections that fall outside mainstream culture's conception of what those relations ought to look like. How do people find and establish compatibility? How could we move beyond algorithms of similarity? How could we break from "swipe" culture? The "game" of dating is very much one of communication, asking questions and telling stories, and setting expectations. How does one make a game about something that is indeed "fun"—meeting someone new who you have that connection or "spark" with—but can also not be fun; rather an experience fraught with doubt, anxiety, and frustration. The world seems to be full of more bad dates than good ones and finding new connections takes time and involves both positive and negative experiences and emotions.

The design goal became to prompt or "simulate" challenging topics and situations that the authors had either encountered themselves or discussed with others. The authors wanted players to engage with challenging topics and situations to discuss and roleplay prior to encountering them later in a relationship when they would have to react to something potentially more threatening or destabilizing to an established relationship. Players could instead have proactive exploratory roleplaying conversations that would investigate these issues beforehand that could ultimately contribute to the courtship process; these conversations being potentially fun, exciting, and meaningful to those that find common ground and compatibility with one another. It was important to the authors to include prompts surrounding ethical and non-ethical (a.k.a., "cheating") non-monogamy as well, in order to (as much as possible) avoid making a game that would fall strictly into more mononormative and amatonormative culture. Encouraging players to imagine and explore a romantic and sexual world outside the traditional narrative was important.

Through this process, however, the authors realized quickly that many people have difficulty just finding friends and connecting with others at the level of friendship, let alone developing romantic or sexual relationships. Thus, *Fellowship of Fools: The (Friendship) Game* (*FoF:F*) became the first game in what was imagined to be a series of games. *FoF:F* was first and foremost a game about consent, vulnerability, interpersonal communication, and establishing connections and friendship between players. Perhaps most importantly, as the authors began to explore academic literature around friendship, romantic and sexual relationship formation, it became critically clear how important friendship connections are for the overall health and wellbeing of people and their romantic and sexual relationships. It was imagined that once friendship was established between individuals, then, if they were interested in exploring romance or sexuality with that person, they could move on to decks focused on those situations and topics. Those two decks became: *Fellowship of Fools: The (Romance) Game* (*FoF:R*) and *Fellowship of Fools: The (Sexuality) Game* (*FoF:S*). In this essay we may also use the shorthand *FoF* to refer to all three of the games collectively considered.

Throughout each deck it remained critical that players engage with issues of compatibility and consent, as well as the additional components of the desired relationship, whether that be friendship, romance, or sexuality. It was also important that LGBTQIA+ concerns be in the forefront of the designer's minds. This was one of the reasons for specifically separating romance and sexuality into different decks, to allow for asexual or aromantic people to still engage with the decks on their own terms. While subtle, this move helps avoid falling into the amatonormative (Brake, 2012) trap. Many of the design elements of *FoF* can be difficult to spot, while others are more heavy-handed. We discuss the reasons for some of those in what follows.

In this chapter we explore the broad literature that we have since connected our work with. However, *FoF* largely sprang from our personal experiences and those of others. We liken the development of *FoF* to a Grounded Theory (Glaser & Strauss, 1967) approach to design. We have only recently returned to the literature to then connect our work to that of others. We briefly discuss some of the literature surrounding interpersonal intimate relationships, we explicitly discuss the technological considerations of the design process and explore various design components of the game. While we do it through the lens of *FoF*, we also connect that work to the broader literature surrounding friendship, romantic, and sexual relationships.

In this essay we use "dating" to be some combination of friendship|romantic|sexual relationship:

$$\text{Dating} = (\text{Friendship} \times (\text{romantic} \mid \text{sexual})) \text{ relationship}$$

Or, less mathematically, that when dating you are establishing some kind of friendship relationship that begins to include some combination of romantic and/or sexual elements over time. Even in a "friends with benefits" (FwB) relationship, it (by its own definition) includes a friendship, and as such is included in our definition of dating. We discuss this reasoning further in the section on friendship, romance, and sexuality. We are not implying that somehow "casual" sexual or solely romantic connections are less important or meaningful to people that engage in those connections, but we are not focusing on it in this essay. However, the *FoF:S* and *FoF:R* decks can be played individually for those specific relationship goals. So, while it is not the focus of this essay, it does not mean that the game itself doesn't actually support these relationship endeavors, it in fact does (Table 10.1).

Dating Games

It has been proposed that historically game play and game design have focused on the "lower-order" needs of the pyramidical Hierarchy of Needs as described by Maslow (1968; Grace, 2017), that is, on physiological needs of survival and broader safety such as security, health, property, resources, and income and hence are largely materialist (Webster, 2013; Hejdenberg, 2005). These are materialist in that they focus on the acquisition of objects and require material inputs to be satisfied (Jackson & Marks, 1999). While the hierarchical structure, pyramidal shape, and interdependence of needs of Maslow's Hierarchy has been found incongruent with lived reality, research has largely corroborated Maslow's categories for universal need predictors of well-being (Tay & Diener, 2011). As such, material needs, the so-called "lower-order" needs in Maslow's Hierarchy, do not have to be fulfilled in order for humans to derive happiness from nonmaterial, so-called "higher-order," needs being filled. We can be insecure in our physiological needs, we can be hungry, and still derive benefits from our affection needs being met, such as the comfort of a friend.

TABLE 10.1 Fellowship of Fools: The (Sexuality) Game—Example "Casual" Prompts

Situations:	Topics:
The High Priestess Upright (2)—You are having sex with a stranger...	Queen of Swords Upright (2)—How do you feel about casual sexual relationships?
The World Upright (2)—You are at a sex party...	Nine of Wands Reversed (2)—How do you feel about the phrase "no drama"?
Justice Upright (2)—You are at a Swingers' event...	Six of Swords Reversed (2)—What are your sex safety protocols?

In "Needs and Subjective Well-Being Around the World," Tay and Diener (2011) found non-material needs to consist of social support and love, feeling respected and pride in activities, mastery, and self-direction and autonomy. These non-material needs can, in principle, be satisfied without any material throughput, rather they are about individual and social psychology, about processes (personal, social, and cultural) rather than objects (Jackson & Marks, 1999). For Huizinga, the "preparation for and introduction to 'love,' which is often made enticing by all sort of playing," He (1955, 42) includes forms of courtship, flirtation, and wooing, the road to sex and, arguably, sex outside of procreation (Paasonen, 2018) as forms of play. While games have historically focused on materialist needs, increasingly game developers are making spaces, crafting stories, opening up player actions, and designing mechanics and tools for players to pursue non-material needs and goals in game play spaces.

In previous eras, romantic relationships primarily served to facilitate the fulfillment of basic material needs, from physical and financial security to a structure for child-rearing. In the current era, however, romantic relationships are expected to satisfy more and more non-material needs, such as social belonging through intimacy and friendship, personal self-esteem and support, sexual gratification and novelty, romantic passion, and assistance with the pursuit of personal development and goals (Vanderdrift, Agnew, & Besikci, 2017). The normative romantic trajectory now is that spouses embrace the "couple companionate ideal" in which each person is expected to meet all the other's needs, including those for close friendship (Rawlins, 2008). This construct plays into the broader hierarchical organization of relationship bonds based on amatonormativity, heteronormativity, sex centrism, mononormativity, and couple privilege referred to as the erotic pyramid (De las Heras Gómez, 2018). Relationships imbued with greater meaning and expectations to fulfill personal needs require greater investment, and this is not reflected in player experiences with affection games. Players are not being asked to give more of themselves and they are not getting fulfilling relationships out of their experiences.

Affection spans relationships with family, nature, friends, as well as romantic and sexual partners (Max-Neef, Elizalde, & Hopenhayn, 1989). Friendship overlaps with, but is also distinct from, romantic and sexual relationships. Friendships are relationships that are voluntary, personal, affective, mutual and tending toward equality, though they occur on a continua (Rawlins, 2008). Love between close friends is often referred to as companionate love, it is a durable affection, fairly slow to develop, and characterized by interdependence, trust, feelings of affection, attachment, intimacy, closeness, and commitment (Hatfield & Rapson, 1993; Vanderdrift et al., 2017). In almost all cultures, people distinguish between companionate love and passionate love (sometimes called "romantic love," "obsessive love," "infatuation," "lovesickness," or "being-in-love") (Hatfield, Rapson, & Martel, 2007, 76). Passionate love is generally associated with passion, sexual desire, excitement, and a variety of other intense emotions such as yearning, jealousy, and anxiety (Aron, Fisher, & Strong, 2006). Part of the meaningfulness of passionate love is the intensity of the emotions involved, the thrill and anxiety of uncertainty and risk, the pains of yearning and jealousy. Romantic relationships are regarded as exhibiting a more overt expression of positive emotions and affection, increased support and mutuality, an increase in commitment wherein dating partners are more likely to commit free time to one another, but, concomitantly, there is also a higher expectation of exclusiveness, to have "sole or preferential access to various mutually involving activities" (Fehr, 1996, 17). However, like friendship, romantic relationships occur on a continua and we should not confuse what is common with respect to relationships with what ought to occur within relationships. In other words, while we do gravitate toward more commitment and exclusivity in our relationships, that is not inevitable or necessarily desirable for many (Tables 10.2 and 10.3).

Studies of (predominantly heterosexual) romantic relationships indicate they typically involve at least a moderate amount of friendship (Fehr, 1996), and those who were friends before they become romantically involved tend to be kinder to each other during troubled times and nicer

TABLE 10.2 Fellowship of Fools: The (Romance) Game—Example Exclusiveness Prompts

Situations:	Topics:
The Emperor Reversed (4)—Someone is being controlling...	Five of Wands Upright (2)—How have you struggled to find balance between your friendships and your romantic relationships?
The Hierophant Reversed (4)—You are considering a polyamorous relationship...	Queen of Swords Upright (2)—How do you feel about dating someone who is ethically non-monogamous?
The Devil Reversed (4)—A relationship you are in is on a break...	Seven of Swords Upright (2)—How do you define cheating?

TABLE 10.3 Fellowship of Fools: The (Sexuality) Game—Example Exclusiveness Prompts

Situations:	Topics:
The Hierophant Reversed (4)—You are considering opening up a relationship...	Three of Wands Reversed (4)—How would you feel about someone wanting to cheat with you?
Justice Reversed (4)—Someone suspects cheating...	Seven of Swords Reversed (4)—What do you think ethical non-monogamy could look like for you?
The Star (4)—You and a partner are looking for a third...	Five of Cups Reversed (4)—What makes you feel jealous and how do you manage those feelings?

to each other if their romantic relationships end (Rawlins, 2008). Those individuals who see their companionate love as central to their passionate love report experiencing greater friendship with their partner and better overall relationship quality, and the amount of importance placed on friendship needs is positively associated with increased commitment, experienced love, and sexual need fulfillment both concurrently and over time. In contrast, those individuals who place greater importance on passion do not report a greater experience of passion than those who place a lesser importance on it, rather, the experience of friendship within a romance is positively associated with experiencing greater passion in the romance and satisfaction with the romance and life generally (Vanderdrift et al., 2017). Indeed, most neuroscientists seem to agree that all of the brain systems for passionate love, sexual desire, and attachment in fact communicate and coordinate with one another (Horstman & Staff, 2011) (Tables 10.4 and 10.5).

Friendship, or companionate love, then, is particularly beneficial to romantic and sexual relationship satisfaction. Yet, romantic, or passionate, love is culturally considered to be the peak of the relationship hierarchy,

TABLE 10.4 Fellowship of Fools: The (Romance) Game—Example Passion Prompts

Situations:	Topics:
The High Priestess Upright (2)—Someone has caught your eye...	Page of Cups Reversed (4)—How do you flirt?
The Devil Upright (2)—You are feeling addicted to someone...	Nine of Cups Upright (2)—What qualities attract you to someone?
The Moon Upright (2)—You are imagining a future with someone...	Ace of Coins Upright (4)—How have you found people beautiful in the past?

TABLE 10.5 Fellowship of Fools: The (Sexuality) Game—Example Passion Prompts

Situations:	Topics:
The Fool Upright (2)—You are fooling around with someone for the first time...	Nine of Cups Upright (4)—What things sexually excite you? What repels you?
The High Priestess Reversed (2)—You are not in the mood for sex...	King of Cups Upright (2)—Describe a time you moved very quickly with someone...
Strength Upright (2)—You are feeling lustful...	Knight of Cups Upright (4)—How much do you think love matters with sex?

of the erotic pyramid, widely encouraged, institutionalized, normalized, represented, incentivized, and positively sanctioned religiously and legally through marriage, whereas other relationship forms are seen as less valuable and expendable (Rawlins, 2008). This disproportionate focus on an amorous, exclusive, and central relationship as a universally shared goal in preference to other types of relationships is amatonormative, and erases the value of, and encourages the sacrifice of, other types of affective bonds. This phenomenon is known as the dyadic withdrawal hypothesis, that as involvement becomes greater with a romantic partner they become far less involved with their larger network of relationships, and is particularly true for heterosexual women (Fehr, 1996; Rawlins, 2008). Heteronormativity adds a layer to this wherein friendship between heterosexual men and women are considered to inevitably become sexual and romantic.

There are multiple possible partner "scripts" for established friends to explore their attraction to each other. The most basic script is that neither person finds the other physically or romantically attractive, so neither is an issue and the friendship continues, they deemphasize their sexuality, romantic feelings and emphasize other qualities important to their friendship (Rawlins, 2008). This requires that friends discuss and set boundaries to establish behavior norms from the beginning, but there is a need for ongoing open communication about a relationship's boundaries and the definition of the relationship as feelings of attraction may change over time. Second, there may be an "attraction conflict," one person wants romance and/or a sexual relationship and the other does not, attraction is asymmetrical. Unrequited feelings of love can cause feelings of emptiness, anxiety, and despair, and in some cases the person with deeper feelings will sometimes demand "all or nothing," which often ends the friendship. This is most often seen in heterosexual relationships where men misinterpret motives of friendship from women as romance, perhaps because men are not used to expressing emotional closeness with their same-sex friends and are socialized to interpret caring from women as romance (Rawlins, 2008). The term "friendzone" linked to the asymmetrical affection script, simultaneously devalues friendship and objectifies our relationships with other people. It erases the many ways these friends can negotiate and fashion their own possibilities for loving and being loved, for care and concern for each other, to learn from each other, and to explore the freedoms this particular kind of friendship between heterosexual women and men lends to enacting alternative scripts of masculinity and femininity (Rawlins, 2008). Third, the attraction is mutual, symmetrical, and acknowledged, the partners then may decide to explore that romantic and/or sexual attraction. They could find they are compatible, in various ways, or that they are not, and so they return, with varying ease, to a good friendship. And fourth, the friendship expands to incorporate sex as another activity that friends do together, also known as an FwB.

While this co-existence of friendship and dating and their overlap and negotiation was once more ubiquitous (Paik, 2010), it has become more common now for relationships to begin and end with casual sex (Albury, 2018), and for young people to think this is the best arrangement available to them (England & Thomas, 2007). Today commonly called "hooking up," where "two people agree to engage in sexual behavior for which there is no future commitment" (Vanderdrift et al., 2017), casual sex practices of interaction have been practiced for some time (Ryan & Jethá, 2010) and allow individuals to expand their sexual repertoires, practice affection and explore their desires. The practice in modern western societies however by and large scripts participants to separate sex from emotion. In doing so, it simultaneously structures and constrains impulses into definable and normative constructs, into "the masculinisation of sex," where the experience of participants comes increasingly to resemble men's. Perhaps more to the point, "just as friendship and love have been increasingly 'feminized,'... masculine notions that sex and love are separate," have become normalized and reified (Kalish & Kimmel, 2011, 138).

Given the importance of friendship for meaningful romantic and sexual relationships, game design that is focused on player's desire for dating should start first with designing for friendship. The authors have defined Friendship Games as: "Games that attempt to, through their narrative, mechanics and/or systems, enable player friendships (new or existing) through facilitation or exploration of the foundational aspects of friendship: voluntary commitment, mutual and personal relationships, affective bonds: requiring care, liking and/or love, tending toward equality between relations and necessitating maintenance" (O'Donnell & Banger, 2019). The design components discussed later are useful for helping players form and maintain friendships, as well as the unique components of passion and exclusiveness that come with romantic and sexual relationships. An explicit goal of dating games is much like the explicit goals of friendship games: to attempt to, through their narrative, mechanics and/or systems, enable player relationships based on negotiated voluntary commitment and exclusivity, mutual and personal relationships of affection and intimacy, tending toward equality between relations and necessitating maintenance.

Technological Considerations

It is important to note that we are not considering in this essay dating simulation games or other human-computer interaction games that include affection. We are explicitly exploring the design considerations around games that connect two (or more) players in such a way to facilitate friendly, romantic, or sexual relations. That isn't to say that some of the discussed design elements might not inform the design of better affection games, but we want to be clear that establishing friendly, romantic, or sexual interest between human players and virtual non-player characters within a game is not the goal of this essay. Broadly considered we see dating simulations falling more in their own adjacent category of game.

FoF was designed as a non-digital card game in part because the authors were frustrated by the "swipiness" and the feeling of disposability of people within existing dating apps. Users of these apps often talk about "playing around with" or "playing around on" these dating platforms. The whole concept of "toying with the idea" of a connection with others eventually became a reason to avoid digital systems. In our definition of Friendship Games (outlined above and detailed below) the notion of "commitment" or "intentionality" became core. When playing a Friendship Game or Dating Game, the commitment to coming to the game with voluntary intent to establishing new or deepening existing connections is critical. Often with platforms like *OKCupid*, which does more than other platforms to try to be more inclusive of difference and LGBTQIA+ concerns, and other dating apps, the platform itself seems to get in the way of people *really* getting to know one another. Many connections barely make it past an initial message let alone to the handful of messages that so often drifts away in the end. Designing a non-digital game solves one of the key difficulties in creating relationships: voluntary commitment and its underlying subcomponent, proximity.

This isn't to say that digital Dating Games are impossible or even undesirable, the authors themselves want to bring some incarnation of *FoF* to digital platforms. Rather, that by making a non-digital game it helps players with two key components needed for forming a friendship, romance, or sexual relationship—proximity and a level of voluntary commitment to engage and connect with another person. The likelihood of physical proximity of residence, work, or school is higher by the fact that players must meet in person to play with each other. Non-digital games offer a greater chance of constructing a sense of commitment because one must make time to co-occupy time and space with another person in order to play. Also, for conversations, responsiveness and mutuality are often easier face to face. For most people, reading cues and responding in kind to the person you are playing with comes more naturally in person. While this lends itself to helping with the initial barriers of relationship formation, the potential of digital games breaking these limitations should not be discounted, but nor should their disadvantages.

The digital space provides players with more opportunities and capabilities for conversation, but it lacks the support for continuity that makes the physical space so precious (Turkle, 2015). In non-digital games, people don't easily come and go, log off or drop out, there is greater investment and commitment inherent in showing up in person to engage in play or conversation with another person. Conversation gives players a range of information to read and interact with—body language, posture, gestures, tone, facial expressions, inflection, silences, and so much more—beyond the content of the words exchanged. Conversation, like storytelling, is a space for exploration rather than exchange, where players are interested in hearing about how another person approaches the world. We are more likely to understand opposing viewpoints when it is transmitted through the human voice (Schroeder, Kardas, & Epley, 2017), whereas over text communication we overestimate our ability to correctly interpret sarcasm, humor, or sincerity (Kruger, Epley, Parker, & Ng, 2005). The authors would press for a single example of a digital multiplayer dating game that doesn't rely on text communication, other tools commonly used are personal profiles, a virtual space for avatars to interact and communicate, and the use of roleplaying. The relatively small number of examples of dating games the authors have found are non-digital and role-playing centric to encourage interpersonal connection and exploration.

In fact, one of the greatest inhibitors of exploratory conversation may even be our digital devices: "the presence of a smartphone, even when off, can reduce the cognitive capacity by taxing the attentional resources that reside at the core of both working memory capacity and fluid intelligence" (Ward, Duke, Gneezy, & Bos, 2017). Our phones are psychologically potent devices that change what we do, as well as who we are, with others: we find it hard to turn back to each other, it signals our attention is divided, it limits how much we listen, what will be discussed, the degree of connection we will feel (Turkle, 2015). While the presence of phones inhibits our ability to communicate, to commit to the interaction and connect with each other, similarly, people who compulsively use mobile dating apps are found to have a high rate of loneliness and social sadness, as well as a preference for online social interaction over personal interaction (Coduto, Lee-Won, & Baek, 2019). Digital social interaction comforts players that they are in touch with other people, but they are emotionally kept at bay, interaction is moved from conversation to the efficiency of mere connection that is made legible by binary systems and signals.

Our reliance on digital stimuli and communication threatens our human faculty of sensibility, our ability to make "empathic understanding possible, the ability to comprehend what words cannot say, the power to interpret a continuum of non-discrete elements, non-verbal signs and the flows of empathy" (Berardi, 2011, 17). Sensitivity involves difficult, awkward, ambiguous encounters in-person between ambiguous beings, encounters that are perhaps pleasant or difficult, or both, that require time, attention, and effort of sensing. Due to the effort, the two might come away from the encounter a bit different than they went into it.

DESIGN COMPONENTS

Numerous design components plug into what makes a multiplayer Dating Game. We are forefronting elements around those components that connect human-to-human and less-so human-to-computer/game. We break these design components down into Consent and Code of Conduct, Situational Design, and Design for Emergence. However, many of these elements could inform the design of Dating Simulators and single-player affection/dating games, which in many respects can have the same positive or negative impacts on how people understand things like dating, romance, sex, and consent. Design (and who is doing the designing) matters deeply in this case. Without explicitly designing against dominant cultural norms, Dating Games or Dating Simulation games will largely reinforce broader hegemonic ideas about dating, romance, and sexuality. Dating Games perhaps risk even more, because as formulated here, they explicitly attempt to facilitate, coordinate, connect, or otherwise engage players in increasingly deepening connections with others, which carries with it the risk of both pleasure and pain.

Consent and Code of Conduct

It would seem that the most difficult aspect of consent is that people largely understand it differently the moment you no longer use the word "consent." While proponents of consent culture, and likely those with a deeper understanding of the word, use phrases such as "consent is sexy," the broader heteronormative/mononormative world views the term largely as one wrapped up with legal considerations around "legal" or "illegal" sexual acts. When people are asked what consent is, it is largely viewed as a single event or agreement (or often problematically "irrelevant" in partnered relationships), which then becomes a kind of blanket acceptance of whatever follows (Beres, 2014). Yet, when the same individuals are asked about how they negotiate sex, they develop much more nuance. Suddenly consent (without the use of the term) is no longer an event, but an ongoing discussion with the person(s) involved in the encounter. Perhaps most interestingly, the majority of people talk about sexual "negotiation" in relationships much in the way that feminist scholarship talks about consent, the word consent is simply absent from partners' vocabulary. More importantly, research indicates that heterosexual men DO understand and recognize women's indications (verbal or non-verbal) of assent or dissent (Beres, 2014). The question of whether those same men then accept or ignore those indications becomes the more important concern. Research largely seems to indicate that "contemporary sexual relations remain defined by male-privileging ideals and are constrained by implicit pressures in ways that make the sexual freedoms which were bestowed upon young women inherently difficult to embody and enact in everyday practice" (Burkett & Hamilton, 2012, 816).

With this in mind, while advocates of consent culture may cling dearly to the word itself, it is possible that using the word may immediately put the majority of players in the wrong mindset. This prompts them to then see agreement to "play" a game as blanket consent rather than an ongoing conversation that can be adjusted or ended at any moment by any party at any time. Even among sexual sub-communities (in this case a BDSM community—a.k.a., "kinksters") much more informed and embracing of consent culture, the notion of consent as an event rather than process or conversation persists (Fanghanel, 2019). While it may be difficult to swallow for proponents of consent culture, at least for the time being the use of the word may prove difficult for game designers to use without additional scaffolding.

For the purposes of this essay, we embrace a more intersectional (and kinky) form of consent, defining it as a process or ongoing conversation: "An ethical consent praxis, which understands consent as a flow of implicit, explicit, intersubjective negotiation, helps us to perceive the power structures at play in the encounter. It opens up the possibility of enacting different ways of engaging with these politics, and of talking about (and not talking about) consent" (Fanghanel, 2019, 15). In many respects we see the role of games in this domain as ideally helping people understand consent through experiences with it as a broader process fraught with power dynamics that people are often unwilling or unable to engage with in their own personal realm of praxis. Games dealing with romantic or sexual encounters can help players actually learn to do better, but by the same token, designed poorly, they can likely reinforce existing characteristics of rape culture.

Particularly for Dating Games, it is critical that designers disclose their overt design goals. Players must knowingly consent to playing Dating Games as the player bears the risk of having connections established or deepened in/through the game. Designing for friendship, romance, or sexual relationship formation starts with designing for consent in mind. These are connections that we (should) enter into voluntarily, not something that is forced upon or expected of us. Unlike "stealth" (learning or otherwise) games, because there are real mental and health risks in extending one's self to others, players must knowingly consent to Dating Games. A player who knows that they have no time or resources to commit to a new potential relationship would then be discouraged from playing a Dating Game, unless they were using it to maintain or deepen an existing relationship. The reality is that we can really only accommodate a limited number of close relationships, and particularly those that are more central take the most time to establish and maintain (Dunbar, 2010). Friendships and romantic and sexual relationships that grew out of friendships take significant time to establish and maintain (Hall, 2018). Players need to be honest about the number of "spoons" that they have and rushing off to make new connections when one does not really have the ability to commit time to others, is its own kind of betrayal to playing these games.

Behavioral Norms

Rather than explicitly using "consent" in the authors' own work, they turned to the language of a "Code of Conduct" (CoC), which, in a sense, lays the ground rules for how players should play with one another. The CoC for *FoF* was identical between friendship, romance, and sexuality versions of the game. It informs the players that relationships are all voluntary, and that the voluntary nature of the relationship is ongoing rather than an "event": "Players do not have to play every prompt drawn or asked of them" and "Players can at any point exit gameplay or choose to sit out a round." The CoC also focuses the player on their own actions and behaviors rather than on those of other players, on what they can control. A CoC asks players to come into the game on its terms rather than on their own. It also makes players accountable to one another for their actions. If a player is not respecting the CoC then the other players should no longer play with them or offer them feedback on how they are violating the CoC.

In the playtesting of the author's own dating game, many players (often cisgendered heterosexual men) discussed an inability to read well, in the moment, what was welcome or unwelcome, even though the research indicated above would indicate otherwise. While in some cases this could be attributed to a lack of socioemotional skills or neurodiversity, it was also too pervasive to chalk up to this reason alone. What this would seem to indicate is that what many (cishet male) players are looking for is a way to turn a "no" or a "maybe" into a "yes." Dating games should avoid falling into this trap at all costs, as promoting male-privileging sexual ideals and implicit pressures perpetuate a broader rape culture. Instead the focus should be on meeting others where they are at and establishing ground rules, behavioral norms, and boundaries that discourage coercion. Nor should Dating Games discourage the importance of friendship. Indeed, an initial friendship is often critical to the success of a subsequent romantic or sexual relationship (Vanderdrift et al., 2017). Nor should friendship be seen as "leveling up" into romantic or sexual relationships. Friendship has its own importance and Dating Games should not instill the idea in players that simply if enough "friendship coins" are inserted into another player that "sex or romance will pop out" (a.k.a., "the friend zone" or "sex slot machine" falacies). Such an idea discounts the value of friendship and objectifies relationships. Tit-for-tat interactions and the explicit tracking of exchange promotes relationships of exchange and can be detrimental to communal-type relationships of care and maintenance such as friendship, romance, and sexual relationships (Neyer, Wrzus, Wagner, & Lang, 2011; Berg & Clark, 1986). Dating Games should avoid mechanics that track inputs, outputs, costs, benefits, favors and resources, of earning or losing points and leveling up (Figure 10.1).

The Code of Conduct of *FoF* asks players to engage in the spirit and components of friendship: personal and self-disclosure ("Play as Yourself"), mutuality and self-disclosure ("Be Vulnerable"), commitment, mutuality, and affection ("Be Fully Present"), commitment

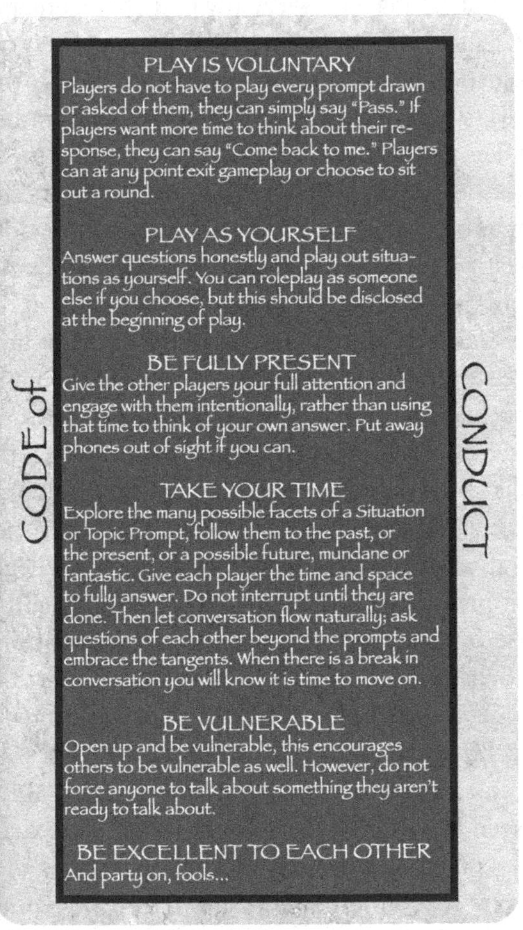

FIGURE 10.1 Code of Conduct from *FoF*.

("Take Your Time"), and finally mutuality and equality ("Be Excellent to Each Other"). It encourages behavior that constitutes what "playing well" looks like: "Give the other players your full attention and engage with them intentionally," "Open up and be vulnerable," "Do not force anyone to talk about something they aren't ready to talk about," "Ask questions of each other beyond the prompts and embrace the tangents." Having a Code of Conduct establishes shared behavioral and communication norms for the gamespace and the players, but it is up to players to agree to and follow them.

While fans of Consent Culture may love phrases such as, "Consent is Sexy," as research already cited indicates, this may actually turn off players that need the education the most. Rather, by emphasizing that ongoing connections with others must be mutual, they remain ongoing. Either player can terminate or de-escalate the connection at any time. Having a CoC creates a player guide for behavior that frames what kind of behavior players are consenting to during play and also authorizes players to extract themselves without penalty from play. The only way a player "loses" in *FoF* is when the other player(s) doesn't want to play with them or does not consent to play with them any longer. The ongoing consensual nature of our relationships and the behavior that constitutes them needs to be at the core of all Dating Games.

Socioemotional Learning

In many respects one of the potentials the authors see in Dating Games is the ability to scaffold and help players better understand what goes into forming close relationships such as friendships, romance, and sexual relationships. Some have categorized this as Social and Emotional Learning (SEL), or socioemotional learning. These include an intrapersonal understanding and managing of the self and the interpersonal skills of establishing and maintaining positive relationships that underpin both personal resilience and healthy relationships (Hromek & Roffey, 2009). SEL has emerged as a possible learning outcome that (serious or otherwise) games could have, those outcomes can be either leveraged from existing games or designed for explicitly. Games used for socioemotional learning are primarily cooperative or collaborative small-team based play rather than competitive games or single-player games, featuring play that include discussion, learning games, role-play, and problem solving to engage players in solving social dilemmas while practicing social and emotional skills (Hromek & Roffey, 2009).

The category of SEL is quite broad, with desired learning outcomes ranging far and wide across the prosocial spectrum. Some of these goals include: recognizing and labeling personal feelings, strengths, and values; knowing how to regulate and express feelings effectively and safely; not prejudging but having a prosocial orientation to others; being responsible to oneself and others; making ethical decisions; personal coping and problem-solving interpersonal conflict; being able to negotiate fairly, to deescalate confrontation and to manage conflict; being able to admit mistakes and seek help; respect for others; treating others with care and compassion; and how to establish, develop, and maintain healthy relationships (Hromek & Roffey, 2009). SEL sees these competencies as dynamic and overlapping, that individual well-being helps with the development of healthy relationships as well as that of caring communities. Many of these skills may be a byproduct of many Friendship Games or Dating Games, but SEL can occur outside of these kinds of games. SEL elements can certainly aid players in this space, but nor can it be subsumed into the broader category of Dating Games.

Most important for Dating Games, adolescents' friendships also serve as training models to prepare them for intimate romantic relationships (Wrzus, Zimmermann, Mund, & Neyer, 2017, 22–23). The reality is that many people, for a variety of reasons, do have to live with a variety of constraints around how good they are at "peopling." Children's social competence develops in the context of interacting with their peers (Burdette & Whitaker, 2005), and our education system may be in many ways to blame for its focus on standardized tests, memorization, intensification, and discipline. A certain definition of intelligence has been privileged and guided the structure of our lives, but *intelligence* "used to include sensibility, sensitivity, awareness, discernment, reason, acumen, and wit" as well (Turkle, 2015, 51). Other education models, such as the Finnish model, emphasize learning how to learn, a slow pace, the development of social and interactive skills, encouraging students to pay attention to other people's needs and interests, to care about others and have a positive attitude toward them, and increased independence to take care of oneself (Niikko & Havu-Nuutinen, 2009). Studies show people are most likely to pursue a friendship with someone who is socially skilled, responsive, and not shy, and that we are also more likely to befriend someone who is similar to us in a variety of ways (Fehr, 1996). Shy individuals in particular are slower to reply to other's comments, smile less, make less eye contact, initiate conversation less often than nonshy people, leading their interaction partner to infer that they do not wish to interact (Fehr, 1996, 56). The kinds of skills designers can look to encourage in players are ultimately about responsiveness, or mutuality of attention and affection, whether verbal or non-verbal, using exchange to indicate and negotiate interest and care for social norms and the other player. These skills are beneficial to players' well-being as well as their interpersonal relationships.

Often in the authors' discussions with players of *FoF*, many players indicate difficulty in some of these socioemotional skills, which is why things such as scaffolding turn-taking measures can provide some level of assistance to those that struggle with it. Most "conversation" or "ice-breaker" games, such as *Table Topics* or *Our Moments*, be they for families, romantic/sexual couples, strangers or friends, provide no rules that encourage turn-taking norms. Rather, the game is presented as a pile of cards with prompts to start conversation and players are left to navigate the play space and the behavior norms that govern it. In the simplest gameplay Mode of *FoF*, called "Conversation Mode," it mimics these "conversation" games by using only the Topic Cards within the deck. Players shuffle and draw a card, then either answer one of the card's prompts themselves or direct it at another player to answer. If the player who drew the card directs the prompt at the other player, that player can answer if they choose and then should ask it back to the first player. These rules of gameplay encourage learning conversational turn-taking norms and mutuality of self-disclosure, that if one asks a question of a conversation partner, one should expect to answer it themselves. And for the other partner, when one is asked a question to then ask that question back to keep the conversation flowing and reciprocal.

Designing for interpersonal SEL encourages conversation a behavioral and turn-taking norms in game rules, encouraging affective attitudes, behavior, and communication through a Code of Conduct and facilitating empathetic feedback and conflict resolution between players. With that foundation, players should be given opportunities to build relationships with low-cost (low-disclosure and low-commitment) trust building "reciprocation loops" (Youngblood et al., 2018). Effective relationship games have built into their core design scaling reciprocation loops that provide players the opportunity to either scale up or down the intimacy of their play. In *FoF*, the game has both gameplay "Modes" and "Mods." Modes are different overall ways to play the game, while Mods modify player activity within a Mode. Each "level" of Mod increases the possibility of deeper self-disclosure, greater information gathering and possibly affectionate communication, as well the risk of a harder prompt and the possibility for conflict. Numbers next to the prompts indicate if they are "easier" (2) or "harder" (4) [more intimate] prompts to play. With this, players can more easily distinguish more "superficial" or "easy" prompts—better suited for early in the relationship formation process—from the "risker" moves among their options. The game has players think about what prompts are most appropriate for the current depth of the relationship they have with the other player(s) as well as which are more appropriate to the Situation Prompt in play, encouraging players to learn to read social context and to gradually and mutually increase self-disclosure. It puts reciprocation loops in the players' hands and provides mechanics that helps players read and construct those loops themselves.

An important component of SEL is play to encourage intrapersonal (self) knowledge, understanding, and management. *FoF* offers multiple Gameplay Modes for single-player play, many of these Modes involve story prompt and journal prompt generators, doing so increases player familiarity with the game, and player self-knowledge and comfort with answering the prompts by answering them alone first. Games directed toward interpersonal play should make space for SEL through "non-social solitary play," identified as one of the four types of play that children move through by developmental psychologists (Grace & Spangler, 2014). Solitude seems anathema to our current age, where people often become anxious without a constant feed of online stimulation. Solitude, rather than being lonely, is a state of gathering the self, going inward to daydream, wander, reflect, muse, meditate, and play. It is a conscious retreat, where one can better come to know who one is. Yet, having a capacity for solitude and non-social play makes us more fully able to experience others as who they are and create authentic relationships (Turkle, 2015).

Other types of developmental play include "parallel play" involving individuals playing next to each other, but without direct interaction or any type of sharing. The single-player Modes of *FoF* can be played in parallel with players choosing to not share their individual play experiences—journaling or writing stories side by side using prompts from the game. "Associative play" occurs where players play near each other and share objects of play but not the same goals of play, and is offered in *FoF* in Lightning Mode and GM Directed Mode. Here game prompts are shared between players, but they use them to create their own stories separately or to share their own particular experiences based on the prompts. Lastly, "cooperative play" requires players to share the objects of play as well as the goals of play. This type of play can be pursued with RPG Mode, In-Depth Mode, Signifier Mode, and Improv Mode, where players cooperate toward the same goals and assist each other, be that for roleplaying and co-creating a good story, exploring a shared problem or situation, or to create a cohesively acted and improvised scene. Ideally, games that are aimed at improving players' relationships should offer multiple types of play that give players the opportunity to play alone to better know themselves and explore in safety; to pursue low cost, low risk, trust-building reciprocation loops; and higher cost and higher reward reciprocation loops with other players to build various kinds of relationships.

Promoting Components of Friendship

Ultimately, Dating Games *are* Friendship Games, and as such they incorporate many design components in common (O'Donnell & Banger, 2019). As noted above, the qualities of friendship are voluntary commitment, personal and mutual, self-disclosure and affection, equality and requiring maintenance. We will outline briefly here what design components Friendship Games can use to encourage these qualities of interaction between players and some of the foundations for design, but much more detail can be found in that work.

Voluntary commitment is one of the first design components that promotes friendship formation and deepening within games, and goes hand-in-hand with the importance of consent. One should not play a dating game unless one is interested and desiring of new or deeper connections with other players. The authors like to see this as antithetical to the idea of "playing around" that goes on with many dating apps or websites, or inactivity on the platform but checking it periodically to get a boost in self-esteem through new messages and likes. This connects to the idea of commitment. Players when playing are making a voluntary assertion that they have the time, desire, and interest in forming new or deepening existing relationships. Within this you also have things like propinquity, or physical proximity, that makes commitment possible or likely. As discussed earlier, the use of non-digital games ensures some level of proximity and commitment from both players that digital games will have to contend with. Games rules or CoC that encourage intentionality of play—such as putting away any phones or other devices and being present and engaged in play—can also encourage voluntary commitment to the process involved in games geared toward relationship formation or maintenance.

In studies of communal relationships (friendships, romantic relationships, those concerned with one another's needs, and those that benefit one another in response to needs) versus exchange relationships (acquaintances, business relationships, people with no special responsibility for the other, and those relationships that benefit one another in response to past benefits or with the expectation of receiving comparable benefits in return), manipulations that primed dyads or groups for one or the other relationship found subjects *immediately* express preferences for distinct relationships, preferences for following distinct social exchange norms, and that those subjects behaved in ways consistent with those distinct social norms (Miell & Duck, 1986). When making Dating Games, because the developer has disclosed to the player that it is a Dating Game, players that commit to these games enter the game space viewing other players as a potential friend, romantic partner, or sexual possibility and will adopt prosocial behavior and norms. This is a massively different stance than how players view those that they play other games with (digital, non-digital, physical, or otherwise). Here, the other players are viewed as simply strangers or possible vectors of exchange.

Commitment also acknowledges that in many situations people make snap judgements about the friendship or other kind of relationship possibilities with new people. Friendship is a personal relationship, person-qua-person, initiated and maintained for the other person's sake (for who they are) and not because of their membership in a group. Because we cannot date or befriend or sleep with everyone we come in contact with, we begin to make judgements about others and their potential for a relationship, making first exclusion judgements of dislike and disregard based on our individual criteria (Rodin, 1982, 32). After we make rapid "exclusion" choices, we make inclusion choices about what we do want in a friend or relationship. For better or worse this is often dominated by people leaning toward those that are similar to themselves in background and/or attitudes (Fehr, 1996). While these choices can be problematic and it is worth encouraging players to assess the biases in these personal desires, they nonetheless are personal and no one is obligated to return the interest expressed toward them by others (Tables 10.6 and 10.7).

Friendship is a mutual relationship, sustained by a bidirectional flow of communication, association, and support—sometimes called interdependence or reciprocity. While we may think there is great potential for a friendship or other type of relationship and are committed to pursuing it, it is built on the back of mutuality, of freely assumed obligations, and the

TABLE 10.6 Fellowship of Fools: The (Romance) Game—Example Commitment Prompts

Situations:	Topics:
The Star Upright (4)—You are moving in with a partner...	Six of Cups Upright (2)—How do you feel about having children?
The Lovers Upright (2)—A partner is asking you to make a serious commitment...	King of Coins Upright (2)—What does security look like for you in relationships?
The World Upright (2)—You are having a commitment ceremony...	Six of Coins Reversed (4)—Describe a relationship that you thought was one-sided...

TABLE 10.7 Fellowship of Fools: The (Sexuality) Game—Example Commitment Prompts

Situations:	Topics:
Justice Reversed (4)—Someone suspects cheating...	Seven of Coins Upright (2)—What does enthusiastic consent mean to you?
The Empress Upright (4)—Someone is pregnant...	Six of Swords Reversed (2)—What are your sex safety protocols?
The Lovers Upright (2)—A partner is asking you for a monogamous commitment...	Five of Coins Reversed (4)—How would you feel about a partner pursuing unmet needs outside of your relationship?

enmeshing of lives and activities. Game designers can scaffold mutuality with various mediums of bidirectional flow between players (in-person, voice, video, chat, emotes or signaling, visual spaces with movement, trade systems for exchange and gifts) and for various forms of resources (verbal and non-verbal affectionate communication, self-disclosure, support, assistance, status, information, money, and goods). Encouraging a greater in-game and beyond-game cultural acceptance of dependence and interdependence, seeking support, providing support and altruism over more established narratives of competition and fight or flight are needed to improve player relationships (Yee, 2009). *FoF* is played in-person, as such there is a higher continuity of communication than is typical over digital platforms. The "resource" exchange promoted by the game is primarily self-disclosure, but as players scale up their mutual self-disclosure however, other resources are exchanged such as support, assistance, information, and verbal and non-verbal affection.

Mutuality is intrinsically tied to the bi-directional flow and upward spiral of self-disclosure and affectionate communication, both of which are considered "striving behaviors" central to developing close friendships (Hall & Davis, 2017, 31). Dating Games ought to encourage these behaviors, but they must scaffold it on reciprocal structures ranging from low to high commitment and risk. Starting with low-commitment and risk activities can encourage low-self-disclosure and low-affection early on when players are connecting with one another and discourage premature high-self-disclosure or high-affection. In multiplayer forms of playing *FoF*, the lowest striving behavior structure occurs with Conversation Mode, and can be minimized even further by using the Intentional Mod to give players the choice between the two prompts on a drawn card, or with the Signifier Mod which lets players choose any Topic Prompt they wish. This gives players direct control of the prompt they ask (and thus are expected to answer by the rules) to better modulate the amount of self-disclosure and risk in these early interactions. The different card prompt difficulties, the various multiplayer Gameplay Modes that offer associative or cooperative play, and the variable randomness and uncertainty offered by different Mods offer multiple ways to scale up or scale down self-disclosure, affectionate communication, risk, and uncertainty.

Affectionate communication can be verbal or non-verbal and indicates and negotiates interest and care for shared social norms and the other player. Questions asked to encourage greater depth or breadth of conversation indicate interest and is encouraged in *FoF*'s CoC: "Let conversation flow naturally from the prompts, ask questions of each other beyond the prompts and embrace the tangents." Intermediate feedback, so much more detectable in in-person conversation than in digital text exchanges, is often found in physical responses such as head-nodding and sub-verbal feedback such and "hmms" and "yeahs" (Fehr, 1996, 86). The most involved Mod of the game, the Feedback Mod, optional in most multiplayer Modes and required in only one, provides quantitative and qualitative feedback to players on their answers and choices that can range from the affectionate to the critical. Thus, mutuality scales up and down in relationships, and games for friendship or other close relationships need to provide pathways for players to negotiate, ratchet up or ratchet down self-disclosure, affection, and mutuality. However, we often imagine relationships scaling increasingly up like an escalator, but the authors prefer to see a continuum or "flux" within relationships managed by its participants rather than a kind of "relationship escalator" (Veaux & Rickert, 2014, Chapter 15).

Friendship is a private moral sphere where we test the constraints of cultural and public moralities; wrestle with issues of equality, difference, and power; and negotiate affection and respect. The most common instigators of conflict in friendships were identified as including rebuff and rejection, being mocked or minimized, cumulative annoyances, negligence or lack of consideration, unwarranted criticism, and betrayal of trust (Fehr, 1996). Many of these instigators come from the inversion of what makes friendships powerful: minimizing or mocking the other instead of being supportive and caring, rebuffing and rejecting someone rather than liking them for who they are, caring about their needs, committing to being in a relationship and caring about them. Being negligent of the relationship as opposed to voluntarily engaging in it with intention and commitment, treating someone with a lack of consideration rather than striving to treat them as an equal and how they have asked to be treated.

The most common response to disagreements and conflict in friendship is, by and large, to bury one's head in the sand (Fehr, 1996), but ambivalent friendships can be harmful to our health (Hibbard & Walton, 2017) and successfully weathering conflict can create a stronger friendship bond (Fehr, 1996, 165). Integrative tactics have been shown to be the most effective for this, having an explicit discussion about the conflict without distributing blame or demanding concessions (Fehr, 1996, 165). These can be encouraged in design that facilitates this kind of behavior, as *FoF* attempts to do with the verbal feedback in the Feedback Mod, which adds a "whole new layer of challenge and intimacy to play" (Banger & O'Donnell, 2018a). Further guidelines are given on the game's website for the Feedback Mod that encourage an integrative experience between players, such as: "feedback should be used to serve the person to whom you're giving it, and also as a way for you to draw and communicate your boundaries—what you like to do, how you prefer to communicate, your personal preferences" (Banger & O'Donnell, 2018b). These guidelines advocate that players identify their own biases, any self-centered agendas they may have, and try to set them aside, to keep feedback clear, concrete, and actionable. Players receiving feedback are encouraged to sit with the feedback and try not to react immediately, to consider it as if they had discovered it themselves, to not take it too personally or blow it out of proportion, to try to trust the good intentions of those giving them feedback, yet also to be critical of their possible biases and communication skills. Friendship Games should try to give players the tools they need to construct their own meaningful relationships and to manage conflict within them, and this means game design will need to look to other work with human relations such as non-violent communication, mediation, facilitation, and so on.

Finally, it is important to discuss maintenance. The maintenance of friendship is as important as its establishment and the key components of friendship formation help ensure its continuation. One of the primary limiting factors for close friendships, however, is decreased interaction (Fehr, 1996), interaction being a measure of commitment to the shared activities that maintain a friendship—such as conversation, self-disclosure, shared activities, support, and affective communication. At the lowest level, "laughing and joking, hanging out and catching up," serve as the most basic level of friendship maintenance. The stronger the relationship, the more important other forms of everyday talk become: gossip, meaningful talk, self-disclosure, and affectionate talk (Hall & Davis, 2017). Lower self-disclosure forms of everyday talk—such as small talk that limits the diversity of topics, the frequency and duration of talk and the quality of talk—often represent the declining importance or investment in a friendship (Hall, 2018; Fehr, 1996, 166). The causes for this often rest on differing personal characteristics of an individual partner or of the relationship itself, deterioration of openness, communication and/or trust, or the mutuality of outcomes and future plans may have changed (Levinger, 1980). Friendship Games, and Dating Games as well that focus on the centrality of friendship for romantic and sexual relationships, need to support friendship maintenance with game design that facilitates meaningful conversation, self-disclosure, and affectionate communication between players. More importantly, players need ways to discuss their differences, to approach deterioration in relationship openness, communication, trust, and their mutuality of future plans through integrative tactics that do not place blame or demand concessions, but work toward mutually remediating the relationship.

Situational Design

Situational Design (SD) is a player-centric approach to game design that recognizes a range of player goals and motivations besides "winning"—such as, interpretation, introspection, exploration, integrity, authenticity, coherence, expansion, and closure—and therefore includes designs for situations that open up a play space for players to include their own attitudes, personal history, and intrinsic motivations (Upton, 2017). SD, in many respects, is the player-centric consideration that players most often describe as lacking from contemporary romance games. Player affection needs can be better served through more options and content—more gender and sexuality options for character creation, deeper, more well-written romance content that continues after sexual encounters and has larger consequences on the characters and/or the game—this would require greater investment in narrative designers and storytellers and an excess of content (McDonald, 2015). This still situates the nexus of play between the player and the game, with the game transmitting meaning to the player. Instead, SD situates play in the mind of the player, seeing meaning emerge from the experience, where "Some of the moves the player makes will affect the external state of the game, but others will affect their internal understanding of the game, or even their understanding of themselves and the world at large" (Upton, 2017, 6). Rather than focusing on content and options, SD encourages the design of a system that will generate fresh situations by using a variety of elements or objects that are distinct and designed for reuse.

Coherence, Exploration, and Closure

SD conceptualizes the play experience as a chain of situations, each being an interval of play that contains a choice of moves, the move chosen determining the player's next situation (Thomas, 1999). SD sees interactivity and winning as two useful strategies for the construction of playful situations, but not as foundational to play. Rather, it recognizes the existence of a range of player motivations for play, and so the "best move" is not necessarily one that moves the player toward some win state, but instead ones that shift player attitudes or feelings, that are personally significant. These moves advance players toward their intrinsic goals, the three we will focus on here are that of coherence, exploration, and closure.

In play with goals for coherence, players privilege an internal constraint as off-limits to any kind of strategic shift (Upton, 2017). For dating games, this means that players should privilege the constraints of their real-world identities and play in such as way that minimizes disruption of their sense of self. This can encourage introspection and principled play that reinforces the player's sense of who they are. In *FoF*, players are asked in the CoC to "Play As Yourself," to play as their real-world identities since they are trying to make real-world relationships. "Take Your Time," promotes another interpretation of coherence, to playfully and almost aimlessly explore yourself (and other players) through the game. Players are encouraged to "Explore the many possible facets of a Situation or Topic Prompt, follow them to the past, or the present, or a possible future, mundane or fantastic."

Using the prompts imaginatively can reinforce players' "sense of self" as well as open a space for them to explore and experiment with their sense of self in a series of "What would it be like...?" thought experiments and stories. Alongside personal coherence is the goal of coherence of the other player, to get to know their real-world identity through play, learning about their background, interests, values, and so on through playing the game strategically to uncover new information and engaging them more with follow-up questions. Self and other coherence can be a mutual goal of players prompting mutual self-disclosure. Playing for coherence goals in dating games is especially important for promoting self-disclosure and exploring previous behavior and current expectations regarding those aspects central to dating: commitment, exclusivity, and passion (Tables 10.8 and 10.9).

Expansion on the other hand, is play that weighs the options according to how they open up the play space and privileges the moves that look to increase the number of future moves available (Upton, 2017). This can mean literal exploring, be that the multiple Situation and Topic combinations *FoF* can offer, or playing with an unfamiliar player, or roleplaying as an unfamiliar character (which is allowed, but players are asked to

TABLE 10.8 Fellowship of Fools: The (Romance) Game—Example Coherence Prompts

Situations:	Topics:
The Magician Upright (2)—You are making a couple's costume...	Ten of Cups Upright (2)—How do you feel about marriage?
Justice Upright (2)—The check just came at dinner...	Six of Cups Upright (4)—How do you feel about having children?
The Sun Upright (2)—You are seeing someone with a child from a previous relationship...	King of Wands Reversed (4)—What does patriarchy mean to you?

TABLE 10.9 Fellowship of Fools: The (Sexuality) Game—Example Coherence Prompts

Situations:	Topics:
The Chariot Reversed (4)—A new partner tells you that they have an STI...	Eight of Wands Upright (4)—How much time do you spend having sex and masturbating each week?
Temperance Upright (2)—You are attracted to someone very different than your usual type...	Five of Wands Reversed (4)—What is your preferred size for a partner?
Wheel of Fortune Reversed (4)—A barrier protection has broken...	Page of Cups Upright (2)—How and where do you like to be touched?

disclose this to other players at the beginning of play). It's the unfamiliarity of these situations, the unknown constraints, that make them feel so open and inviting. Expansion play can also mean choosing a familiar Situation Prompt if the player feels that they know that situation well and so it offers the player many opportunities to act and interact. Like coherence play that expands sense of self or other, expansion play has an aimless quality to it, where players don't know where they are headed, but they expect it will be interesting and they will expand their horizons by following where the most open situations lead them, but it can come at the expense of coherence. Players with these goals may not play true to their real-world identities or focus on learning about the other player, they may go against their natural tendencies and transgress their personal principles in order to pursue new paths of play. This can be particularly powerful though for more transgressive questions that are out of their known and comfortable boundaries (Tables 10.10 and 10.11).

While players who play for expansion and exploration want to open up the possibilities of the play space, those who play for closure wish to shut them down, to accomplish a feeling of completeness. Closure is the sense that players get when anticipatory play has been suspended for long periods or shut down altogether (Upton, 2017). With closure comes the feeling that

TABLE 10.10 Fellowship of Fools: The (Romance) Game—Example Expansion Prompts

Situations:	**Topics:**
The Fool Upright (2)—You are going on a first date...	Three of Cups Upright (4)—How do you feel about being in a triad relationship?
The Magician Reversed (4)—You are playing on a dating app...	Seven of Wands Reversed (4)—How do you feel about being single?
The Hanged Man Upright (2)—You are in a non-traditional relationship...	Three of Wands Reversed (4)—When have you let your imagination get ahead of you in a relationship?

TABLE 10.11 Fellowship of Fools: The (Sexuality) Game—Example Expansion Prompts

Situations:	**Topics:**
The Magician Upright (2)—You are visiting a sex shop...	Ace of Swords Upright (2)—How do you feel about toys?
The Fool Upright (2)—You are fooling around with someone for the first time...	Five of Wands Upright (2)—Describe your ideal orgy...
The Sun Upright (2)—You are experiencing a long-awaited fantasy...	Seven of Cups Reversed (2)—What kind of porn star would you be?

whatever questions we were asking ourselves have been answered and no more remain. This could be caused by the game, for instance, during *FoF* players could have a heated disagreement or players disabused each other, or when Feedback provided was not helpful, was poorly delivered and/or poorly received. At such a point, the challenge of the interaction and continuing the relationship is high, anticipatory play shuts down and players no longer want to interact or try to learn more about the other player, but rather to cease interaction altogether and possibly the relationship itself.

Or, the game can be used to try and bring closure and resolution to the disagreement, as a conflict management and resolution tool, especially when played with a therapist, mediator, or game facilitator. In Signifier Mode players can work through a specific topic or situation that has been mutually challenging, choosing a signifier prompt that signifies the issue and drawing Topic Cards and choosing Topic Prompts to play within the signified challenge. Each player gives each other space and time to give their answers to each prompt, and then reply as they choose to each other's drawn Topic Prompts and/or the responses the other player gave to them. A desire for closure can also come when the feeling of progress (in the game, or in the relationship) slows, when players feel like there is nothing to do, they can accomplish less and less together, or their actions together no longer feel meaningful. Dating games need to open up a space for players to discuss these personal issues, to find closure and resolution. Multiple Situation and Topic Prompts in *FoF* deal with issues of falling out of love, boredom, of stagnating or changing desire. With various Gameplay Mode rules to constrain interaction and encourage listening, feedback mechanisms to cue each other directly, and a Code of Conduct to establish base shared behavioral norms, dating games can make the process of finding closure and dealing with change in a relationship easier (Tables 10.12 and 10.13).

TABLE 10.12 Fellowship of Fools: The (Romance) Game—Example Closure Prompts

Situations:	**Topics:**
The Chariot Reversed (4)—Someone is slowing things down in a relationship...	Three of Swords Reversed (2)—How do you give yourself closure after a relationship ends?
Judgement Reversed (4)—A previous partner is seeking closure...	Knight of Coins Reversed (4)—Describe a relationship that you felt bored in...
The World Reversed (4)—You are feeling trapped in a relationship...	Two of Wands Reversed (4)—Describe a relationship where you realized you wanted different things...

TABLE 10.13 Fellowship of Fools: The (Sexuality) Game—Example Closure Prompts

Situations:	Topics:
The Lovers Reversed (4)—You aren't sexually compatible with someone...	Page of Coins Reversed (4)—How do you deal with boredom in sexual relationships?
The Emperor Reversed (4)—You are revoking your consent for...	Eight of Cups Upright (4)—How do you know when to stop having sex with someone?
Judgement Upright (2)—A partner has cheated...	Four of Cups Upright (2)—Describe a time you rejected someone's advances...

Constraints, Cues, and Strategies

In *FoF*, the objects are tarot cards, a deck of 78 cards with 5 suits that has been in use since the fourteenth century for games and since the seventh century for divination. Four of the tarot card suits closely resemble traditional playing cards, but the highly symbolic fifth suit of the Major Arcana was introduced by a reclusive Italian Duke Filippo Maria Visconti of Milan as a likely allegory of the events circling his life (Farley, 2009). The authors of *FoF* focused on designing a system that would generate a variety of complex and open situations, using the Major Arcana to create 44 Situation Prompts for each deck of Friendship, Romance, and Sexuality. The Minor Arcana, the other four suits, were used to create a significant number of constraints that would narrow the possible moves and player choices within these situations, with 112 Topic Prompts for each deck. Together, these generate fresh situations with constraints, and further game components add to this. There are also the external constraints of the Code of Conduct of the game which establish the behavior norms of the players, constraining what is "acceptable" play. Different Gameplay Modes and their rules constrain players further, some are single player which can be played alone or in parallel play, others are multiplayer in which different Modes structure for associative play or cooperative play.

As players explore the game prompts, they go back and forth between immediate play and anticipatory play, between doing and learning. In immediate play, the player's understanding of the game and the other player allows them to pick what they think is the best move for the situation and discuss it. These moves need to feel meaningful, with a tension between uncertainty and predictability that can be balanced by the familiarity of the player with the situation and topic and the move they are choosing, their assumptions about their strategies, and the uncertainty of the hidden information of the other player, their preferences, and their reaction to the move. Anticipatory play on the other hand occurs in the mind of the player, and so requires stillness and time to mentally explore the possible situation tree of past and future situations; consider moves and their ramifications; think about what it is possible to do; learn how to better play the game or how to play well with the other player. These are those short periods where players can decide on the constraints, which Modes and Mods to play, which Situation Prompt to play, the Topics Prompts to play within the Situation Prompt in play, and in how they will answer the prompts in play.

Another game constraint are the Mods, which can alter the uncertainty with which the prompts are chosen on the card, possibly asking players for more self-disclosure or responsiveness or to play a situation or with a constraint that would not have been their preference. The other significant external constraint are the players and their own internal constraints that they bring to the game. These internal constraints can include the player's understanding of the game, their goals for the playing, their background knowledge, their socioemotional skills, their experience and proficiency with conversational turn-taking norms, with building friendship and/or intimacy with others, the strategies they've learned for doing so, the similarities and differences of the players, their ability and willingness to manage difference and disagreements, their willingness to play well with each other, to be responsive and mutual, their attraction to each other, their commitment to each other and to playing the game to get to know each other, their expectations for exclusiveness and commitment in dating, and so on.

Each player's goals for play are an internal constraint which give them a reason to prefer one move over another, and so makes those choices feel meaningful. An explicit goal that most players will have coming into a dating game such as *FoF:R* and/or *FoF:S* is to find a romantic and/or sexual partner, to determine through gameplay if players are compatible for such a relationship, to help that relationship to form/develop/deepen and to maintain that relationship after it is established. Partners seek information about each other to determine if there is mutuality in the relationship and if they are safe in interdependence. This information is called "symbolic outcomes" (Vanderdrift et al., 2017). Symbolic outcomes are the result of interaction and their broader implications about the other player's dependability, their willingness to compromise or sacrifice for the other player, the degree to which they are selfish, impulsive, or self-reflective, their readiness to be relied upon. These outcomes are more apparent specifically from situations that ask players to play altruistically, out of line with their self-interest and instead in line with the other's best interest (Vanderdrift et al., 2017). These situations help players to build mutuality, the bi-directional flow of communication, support and association, concrete outcomes and symbolic outcomes of mutuality, and they can provide the impetus for transformation of motivation, where an internal constraint of player motivation changes (Vanderdrift et al., 2017; Upton, 2017). Situational design used for cooperative multiplayer games is particularly effective at this because of the mutual, interdependent nature of a committed and intimate relationship, an individuals' thoughts, feelings, and behaviors are impacted by another's and vice versa, there is vulnerability as well as shaping and becoming.

An important additional component of SD is the addition of "cues," a tool for shaping the player's internal constraints and thus how they will play and interpret the game, and how they will play with and interpret the play of the other player. Early moves as players learn the game should not be cued, then when cues are introduced they need to follow immediately after moves, directing attention to the consequences of the move and its significance. Intermediate feedback in conversation and storytelling is often found in physical responses, such as head-nodding, and sub-verbal feedback, such and "hmms" and "yeahs" (Fehr, 1996, 86). Free-flowing dialogue and asking further questions is also encouraged in the Code of Conduct, "Let conversation flow naturally from the prompts, ask questions of each other beyond the prompts and embrace the tangents. When there is a break in conversation you will know it is time to move on." As players receive intermediate feedback and questions and comments from other players, these function as cues that the other player wants to expand the breadth and depth of the conversation or story and the directions in which that is desired.

The Feedback Mod, however, provides the most satisfactory way to deliver social cues between players. It was designed to assist players with better communicating and negotiating their personal preferences and boundaries, as well as a tool to help players remind and reinforce the behavioral and communication norms established in the Code of Conduct. This Mod makes use of a "Character Sheet," which players use to take notes about the other player (rather than for themselves as might be done in a traditional role-playing game or with the use of profiles on dating websites/apps), to write down what they learn about the other player's "Attributes," "Abilities," "Interests," and "Background" as they self-disclose through play. Players provide verbal feedback to the other player after a move. Recommendations and guidelines for the giving and receiving of feedback is further guided and scaffolded in an expanded post on the game's website (Figure 10.2).

Players also award or detract "Experience Points" on their Character Sheets for each other, and communicate that score to each other for direct quantitative feedback. These experience points are bi-directional, each

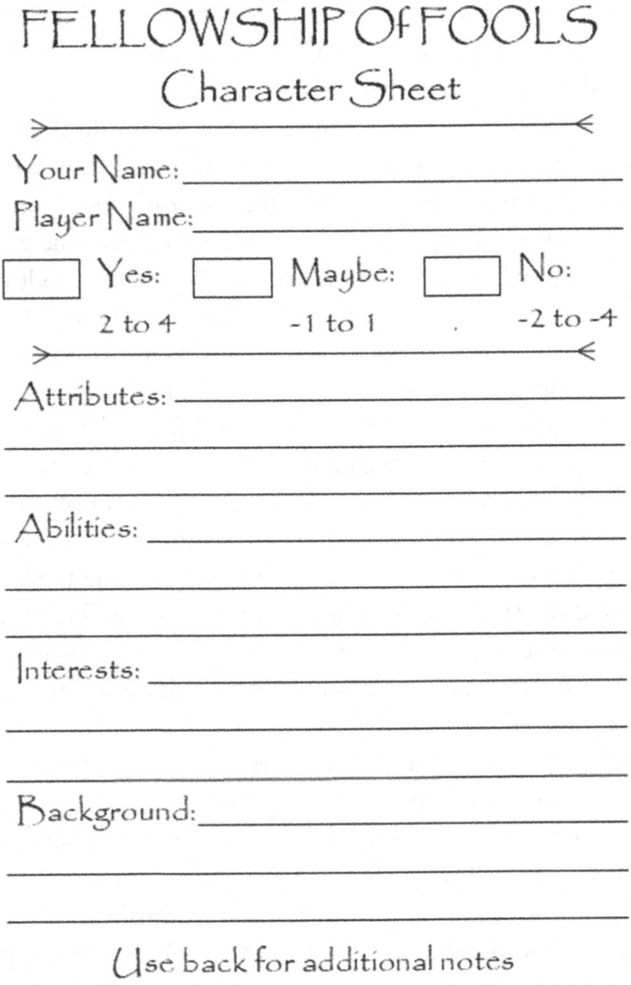

FELLOWSHIP OF FOOLS
Character Sheet

Your Name: ______________________
Player Name: ______________________

☐ Yes: 2 to 4 ☐ Maybe: -1 to 1 ☐ No: -2 to -4

Attributes: ______________________

Abilities: ______________________

Interests: ______________________

Background: ______________________

Use back for additional notes

FIGURE 10.2 Character Sheet from *FoF*.

player has built up a different amount of Experience Points with each other based on their own criterion, and players have significant flexibility in deciding the criterion for these judgements and those criteria can vary with each move. The rules state they should communicate their reasons to the other player as part of the feedback, and so the more feedback players give each other the more they learn about the various criterions of judgements the others use and their relative significance and relation to their own moves. This gives players quantitative and qualitative cues of how to play well with the other partner, enabling them to reevaluate their moves and the internal constraints that shape them. The experience points are cumulative, but also split into the categories of "Yes," "No," and "Maybe," so that players can see the overall trend in their compatibility and their adaptation to cues/feedback. In the real world, we're often unsure of the ramifications of our actions, how others interpret them, or judged us for them. Relationships are particularly murky to navigate, filled with unforeseen setbacks and unintended consequences and meanings. Part of what makes games playful is our ability to learn them, to find a degree of predictability and causality that brings a clarity to game worlds that the real world lacks. The Feedback Mod attempts to enable some greater clarity for players on the impact of their play, to more easily gauge how well they are "playing well with" others and how to "play better" with them.

As the players traverse the game's and their relationship's possible narratives, they use cues to modulate, or regulate, the disposition of the other player toward them and/or between themselves, thereby intentionally crafting the relationship and each other's behavior (Cardoso & Carvalhais, 2013). With the Feedback Mod, players communicate their assessments of the moves of other players and give feedback based on their own particular and varying criterion, giving their justifications verbally to the other player to choose whether or not to alter their behavior. For instance, players could receive less experience for a move based on different preferences, or for giving an answer that was "safe" and did not disclose much or that seemed disingenuous, or by making a choice or comment that showed a low regard for equality, and so on. The open qualitative aspect of the Feedback Mod helps players to modulate their behavior and to shape their relationships, to negotiate their relationship with this small ritual of feedback. This scaffolds player opportunity to change, whereby they can acquire more experience, develop more or less patience, concern, understanding, and empathy for others, and so forth. This "ritual" can make expressive cooperation work, can enable communications that address ambiguity and establish mutual respect, as a practice it can become structured and focused in time, a self-renewing habit that promotes reflexive self-criticism and imbues our bodily gestures and words with dense meanings (Sennett, 2012). Ritual's role in all human cultures has been as a multivocal medium, a joint performance, used "to relieve and resolve anxiety, by turning people outward in shared, symbolic acts" (Sennett, 2012, 280) that are structured, choreographed, gestures both physical and verbal so that they can be repeated, performed, again and again and pay homage to some sacred object, such as a relationship (Goffman, 1967).

Satisfaction for players comes from fulfilling particular goals and also when players sense a shift in their internal constraints—their understanding of the game, of themselves, of the other player—and now they know what to do and how to do it. This often comes after the player faces a crux, a sense that their understanding of the game, or the other player, is insufficient for them to make an immediate move in the current situation, because something is unfamiliar to them, play or the other player has unfolded to them in an unforeseen way, or because a previous move failed to yield the outcome predicted (Upton, 2017). This comes from an uncertainty with our predictions, with our interpretations of the game and the other player. They are doubts about their moves, their goals, their interpretations of the choices and/or behavior of other players and themselves, their correctness, their ramifications, their implications.

> "If we design game systems to make use of a player's existing attitudes toward the world, then the strategies they adopt as they play the game will affect those attitudes. The game changes the player, not because it tells the player something new, but because it gives the player a space to inhabit in which a new way of being is an effective strategy" (Upton, 2017, 9).

Dating Games that are player-centric and focus on generating the desired experiences players can have—the various situations they may face at some point—can provide a space for players to inhabit individually and with others to explore the various goals and effective strategies that come with dating. Growth is an inherent potential between organism and environment, free interaction can stimulate reflection and experimentation, horizons are expanded, connections deepened, meanings enriched, and it is best done as shared experiences. If we design systems that make use of player's existing socioemotional skills, attitudes and strategies toward the world, and provides a space in which they can play with those and find more effective strategies that other players genuinely respond to, these games have the potential to change player social behavior outside of the game.

Design for Emergence

Designing for intentional emergence facilitates player-to-player relationship formation, maintenance, and socioemotional practice. Intentional emergent design components that contribute to emergent play examined here are agency, abstraction, complexity, dialogue, and narrative. Emergence is not determined by any one constituent part at the lower level, but rather is the result of the non-linearly combined interactions between parts and/or agents in a system that creates a higher level of organization. These parts should be abstracted and interact in complex ways, giving players greater agency (Holmes et al., 2018). Emergent game design has enabled more engaging experiences where players don't focus on content or rules but rather create experiences around the game's systems and constraints.

The Emergent Dialogue Model

The model of Emergent Dialogue is a relatively new one coming from within sustainability research and has thus far been primarily used as a design model for social mobilization in support of collective behavior change in Serious Games (Antle, Warren, May, Fan, & Wise, 2014; Tanenbaum, Antle, & Robinson, 2013). However, the authors of this work believe it can be useful for individual attitude and behavior change as well. The Emergent Dialogue model within Serious Games is positioned against the Information Deficit and Procedural Rhetoric models, though there is no empirical evidence that any one model is more effective than any other (Tanenbaum, Antle, & Robinson, 2013). The Information Deficit model focuses on persuasion through delivering the "correct information" and so is limited by a preset story to deliver that information in a top down, unidirectional flow. In the Procedural Rhetoric model, the message is encoded into the game, players interpret the message through interacting with the system and experiencing the consequences of one's actions, but it is limited to what can be encoded within a computational system. In contrast, in the Emergent Dialogue model the message is not communicated or encoded in the game; instead, the game interface or mechanics indirectly or the content directly motivate player dialogue and participation that

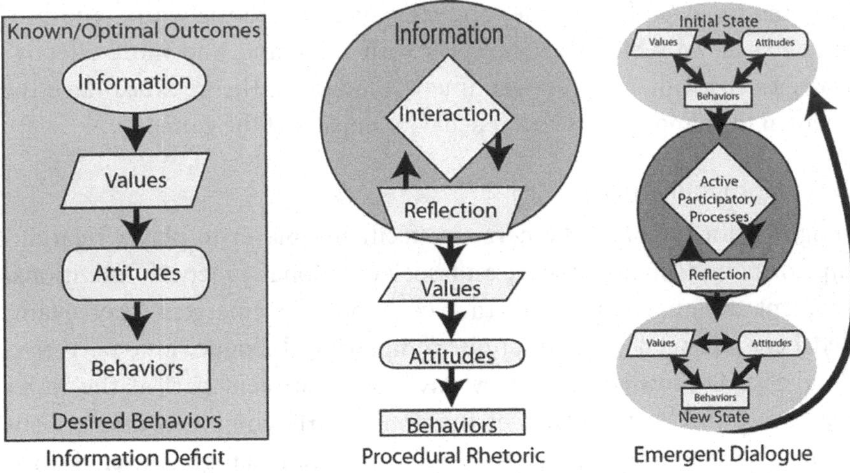

FIGURE 10.3 Image from Tanenbaum et al. (2013). (Reprinted with permission from Tanenbaum, J.G. et al., Three perspectives on behavior change for serious games, *Proceedings from CHI 2013: Changing Perspective*, Paris, France, 2013.)

leads to new understandings (Antle et al., 2014). Information flows in a bi-directional manner between players, new and original content emerges through dialogue, and the game provides context and space to create new information and outcomes through the iterative process of ongoing engagement, feedback, negotiation, and reevaluation (Figure 10.3).

Both the Emergent Dialogue and Procedural Rhetoric models provide players with an opportunity to arrive at their own conclusions by experiencing the issues through an active process (Tanenbaum, Antle, & Robinson, 2013). Like Situational Design, the Emergent Dialogue model is concerned with the player's personal history, attitudes, and goals related to the game's subject. The game provides situations and opportunities to explore, reflect, and discuss these and make meaning. The card prompts of *FoF* directly create openings for players to explore their own expectations and experiences on various topics and situations related to relationships such as commitment and exclusivity, compatibility and difference, ethics and conflict, attraction and passion. The Emergent Design model has no fixed win or lose goals. They can include learning outcomes such as socioemotional learning for relationship games, but they are primarily to support players to "determine their own game goals in line with their personal values" (Antle et al., 2014, 46). *FoF*'s only explicit goals are "self development and developing relationships with other players," which correlates to socioemotional learning through single-player Modes of play and dialogue-based play with others. It does not present a "closed" or fixed interpretation to players of what relationships they should pursue and what they should look like, or what the "right" or "correct" behavior should be within relationships (only within the game space), that is left up to the players to navigate and negotiate.

Scholars of communication and relationships have tended to ignore the positive functions of difference, or have tended to frame difference exclusively as: conflict, incompatible goals, morals, stylistic variation in approaches to conversation and conflict management (Fehr, 1996). When difference is framed only as conflict, it is conceptualized only as something to be managed or resolved. Differences can, however, be the foundation for individual growth in each partner by exposing each other to different perspectives, interests, and approaches for, "to engage in dialogue, voices interpenetrate one another and thereby constitute and change one another" (Baxter, 2004, 19). Through being exposed to differences and perceiving and remarking upon difference, we participate in social construction and individuation, we are better able to know ourselves through knowing others. When dialogue extends into storytelling, players are given an opportunity to perceive others in the context of their own life rather than abstractly or categorically, difference is dramatized and similarities unveiled (Rawlins, 2008). The individual human being is the preferred object of affection, not the larger community or the mass of humanity. Without the concreteness of persons, of sharing our stories and sharing affection, we risk abstracting individuals and losing direct "fellow-feeling." Without this, our morality and values become based on abstract ideals, and the arguments that support them have "no surer touchstones for belief and conduct, morality easily becomes a sometime thing, superficial and transitory, and may readily be used, in systematic ways, to justify evil in the name of the good" (Selznick, 1994, 197).

When difference does result in conflict, it can motivate discussion that involves values and can further game play to try out alternatives, to negotiate issues of equality and shared behavioral norms and find compromises (Malone, 1981). Similarly, seemingly undesirable or harmful interactions in collaborative tabletop settings can provide productive learning opportunities for players by triggering further discussion, in terms of elaborations, justification, and explication (Fleck et al., 2009). Negotiating difference and trying to cooperate is often navigated through two distinct ways of conversing: the dialectic and the dialogic. Dialectic conversation deals with the explicit meaning of statements, it tends to use assertions and a process of point and counterpoint (thesis and antithesis) to find an agreement via conflict and tension (synthesis) (Sennett, 2012). In contrast, the dialogic was coined by the Russian literary critic Mikhail Bakhtin to name a way of conversing where shared agreement is not the goal, rather, listening is just as important as speaking, and "through the process of exchange people may become more aware of their own views and expand their understanding of one another" (Sennett, 2012, 19). Dialogue is an emergent and indeterminate process for Bakhtin, where "the interplay of utterances takes the interactants to places unforeseeable at the beginning of the conversation and in unscripted ways" (Baxter, 2004, 11). The dialogic skills that help navigate difference and encourage cooperation are much akin to socioemotional learning goals, they include curiosity, empathy, listening well, behaving tactfully, avoiding frustration in a difficult discussion, finding points of agreement and managing disagreement without needing to find closure or resolution (Sennett, 2012; Hromek & Roffey, 2009). Cooperation, participation and empathy are both the ends and means of the dialogic process. These skills can be encouraged through game content that directly or indirectly encourages participation and discussion, with game behavioral norms such as Codes of Conduct. They can also be supported and scaffolded with mechanics that encourage conversational turn-taking, negotiating behavior through systems of feedback or cues, and providing rewards for player participation, engagement, and commitment to the process.

A critical limiting factor of the Emergent Dialogue model is a similarly limiting factor for forming and maintaining relationships, that of commitment. Dialogue, so important to relationships as a medium to express affection, to self-disclose, discover compatibility through sharing similarities and differences, establish mutuality through engaging, listening, evaluating and reevaluating, negotiate behavior and equality through renegotiation and giving and receiving feedback, all depend on the effort and commitment of the participants to the process and each other. In Emergent Dialogue oriented design there are no pre-defined objectives that the system can easily measure quantitatively, rather the motivation of the players and their authentic engagement and participation in the process of dialogue is the focus. Players have internal motivations and goals of their own for social support and love for their greater well-being however that bring them to this kind of gameplay and keep them engaging in it. The path to these goals that players traverse is less clear, and the outcomes are in no way predetermined, players take different pathways through the same game space, determine where and when to stop, and whether or not and how they want to keep playing with each other (Cardoso & Carvalhais, 2013). Players can find reward through emergent dialogue play in a number of ways that rely on their intrinsic social motivations and needs, but *FoF* also provides a mechanism to reward authentic participation both quantitatively and qualitatively through the Feedback Mod. The use of verbal feedback gives players verbal rewards and cues for better strategies to play well together, the awarding of Experience Points quantifies each interaction and the relationship in general. Lastly, the use of Character Sheets for players to note what they learn about each other rewards authentic participation with a living document that is shaped by and can continue to shape the players' relationship.

Agency, Abstraction, and Complexity

Agency is an approximate measure of the number of choices available to the player, often measured by how many verbs players have to use in the game. Grace (2017) found the most common verbs of digital affection games to be flirt, hug, kiss, and make love. With many gameplay Modes centered around conversation, *FoF* takes away much of the pressure of performing actions and offers a multitude of verbs for players to use for storytelling and dialogue, many of which give players more agency for coherence and exploration of self and others. The verbs used in *FoF:R* include: feel, think, make, meet, talk, are, being, approach, ask, start, imagine, moving in, moving away, take, struggle, handle, prefer, describe, look, deal with, need, worry, experience, check in, ask for, ghost, spoil, pretend, compete, cheat, recharge, communicate, expect, compromise, struggle, help, act, convince, lie, fear, get over, and manipulate. Verbs used in *FoF:S* include: feel, learn, get, had, assert, find, am, describe, be, are, encounter, try, prefer, establish, deal with, feel about, struggle with, like, mean, break, cheat, experience, avoid, initiate, give, receive, handle, pursue, think, visit, fool around, make, masturbate, tell, behave, look, renegotiate, revoke, offer, understand, violate, change, and teach.

There are a significant amount of verbs in *FoF:R* and *FoF:S* for the player to have interesting, non-trivial choices, stories to relate or create, and dialogues to have. As a conversation game, these verbs are just jumping off points for players, they can bring in other verbs through their interpretation of the card prompts and their own personal history and attitudes they bring with them to the game. Because the game limits how many cards can be drawn in a round, there are not so many verbs presented that the game overwhelms players with too many choices and unknowns at once, their cognitive or expressive abilities to interact with the game are not overwhelmed. Additionally, the authors have tried to keep cultural idioms and slang to a minimum to promote clarity for players and to make it accessible for a diverse set of players.

The next component, abstraction, covers how well the player can "read" the game in terms of universally applicable forms. This can be the visual aspect of the game, but this can also include "incorporating resonant themes and archetypes, but without tipping over into idiosyncrasy, cliche, or overused tropes" (Holmes et al., 2018). A game that is too low on abstraction can be too specific for emergent interpretation and play, whereas a game that is too high on abstraction feels flat and carries no symbolic content for building meaning. The authors intentionally wrote the Topic and Situation Prompts with a certain amount of vagueness and openness in mind, so that players could more easily make connections between the prompts and their own lives. For instance, *FoF:S*'s Five of Wands Reversed Topic Prompt asks, "What is your preferred size for a partner?" is intentionally a nonspecific question, the size of a certain body part, of their entire body? How the player chooses to answer these questions speaks more to how they interpret the prompt and what is important to them personally, and gives other players that insight as well. Instead of relying on cliches, prompts ask players to explore them to find personal definitions and share them, such as *FoF:R*'s Seven of Swords Upright Topic Prompt: "How do you define cheating?" This takes an abstract and loaded concept that has been heavily cliched in culture and asks players to think about and discuss their personal and specific understanding of what constitutes "cheating." The art itself of *FoF* is resonant with archetypal symbols, most obviously in the Major Arcana with cards such as the fool, the lovers, death, the devil, and judgement among others. The prompts for these are abstracted to get at the point of the archetypes but leave them open for player interpretation and agency (Table 10.14).

Similarly, the game does not generally have questions that ask players their "labels" to categorize their sexual, gender, or relational orientation and gender identity as so many dating sites/apps do. Instead, the prompts invite players to explore what that means more intimately and personally to them with Topic Prompts such as in the *FoF:S*'s Ace of Wands Upright

TABLE 10.14 Example Archetypal Prompts

Fellowship of Fools: The (Romance) Game:	Fellowship of Fools: The (Sexuality) Game:
The Fool Upright (2)—You are going out on a first date...	The Fool Upright (2)—You are fooling around with someone for the first time...
The Fool Reversed (4)—You are in an uncertain relationship...	The Fool Reversed (4)—Someone does not want to use barrier protection...
Death Upright (4)—A partner has to move away...	Death Upright (2)—You are exploring your sexuality...
Death Reversed (2)—You have decided that it is time to end a relationship...	Death Reversed (4)—A partner has said they no longer find you sexually attractive...
The Devil Upright (2)—You are feeling addicted to someone...	The Devil Upright (2)—Someone is acting jealous...
The Devil Reversed (4)—A relationship you are in is on a break...	The Devil Reversed (4)—You are considering sex work...
Judgement Upright (2)—You are making a decision about a current relationship...	Judgement Upright (2)—A partner has cheated...
Judgment Reversed (4)—A previous partner is seeking closure...	Judgement Reversed (4)—A previous partner has made an accusation about your past sexual conduct...

"How do you feel about penises?" and the Ace of Cups Upright, "How do you feel about vulvas?" The openness and abstraction of these questions invites players to answer it a number of ways, how do they feel about their own genitals, about the genitals of those they are attracted to or not attracted to, about preferences in their variation of appearance, and how does that figure into their attraction and preferences for activities? *FoF:S*'s Queen of Cups Upright asks, "What kinds of feminine qualities are you attracted to?" While *FoF:S's* King of Wands Upright asks, "What kinds of masculine qualities are you attracted to?" These questions are not meant to essentialize but to probe players to think about what they define as masculine or feminine, how those have variously manifested in those they have cared about, which of those qualities were most attractive to them. They encourage a dialogic conversation about difference that shares views and experiences in an open-ended way, where players can become more aware of their own views and expand their understanding of one another without the compulsions of the dialectic norms of conversation (and many non-digital games) to categorize, convert, synthesize, or convince.

The third dimension of intentional emergent design in games is that of complexity (Holmes et al., 2018) and of how and how much components interact. Each object should be distinct and should interact locally. It shouldn't affect the state of another object far away nor the larger group of objects. In *FoF*, the objects are tarot cards, which has several overlapping taxonomies. Individual card meanings (or prompts toward meaning-making in FoF) are only one taxonomy, the most important for the tarot and for *FoF*, and each card has two individual meanings, dependent on the taxonomy of orientation, whether the card is drawn upright or reversed. There are also the taxonomies of Minor vs. Major Arcana, these three taxonomies are emphasized the most in *FoF*, but there are additional taxonomies of art, and how the taxonomies layer. Other taxonomies are present, such as the card's number, the court cards, the suit, the progression or regression of these in the layout, which all provide a larger semantic web (Manning, 2019). These forms of complexity are always accessible, they are present in the external state of the cards, and are read locally within the card taxonomies or with or against other cards drawn in a round. Many of these taxonomies are only discernible as meaningful moves to those players of a different skill level, with the ability to read them as significant and to interpret their significance. They are more advanced moves of interpretation, furthering player introspection play, but their complexity is masked from beginners and present only to those with the ability to read them more deeply, and so constitute deep play (Upton, 2017, 31).

If objects do not interact enough there is only unremarkable stability and repetitive content (i.e., not much to do), when they interact too much players can struggle to make a cohesive mental model for predictions about the game or finding meaning within the game (i.e., much ado about nothing). The tarot is a powerful procedural generator and quick medium through which to build intimacy, there is an algorithm to play, "cards are drawn and placed into position according to the system the reader has chosen. The results are then read as a whole, both meanings of the individual cards and the interplay of patterns coalescing" (Manning, 2019, 339). To limit complexity, *FoF* limits the number of cards drawn in a round, which varies based on the number of players and the chosen system or "Gameplay Mode." These also determine the rules of player interaction and can limit the next system of choices, the "Mods," that determine how the prompt to be played will be determined, and with it the higher or lower risk and uncertainty of a harder prompt, asking for higher self-disclosure between the players. The majority of the Mods are modeled after different preferences among Tarot readers to read their cards as having either two distinct meanings depending on the card's upright or reversed orientation

("Magick Mod"), or as simultaneously present with personal choice determining the card's meaning ("Intentional Mod"), as well as to pick a specific card to signify a particular person, problem, or situation ("Signifier Mod"). Additionally, players are encouraged on the game's website to fool around with the game and find new ways to play, encouraging co-design or participatory design (Taylor, 2006; Manzini, 2016).

Emergent Narratives

The author Italo Calvino described the Tarot as "a machine for constructing stories" (Calvino, 1979, 126). The Tarot is a system rich with symbols, resonant themes, and archetypes that are open to player interpretation and manipulation. Our minds are naturally inclined to assign meaning to chaos, to find patterns and themes, to create personal and profound stories (Jeffries, 2008). Using the Tarot as the backbone of *FoF* enabled the authors to relinquish authorial control of the stories that players would create, assured they would morph and manipulate the broad symbols and vague prompts to construct meaningful stories all by themselves. The meaning players create is far more powerful than any the authors could try to construct, each card prompt elicits a vignette that connects and relates to the larger story of their lives, their selves, and the players' relationship and knowledge of each other, and players will take care of any flaws in the story the cards project at them. With enough potent symbols and willing, engaged participants, there need be little authorial control over the narrative at all, rather the players will create the story for you (Jeffries, 2008).

Players, through repeated interactions with each other by/through/with *FoF* develop unscripted, multi-authored shared emergent narratives of their relationship. Emergent narrative is a character/player-based approach, rather than a plot-based approach. This is fundamentally opposed to the Aristotelian classical view of narrative and argues that for interactive performances, participation and play, character should be more emphasized than plot, particularly focusing on character definition and player ability for articulation and agency (Louchart & Aylett, 2004). Players are motivated by their own and each other's personality traits and personal characteristics to build the story as they interact with each other, and through their interactions the storyline emerges. The players are not spectators or authors, but are participants in the narrative process in a highly flexible game environment where story development is largely managed by the players and dependent on their interactions between each other and the game environment.

Each interaction from a single game prompt could be regarded as one linear development, a thread, a vignette, the larger gameplay mode round that contains it a sequential grouping of threads into a scene inside the larger story of the relationship between the players (Louchart & Aylett, 2004). The stories shared between players each consist of a setting in time and space, characters and events (plots), but are non-linear, similar to the real development of events where multiple stories are happening at the same time and can be told from different perspectives, and the interaction of these multiple stories and perspectives facilitates greater coherence and information sharing (Louchart & Aylett, 2004). Moreover, the non-linear and multi-linear stories shared reflect the character of player's minds and the path of dialogue, which are often making associative leaps, dwelling on the past and imagining possible futures or the consequences of our actions or words with subjunctive logic.

FoF constitutes a shared narrative space in that it presents a set of units or scenes that each represent a step in a given direction of developments, where connections are made organically by stories and discourse to form a nonlinear story through the collaboration of multiple users (Colás, Tapscott, Moghnieh, & Blat, 2012). Shared narrative spaces are "a ludic and cultural medium of expression and communication, created, developed, and maintained through the collaboration of multiple users" (Colás et al., 2012, 106). Similar to a narrative, a relationship evolves through sequential storytelling and play, connected and shaped through cause and effect relations of self-disclosure, player choices, receptiveness of/to the other player, commitment to the scene and the larger story/relationship, and the compatibility and mutuality of the players. As players choose how to interact with each other and what aspect of their relationship to focus on through the various Gameplay Modes and game decks, they thereby choose and negotiate how to develop various aspects of their relationship and its characteristics.

These player-to-player interactions, these experiences, cannot easily be re-experienced. There may be some that are somehow very similar interactions, but they are not exactly the same. There are the constraints of the Gameplay Modes and Mods, the randomness of the draw, the uncertainty that the same Situation Prompt and Topic Prompts will be drawn and selected, and the uncertainty of what each player will choose to interpret, explore, and disclose. Nor can the larger experience of constructing the narrative of their relationship through play be re-experienced, the conditions and/or behavior of those involved cannot easily be recreated

(Cardoso & Carvalhais, 2013). Many of the Situation Prompts in *FoF* are based on "turning-point" events, momentous events that can transform a relationship (Baxter, 2004, 11). Together, the players experience them jointly, either first in-game together, or having experienced them out of game they re-experience them by communicatively remembering these events through storytelling, reminiscing, and dialogue (Baxter, 2004). This similarity of shared events emerges over time and enables coordinated interaction between the players, constructing the players' sense of who they are, who they are together, the identity, history and flavor of the relationship. By persistence of play the narrative emerges, the players' perceptions of each other and themselves evolving throughout the game and the game itself evolving for them as they explore its many levels of complexity—different decks, different mods, different modes of game play. The players' selves and their relationship provide the thematic unification and overall coherence for the stories that emerge.

None of these processes should be read to be smooth or linear. That as relationships, self-knowledge, dialogue, stories, or participation proceed, they do so by building incrementally more disclosure, more mutuality, more affection, and are continually able to find a balance and stability. Rather, change, like players' minds, like dialogue and stories, like our relationships, are an untidy process, with turning points constructing the relationship in an erratic process of backward and forward, fits and starts, ups and downs, by an ongoing dialogic flux with no center, just the relationship in between players driving change (Baxter, 2004). Relationship games must keep this in mind and design for the untidy process of change and how to best assist it for players and between players. More important to keep in mind, as Octavia Butler wrote: "Kindness eases change" (Butler, 2001, 47).

CONCLUSION

Dating Games, not unlike dating generally, is a fraught field. Players (or even "Players") bring with them a host of cultural and personal baggage, but, the same is true for all games. We are told that we are not supposed to play games in love and sex, not supposed to be a player, that games and play imply deceit, tricks, shifty maneuvers geared toward manipulation of others. Players do and will have different goals in romantic and sexual relationships, be they exploration, personal discovery, closure, orgasm, relationships, marriage, reproduction or otherwise. There is not just one game being played, but many. Sicart suggests that the pleasures that play offers varies: “Play is not necessarily fun. It is pleasurable, but the pleasures it creates are not always submissive to enjoyment, happiness, or positive traits. Play can be pleasurable when it hurts, offends, challenges us and teases us, and even when we are not playing. Let’s not talk about play as fun but as pleasurable, opening us to the immense variations in this world” (Sicart, 2014, 3). Play, be it sexual or courtship or otherwise, may in ideal be fully free, voluntary, egalitarian and exclusively connected to positive affect (Caillois, 2001, 6–7), but it can occur in games and in human lives on a continuum, and as such it can be asymmetrical, risky, coerced, violent, and damaging (Paasonen, 2018). Play can involve mixed pleasures, acquired tastes, and ambivalent feelings, and on the dark side of play, disrespect and disregard toward established rules and other players’ comfort zones (Mortensen, Linderoth, & Brown, 2015).

Taking the design of Dating Games seriously has the opportunity for designers and players to rethink existing paradigms of how we relate to one another. Rather than falling into traditional heteronormative, mononormative and amatonormative roles and scripts, Dating Games can open up for players alternative modes of relating to one another and provide an opportunity to explore more within ourselves as well as with other players. Principled, ethical play and commitment to treating one another kindly is a challenge in most communities and mediums of communication, but players can learn the importance of it through their play of Dating Games, by failing to “win” their games in any meaningful way, by cues from other players, rituals of feedback for discussing difference and equality, or ultimately they will find that no one wants to play these kinds of games with them. When we are afraid of being ourselves in dating games, of committing to the interaction, of trusting others to be themselves, of playing the game genuinely, the only way to play is not to self-disclose and not to fall in love. The fear of becoming dependent on someone else and the risk that entails, is a failure to trust; instead, one’s defenses rule. When we are afraid of losing romantic games, it means we have little possibility of ever really winning them in any meaningful way.

Dating Game designers can take a player-centric approach that opens up the play space for other intrinsic player motivations such as coherence, exploration, interpretation, integrity, anticipation, and closure. Dating games can allow for player motivations of friendship, romance, sexual gratification, orgasm, commitment, closure, and more. Rather than scripted systems of complete developer control, or open worlds of avatars with free reign to interact and little to no scaffolding to support relationship formation, Dating Games designed as emergent systems provide boundaries and constraints to play but give players the tools to navigate and negotiate their compatibility and goals and how they pursue them. Rather than trying to tightly control player behavior or educate players in a top-down asynchronous model of information, Dating Games can instead motivate players to generate, interpenetrate, reevaluate, and negotiate their views about the type of world they want to live in and generate as both social actors and social participants.

While we have leveraged our own Dating Game(s) in the construction of this chapter, *FoF* was really our first attempt to make games that work against dominant constructions of friendship, romance, and sexuality. There is significantly more work to be done in this space, such as an overview of dating games and dating apps and the ethical considerations for these. We look forward to what might emerge from more designers working to build experiences for players that ethically and respectfully engage with these issues. What we do hope we have done is to leverage our work in a way that connects it to the literature more broadly, giving game designers/developers more tools and resources for approaching Dating Games well. So much has already been done, but there is so much opportunity for more work in the future. We look forward to the new possibility spaces offered here.

REFERENCES

Albury, K. (2018). Heterosexual Casual Sex: From Free Love to Tinder. In C. Smith, F. Attwood, & B. McNair (Eds.), *The Routledge Companion to Media, Sex and Sexuality* (81–90). New York, NY: Routledge.

Antle, A. N., Warren, J. L., May, A., Fan, M., & Wise, A. F. (2014). *Emergent Dialogue: Eliciting Values during Children's Collaboration with a Tabletop Game for Change. Proceedings from IDC '14: Conference on Interaction Design and Children*, Aarhus, Denmark.

Aron, A., Fisher, H. E., & Strong, G. (2006). Romantic Love. In A. L. Vangelisti & D. Perlman (Eds.), *The Cambridge Handbook of Personal Relationships* (595–614). New York, NY: Cambridge University Press.

Banger, H., & O'Donnell, C. (2018a). Gameplay. Retrieved October 1, 2019, from https://fellowshipoffoolsgame.com/fellowship-of-fools-the-friendship-game/

Banger, H., & O'Donnell, C. (2018b). The Art of Giving and Receiving Feedback. Retrieved October 1, 2019, from https://fellowshipoffoolsgame.com/2018/07/02/how-to-give-and-receive-feedback/

Baxter, L. A. (2004). Relationships as Dialogues. *Personal Relationships, 11*, 1–22.

Berardi, F. B. (2011). *After the Future*. Chico, CA: AK Press.

Beres, M. A. (2014). Rethinking the Concept of Consent for Anti-sexual Violence Activism and Education. *Feminism & Psychology, 24*(3), 373–389. doi:10.1177/0959353514539652.

Berg, J. H., & Clark, M. S. (1986). Differences in Social Exchange Between Intimate and Other Relationships: Gradually Evolving or Quickly Apparent? In V. J. Derlega & B. A. Winstead (Eds.), *Friendship and Social Interaction* (101–144). New York, NY: Springer-Verlag.

Brake, E. (2012). *Minimizing Marriage: Marriage, Morality, and the Law*. Oxford, UK: Oxford University Press.

Burdette, H. L., & Whitaker, R. C. (2005). Resurrecting Free Play in Young Children. *The Archives of Pediatrics & Adolescent Medicine, 159*(1), 46–50. doi:10.1001/archpedi.159.1.46.

Burkett, M., & Hamilton, K. (2012). Postfeminist Sexual Agency: Young Women's Negotiations of Sexual Consent. *Sexualities, 15*(7), 815–833.

Butler, O. (2001). *Parable of the Talents: Earthseed #2*. New York, NY: Warner Books.

Caillois, R. (2001). *Man, Play, and Games*. Urbana, IL: University of Illinois Press.

Calvino, I. (1979). *The Castle of Crossed Destinies*. New York, NY: Mariner Books.

Cardoso, P., & Carvalhais, M. (2013). Breaking the Game: The Traversal of the Emergent Narrative in Video Games. *CITAR: Journal of Science and Technology of the Arts, 5*(1), 25–31.

Coduto, K. D., Lee-Won, R. J., & Baek, Y. M. (2019). Swiping for Trouble: Problematic Dating Application use Among Psychosocially Distraught Individuals and the Paths to Negative Outcomes. *Journal of Social and Personal Relationships, Online First*, 1–21. doi:10.1177/0265407519861153.

Colás, J., Tapscott, A., Moghnieh, A., & Blat, J. (2012). CrossTale: Shared Narratives as a New Interactive Medium. *Proceedings from MMEDIA 2012: The Fourth International Conferences on Advances in Multimedia*, Chamonix, France.

De las Heras Gómez, R. (2018). Thinking Relationship Anarchy from a Queer Feminist Approach. *Sociological Research Online, Online First*, 1–17. doi:10.1177/1360780418811965.

Dunbar, R. I. M. (2010). *How Many Friends Does One Person Need?* London, UK: Faber and Faber.

England, P., & Thomas, R. J. (2007). The Decline of the Date and the Rise of the College Hook Up. In A. S. Skolnik & J. H. Skolnik (Eds.), *Family in Transition* (151–162). Boston, MA: Allyn and Baker.

Fanghanel, A. (2019). Asking for It: BDSM Sexual Practice and the Trouble of Consent. *Sexualities, Online First*, 1–18. doi:10.1177/1363460719828933.

Farley, H. (2009). *A Cultural History of Tarot: From Entertainment to Esotericism*. New York, NY: I.B. Tauris.

Fehr, B. (1996). *Friendship Processes* (12). New York, NY: Sage Publications.

Fleck, R., Rogers, Y., Yuill, N., Marshall, P., Carr, A., Rick, J., & Bonnett, V. (2009). Actions Speak Loudly with Words: Unpacking Collaboration Around the Table. *Proceedings from ITS '09 Proceedings of the ACM International Conference on Interactive Tabletops and Surfaces*, Banff, Canada.

Glaser, B. C., & Strauss, A. L. (1967). *Discovery of Grounded Theory: The Strategies for Qualitative Research*. New York, NY: Aldine Publishing.

Goffman, E. (1967). *Interaction Ritual: Essays in Face-to-Face Behavior.* Chicago, IL: Aldine Publishing Co.

Grace, L. D. (2017). Love, Lust, Courtship and Affection as Evolution in Digital Play. *Proceedings of DiGRA 2017*, Melbourne, Australia.

Grace, L. D., & Spangler, B. R. (2014). The Psychology of Play: Understanding Digital Game Evolution Through Developmental Psychology. *Proceedings from Foundations of Digital Games*, Fort Lauderdale, FL.

Hall, J. A. (2018). How Many Hours Does It Take to Make a Friend? *Journal of Social and Personal Relationships*, *36*(4), 1278–1296. doi:10.177/0265407511876l225.

Hall, J. A., & Davis, D. C. (2017). Proposing the Communicate Bond Belong Theory: Evolutionary Intersections with Episodic Interpersonal Communication. *Communication Theory*, *27*, 21–47. doi:10.1111/comt.12106.

Hatfield, E., & Rapson, R. L. (1993). *Love, Sex, and Intimacy: Their Psychology, Biology, and History.* New York, NY: HarperCollins College Publishers.

Hatfield, E., Rapson, R. L., & Martel, L. D. (2007). Passionate Love and Sexual Desire. In S. Kitayama & D. Cohen (Eds.), *Handbook of Cultural Psychology* (760–779). New York, NY: The Guilford Press.

Hejdenberg, A. (2005). The Psychology Behind Games. Retrieved from https://www.gamasutra.com/view/feature/130702/the_psychology_behind_games.php

Hibbard, D. R., & Walton, G. E. (2017). Competition in Friendship. In M. Hojjat & A. Moyer (Eds.), *The Psychology of Friendship* (213–232). Oxford, UK: Oxford University Press.

Holmes, R., Austin, M., Compton, K., Ernest, J., Lee, J., Sellers, M.,...Stevenson, J. (2018). Group Report: Constructing Emergence. Retrieved September 15, 2019, from https://www.projecthorseshoe.com/reports/featured/Project_Horseshoe_2018_report_section_7.pdf

Horstman, J., & Staff. (2011). *The Scientific American Book of Love, Sex and the Brain: The Neuroscience of How, When, Why and Who We Love* (5). Hoboken, NJ: John Wiley & Sons, Incorporated.

Hromek, R., & Roffey, S. (2009). Promoting Social and Emotional Learning with Games: "It's Fun and We Learn Things." *Simulation & Gaming*, *40*(5), 626–644. doi:10.1177/1046878109333793

Huizinga, J. (1955). *Homo Ludens: A Study of the Play-Element in Culture*. Boston, MA: Beacon Press.

Jackson, T., & Marks, N. (1999). Consumption, Sustainable Welfare and Human Needs: With Reference to UK Expenditure Patterns Between 1954 and 1994. *Ecological Economics*, *28*(3), 421–441. doi:10.1016/S0921-8009(98)00108-6

Jeffries, L. B. (2008). How to Make Non-Linear Reactive Stories. Retrieved October 1, 2019, from https://www.popmatters.com/how-to-make-non-linear-reactive-stories-2496131835.html

Kalish, R., & Kimmel, M. (2011). Hooking Up: Hot Hetero Sex or the New Numb Normative. *Australian Feminist Studies*, *26*(67), 137–151. doi:10.1080/08164649.2011.546333

Kruger, J., Epley, N., Parker, J., & Ng, Z.-W. (2005). Egocentrism Over E-mail: Can We Communicate as Well as We Think? *Journal of Personality and Social Psychology*, *89*(6), 925–936. doi:10.1037/0022-3514.89.6.925

Levinger, G. (1980). Toward the Analysis of Close Relationships. *Journal of Experimental Social Psychology*, *16*, 510–544.

Louchart, S., & Aylett, R. (2004). The Emergent Narrative Theoretical Investigation. *Proceedings from Conference on Narrative and Interactive Learning Environments*, Edinburgh, Scotland.

Malone, T. W. (1981). Toward a Theory of Intrinsically Motivating Instruction. *Cognitive Science*, *5*(4), 333–369. doi:10.1016/S0364-0213(81)80017-1

Manning, C. (2019). Tarot as Procedural Storytelling. In T. X. Short & T. Adams (Eds.), *Procedural Storytelling in Game Design* (339–350). Boca Raton, FL: CRC Press LLC.

Manzini, E. (2016). Design Culture and Dialogic Design. *Design Issues*, *32*(1), 52–59. doi:10.1162/DESI_a_00364

Maslow, A. H. (1968). *Toward a Psychology of Being*. New York, NY: D. Van Nostrand Company.

Max-Neef, M., Elizalde, A., & Hopenhayn, M. (1989). Human Scale Development: An Option for the Future. *Development Dialogue*, *1*, 1–136.

McDonald, H. (2015). Romance in Games: What It Is, How It Is, and How Developers Can Improve. *QED: A Journal in GLBTQ Worldmaking*, *2*(2), 32–63.

Miell, D., & Duck, S. (1986). Strategies in Developing Friendships. In V. J. Derlega & B. A. Winstead (Eds.), *Friendship and Social Interaction* (129–144). New York, NY: Springer-Verlag.

Mortensen, T. E., Linderoth, J., & Brown, A. M. L. (2015). *The Dark Side of Game Play: Controversial Issues in Playful Environments*. London, UK: Routledge.

Neyer, F. J., Wrzus, C., Wagner, J., & Lang, F. R. (2011). Principles of Relationship Differentiation. *European Psychologist*, *16*, 267–277. doi:10.1027/1016-9040/a000055

Niikko, A., & Havu-Nuutinen, S. (2009). In Search of Quality in Finnish Pre-School Education. *Scandinavian Journal of Educational Research*, *53*(5), 431–445. doi:10.1080/00313830903180711

O'Donnell, C., & Banger, H. (2019). Friendship Games: The Foundations of Games for Making Friends. Manuscript Submitted for Publication.

Paasonen, S. (2018). *Many Splendored Things: Thinking Sex and Play.* London, UK: Goldsmiths Press.

Paik, A. (2010). The Contexts of Sexual Involvement and Concurrent Sexual Partnerships. *Perspective on Sexual and Reproductive Health, 42*(2), 33–42. doi:10.1363/4203310

Rawlins, W. K. (2008). *The Compass of Friendship: Narratives, Identities, and Dialogues.* Thousand Oaks, CA: Sage Publications.

Rodin, M. J. (1982). Non-engagement, Failure to Engage, and Disengagement. In S. Duck (Ed.), *Personal Relationships: Vol. 4 Dissolving Personal Relationships* (31–49). London, UK: Academic Press.

Ryan, C., & Jethá, C. (2010). *Sex at Dawn: How We Mate, Why We Stray, and What It Means for Modern Relationships.* New York, NY: HarperCollins.

Schroeder, J., Kardas, M., & Epley, N. (2017). The Humanizing Voice: Speech Reveals, and Text Conceals, a More Thoughtful Mind in the Midst of Disagreement. *Psychological Science, Online First.* doi:10.1177/0956797617713798

Selznick, P. (1994). *The Moral Commonwealth: Social Theory and the Promise of Community.* Berkeley, CA: University of California Press

Sennett, R. (2012). *Together: The Rituals, Pleasures and Politics of Cooperation.* New Haven, CT: Yale University Press.

Sicart, M. (2014). *Play Matters.* Cambridge, MA: MIT Press.

Tanenbaum, T. J., Antle, A. N., & Robinson, J. (2013). Three Perspectives on Behavior Change for Serious Games. *Proceedings from CHI 2013: Changing Perspective,* Paris, France.

Tay, L., & Diener, E. (2011). Needs and Subjective Well-Being Around the World. *Journal of Personality and Social Psychology, 101*(2), 354–365. doi:10.1037/a0023779

Taylor, T. L. (2006). Beyond Management: Considering Participatory Design and Governance in Player Culture. *First Monday, Special Issue #7.* Retrieved from http://www.uic.edu/htbin/cgiwrap/bin/ojs/index.php/fm/article/view/1611

Thomas, R. J. (1999). What Machines Can't Do: Politics and Technology in the Industrial Enterprise. In D. MacKenzie & J. Wajcman (Eds.), *The Social Shaping of Technology* (199–221). Philadelphia, PA: Open University Press.

Turkle, S. (2015). *Reclaiming Conversation: The Power of Talk in a Digital Age.* London, UK: Penguin Press.

Upton, B. (2017). *Situational Game Design.* Boca Raton, FL: CRC Press.

Vanderdrift, L. E., Agnew, C. R., & Besikci, E. (2017). Friendship and Romance: A Need-Fulfillment Perspective. In M. Hojjat & A. Moyer (Eds.), *The Psychology of Friendship* (109–122). Oxford, UK: Oxford University Press.

Veaux, F., & Rickert, E. (2014). *More Than Two: A Practical Guide to Ethical Polyamory.* Portland, OR: Thorntree Press.

Ward, A. F., Duke, K., Gneezy, A., & Bos, M. W. (2017). Brain Drain: The Mere Presence of One's Own Smartphone Reduces Available Cognitive Capacity. *Journal of the Association for Consumer Research, 2*(2), 140–154.

Webster, C. (2013). Hierarchy of Needs for Rewards in Games. Retrieved October 1, 2019, from https://www.gamasutra.com/blogs/ChelseyWebster/20130923/200782/Hierarchy_of_Needs_for_Rewards_in_Games.php

Wrzus, C., Zimmermann, J., Mund, M., & Neyer, F. J. (2017). Friendships in Young and Middle Adulthood: Normative Patterns and Personality Differences. In M. Hojjat & A. Moyer (Eds.), *The Psychology of Friendship* (21–38). Oxford, UK: Oxford University Press.

Yee, N. (2009). Befriending Ogres and Wood-elves: Relationship Formation and the Social Architecture of Norrath. *Game Studies*, *9*. Retrieved from http://gamestudies.org/0901/articles/yee

Youngblood, A., Cox, C., Hoffman-John, E., Brink, K., Kim, A. J., Cook, D.,... Hughes, L. (2018). Group Report: Design Practices for Human Scale Online Games. Retrieved October 1, 2018, from https://www.projecthorseshoe.com/reports/featured/Project_Horseshoe_2018_report_section_8.pdf

Index

Note: Page numbers in italic and bold refer to figures and tables, respectively.
Page number followed by n refers to footnote.

O

P

Q

R

S

Printed in the United States
by Baker & Taylor Publisher Services

Printed in the United States
by Baker & Taylor Publisher Services